Devon
Gardens

AN HISTORICAL SURVEY

Edited by Steven Pugsley

ALAN SUTTON PUBLISHING LTD.

DEVON GARDENS TRUST

DEVON GARDENS

First published in the United Kingdom in 1994
Alan Sutton Publishing Ltd · Phoenix Mill · Far Thrupp · Stroud · Gloucestershire
in association with the Devon Gardens Trust

First published in the United States of America in 1994
Alan Sutton Publishing Inc. · 83 Washington Street · Dover · NH 03820

British Library Cataloguing in Publication Data

Devon Gardens: Historical Survey
I. Pugsley, Steven
712.09423

ISBN (hardback) 0–7509–0055–5
(paperback) 0-7509-0662-6

Library of Congress Cataloging in Publication Data applied for

Typeset in 11/14 Perpetua.
Typesetting and origination by
Alan Sutton Publishing Limited.
Printed in Great Britain by
Butler and Tanner, Frome, Somerset.

CONTENTS

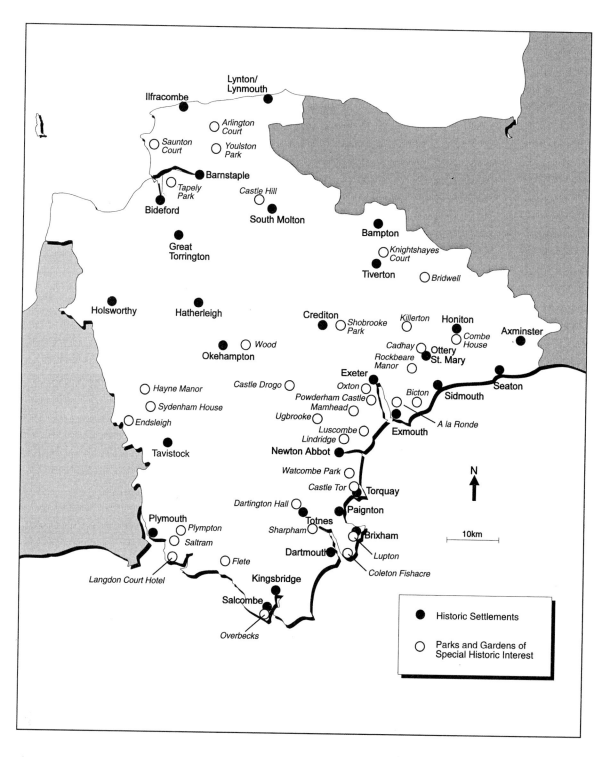

Lynton/
Lynmouth

Ilfracombe

Arlington
Court

Saunton
Court

Youlston
Park

Barnstaple

Tapely
Park

Castle Hill

Bideford

South Molton

Great
Torrington

Bampton

Knightshayes
Court

Tiverton

Bridwell

Holsworthy

Hatherleigh

Crediton

Shobrooke
Park

Killerton

Honiton

Axminster

Combe
House

Wood

Okehampton

Cadhay

Ottery
St. Mary

Rockbeare
Manor

Hayne Manor

Castle Drogo

Exeter

Sydenham House

Oxton

Bicton

Sidmouth

Seaton

Endsleigh

Powderham Castle

Mamhead

Ugbrooke

A la Ronde

Luscombe

Exmouth

Tavistock

Lindridge

Newton Abbot

Watcombe Park

N

Castle Tor

Torquay

Plymouth

Dartington Hall

Paignton

Plympton

Sharpham

Totnes

Brixham

Saltram

Dartmouth

Lupton

10km

Flete

Langdon Court Hotel

Coleton Fishacre

Kingsbridge

Salcombe

Overbecks

● Historic Settlements

○ Parks and Gardens of
Special Historic Interest

FOREWORD

The county of Devon has a splendid gardening heritage. From parks of historic houses to cottage gardens, it represents a tradition of care for the land and regard for its beauty established over centuries. However, land in Devon is coming under increasing pressure for development and road building, and gardens and parkland have no statutory protection in planning law. The Devon Gardens Trust was founded to contribute towards the continuing conservation of this great asset – to encourage the new, to help restore those that have fallen into neglect and, above all, to promote the protection and better understanding of the outstanding achievements of the past.

This is primarily a book about Devon gardens, not about Devon plants. Devon has produced more than its fair share of famous horticulturists, but we are concerned here with the garden demesnes, who made them, who influenced them, not with what grew in them.

The first matter to realize is the huge area the county covers and the enormous range of its climates. At its longest stretch, Devon covers 75 miles; in area it ranks third among the old counties, standing below only Yorkshire and Lincolnshire.

The conditions for gardening vary wildly. At Sharpitor, near Salcombe in the south, conditions are described as 'almost free from frost; sheltered by surrounding trees and on a sloping site protected from west winds; high rainfall but also with a good sunshine record'. Yet in the north, when the great garden of Castle Hill was being altered in 1771, the agent Mr Hilliard wrote: 'I found some difficulty to prevail upon the labourers to face the easterly wind. The most powerful argument was a glass of Cherry Brandy. It is extremely cold with hurricanes of snow.' Castle Hill is only 20 miles south of Tapeley near Bideford, where the Christie family created an almost tropical garden with palm trees and fastigiate Italian cypresses.

As with the diversity of climate, so with the style of gardens. Each century has left its touch. Unlike Cornwall where the image is of camellias, rhododendrons and magnolias, Devon is infinitely unexpected, and is seldom repetitive. The stone gardens of Dartmoor are unrelated to the terraced, seaside delight of Castle Tor or the woody planting of Knightshayes. Lutyens left his mark with his stone backbones in three gardens, but the planting within them has little in common. Rosemoor is Wisley in the west but Dartington, where so many designers have worked, is a garden interpretation of the fourteenth-century hall, with due acknowledgement to the Elmhirsts' 1920s experiment in rural rejuvenation.

The chapters in this book demonstrate the historic aspects of gardens in Devon. The pictures variously show what was there then and what is there now. A gazetteer lists some of the more notable gardens, but only a percentage can be mentioned, and many of these are in private hands and seldom, if ever, open to the inveterate garden visitor. In Devon we have a multiplicity of wonderful gardens of all kinds. The role of the Devon Gardens Trust is to prevent greed and thoughtlessness destroying them.

Robin Fausset
Vice President, Devon Gardens Trust

LIST OF CONTRIBUTORS

ROB ILES

An Inspector of Ancient Monuments for English Heritage.

TODD GRAY

PhD. Research Officer, Devon Gardens Trust, 1992–3. Publications include *Early Stuart Mariners and Shipping: the Maritime Surveys of Devon and Cornwall 1619–35*, and *Harvest Failure in Cornwall and Devon* (1992). He co-edited *Tudor and Stuart Devon: the Common Estate and Government* (1992).

ROBIN FAUSSET

Vice President of the Devon Gardens Trust. Author of 'The Creation of the Gardens at Castle Hill, South Molton, Devon' in *Garden History*, vol. 13, no. 2, 1985.

PETER HUNT

Vice President of the Devon Gardens Trust. Formerly Amenities and Countryside Officer for Devon County Council, and now a freelance planner. Editor of *Devon's Age of Elegance* (1984) and *Payne's Devon* (1986).

RICHARD STONE

Partner Colson Stone landscape architects. He has been heavily involved in formulating the conservation plan for Humphry Repton's garden at Endsleigh and in overseeing its restoration.

AUDREY LE LIÈVRE

PhD. Regular contributor to journals including *Country Life* and *Hortus* on items of garden history and associated interest, and author of a biography of Ellen Willmott.

DAVID MAWSON

OBE, DL, FSA, RIBA, JP. Conservation architect (including to Norwich Cathedral from 1977–90). Chairman of the Norfolk Gardens Trust. Grandson of Thomas Mawson, landscape architect, whose life and work he has been researching for many years.

ROSEMARY ANNE LAUDER

Author. Books include *Vanished Houses of North Devon* and *Picture of Devon* (Hale). Contributor to *Homes and Gardens* and *Country Life*, particularly on items of Devon interest.

DAVID RICHARDSON

Secretary of the Devon Gardens Trust. Architect and landscape architect within the Heritage Section of Devon County Council.

DOUGAL SWINSCOW

Qualified in medicine in 1940. On the editorial staff of the *British Medical Journal* for many years, and at the same time independently engaged in scientific research into lichens, co-authoring the standard work on the lichens of East Africa. A keen student of gardens and an expert photographer, he combined both interests in taking the colour photographs for this book. Dr Swinscow died in 1992.

Chapter One

THE GARDEN AND PARK IN DEVON

S T E V E N   P U G S L E Y

It has been said with justice that Devon, with its remarkable diversity of soils and climate, is gardening England in microcosm. This variety of conditions enables the area to support a surprising variety of plants and a wide spectrum of garden types and styles. While this is substantially true, it is also the case that associated geographical factors have at times limited the development of the art of gardening in the county. Historically, the narrow and not easily crossed land link between Devon and the rest of England, coupled with the difficulties of traversing the characteristically hilly county itself, led to a degree of cultural isolation. This remained largely so until the improvement of transport systems from the mid-eighteenth and particularly the nineteenth centuries, whereupon Devon became integrated with the national mainstream (in gardening terms, at least). The dominant topography of precipitous hills and steep-sided valleys may also have had an influence, in limiting the size of farms and estates and therefore the wealth derived from them that might have been devoted to creating landscapes of pleasure. Apart from a very few great proprietors, Devon has been a shire of small to middling estates from medieval times until the present day; unless some non-agricultural source of funds was available, this has tended to be reflected in similarly sized houses and accompanying gardens.[1]

Devon in the Middle Ages was not well endowed with large baronial establishments. Perhaps the most dazzling in its day was Dartington Hall, built between 1388 and 1399 by John Holand, Duke of Exeter and half-brother to Richard II. Holand was a noted jouster and the so-called Tiltyard – flanked by grass terraces and overlooked by a two-storey viewing gallery – may indeed have been just that.[2] A more sedate household was maintained by Princess Katherine, Countess of Devon, who spent much of her widowhood from 1511 to 1527 at Tiverton Castle. She administered her husband's Courtenay esates from the castle, described in a 1538 survey as:

> the head and chief mansion house, moated, walled and embattled round like a castle, with all manner of houses and offices and lodgings within the same, well kept and repaired and fair gardens to the same belonging.[3]

This description implies that Tiverton possessed a *hortus conclusus* – an enclosed garden. A household account of 1523–4 notes that a man was paid 4d. for two days' work breaking the ground to sow mustard seed, so it is possible that the countess also had some sort of herb garden.[4] These two familiar elements of medieval gardens

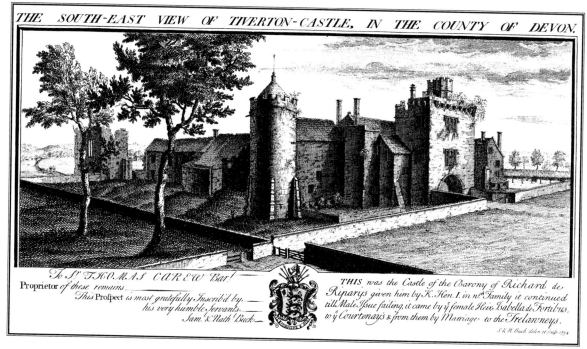

Tiverton Castle (Buck, 1734)

of the somewhat superior type were joined at Tiverton by a third – the park. Usually created for sporting purposes, for the hunting of deer, the park sometimes contained other features such as warrens and fish-ponds for the more direct provision of food. The Courtenays, rather unusually, had two parks at Tiverton, at Assheley and Guddesber.

Although they were the most considerable magnates in Devon in the Middle Ages, in national terms the Courtenays were among the poorest of their degree. Perhaps for this reason, their gardens at Tiverton seem not to have been particularly sophisticated. Similarly, although the Benedictine abbey at Tavistock was the wealthiest monastery west of Glastonbury, it was far from well-off compared to its sister houses elsewhere in the country. Tavistock Abbey appears to have had gardens of utility rather than ornament, with a fish-pond, deer park and orchards to supply the monks' table.[5]

Orchards were an important feature of Devon gardens, monastic and otherwise, for the growth of both fruit and cider apples. At the Dissolution their presence was often noted: at Buckland Abbey Sir Richard Grenville was granted the 'farm of the site with orchards, gardens, meadows, etc';[6] likewise at Totnes Priory, where the farm of the site was sold to Katherine Champernown and others with 'orchards and gardens';[7] and at Forde Abbey, where Richard Pollard purchased the 'Farm of the site, and grange, with orchards, gardens, meadows etc'.[8] Even in the early sixteenth century the tradition of the Devonshire orchard was an old one. In 1285–6 'apple gardens' were recorded on the Earl of Devon's estate at Exminster, Tiverton and Plympton.[9] By around 1600 John Hooker was able to write, in his *Synopsis Chorographical*, of Devon's 'orchards and aple gardens which be stored with all kinds of good frutes' and also of 'the Greate abundans of all kinds of frutes, aples, peares quynces and suche lyke wallnuts, medlers and others innumerable'.[10]

When the barton of Puslinch, some 5 miles from Plymouth, was the subject of a lease in 1641, it consisted of:

the Hall, the Parlour, the two butteries and the chambers over them, the two chambers over the larder, the western end of the barn, the higher stable, a pig house, close called New Meadow, orchard called the Pond garden, with walk or double hedge adjoining, lower herb-garden, the curtilage between the hall and the gate and the ways to them.[11]

Puslinch was, in other words, a fairly typical small Devon squire's house of the time, with an old-fashioned garden whose essential features would not have been out of place several centuries earlier. It is likely that a similar description could have been bestowed on many hundreds of messuages belonging to landowners the length and breadth of the county.

Devon seems to have escaped the expansive and complex tendencies of the Italian-inspired Renaissance garden, beloved of the Tudors and early Stuarts. In part this was due to sheer distance from London; at a period of growth of the centralized state and the waxing of the court at Westminster, Devon was inconveniently situated for the aspiring courtier. The county was thus deprived of the prodigy house and its associated landscape. The one exception might have been Berry Pomeroy Castle, where Lord Protector Somerset embarked on ambitious architectural additions between 1547 and his execution in 1552. These included a Renaissance loggia, described by Prince as

a noble walk . . . supported in the fore-part by several stately pillars . . . behind which were placed in the wall several seats of Freize stone also, cut into the form of an escallop shell in which the company, when aweary, might repose themselves.[12]

The rising lawyer class introduced a dash of sophistication into sixteenth- and seventeenth-century Devon, with men like Sir John Hele, whose house at Wembury – built around 1592, and probably the biggest house of its day in the county – was given a

noble park, well stocked with fallow-deer, whose reflexion, as they were grazing, might be seen in the marble clavels thro' the casements of the chamber chimnies

and

a large and profitable pond, strongly walled and gated; which gate upon the flood opened itself, and the tyde stored it, in its season, with sea fish of divers sorts.[13]

Nevertheless, the keynote was conservatism, and gardens recognizably medieval in form survived right up to the middle of the eighteenth century and later. Even such cosmopolitan figures as the George Trebys, father and son – the former Chief Justice of the Common Pleas and the latter Secretary at War – gave their new home, Plympton House, built 1700–20, a series of walled gardens. One of them was complete with a mount, a device often used in Tudor or even earlier gardens as a means of looking over the garden and out into the world beyond; in this instance, out over the village of Plympton St Maurice and into the south Devon countryside. The gardens at Powderham Castle, home to a junior branch of the Courtenays, were embattled around when they were depicted by Samuel Buck in 1734, and probably remained so until the 1750s. Sharpham, near Totnes, still had several small symmetrical plots, some patterned in the manner of uncomplicated Tudor knots, when it was drawn for an estate survey in 1749.[14] Killerton seems to have

Powderham Castle. The walled gardens (as depicted by Buck in 1734) probably remained in existence until the 1750s

retained its old formal garden right up to the building of a new classical mansion which replaced a Tudor building in 1770; an estate map of 1765 clearly shows a series of small enclosures and an orchard next to the H-shaped house.[15]

However, one aspect of the old-fashioned man-made landscape in Devon began to decline in popularity in the seventeenth century – the deer park. The historian Tristram Risdon, writing in the 1630s, remarked that 'many parks were disparked, and converted from pleasure to profit; from pasturing wild beasts to breeding of cattle, sheep and tillage'.[16] Risdon's comment offers further evidence of the advance of agriculture in Devonshire which resulted in much of the county being enclosed by 1600. Enclosure – in conjunction with Devon's characteristically undulating surface – limited the possibilities for expansive garden layouts. This was particularly so of the French baroque style which became prevalent in England following the restoration of Charles II in 1660. With its axial planning, *parterres de broderies* (elaborately patterned beds of flowers), ornamental ponds and water features, and *allées* (avenues), the French style demanded relatively flat and unbroken areas of ground, and such were at a premium in Devon.

Perhaps because it as a consequence lacked 'showpiece' gardens, Jan Kip and Leonard Knyff overlooked Devon when they compiled their invaluable book of views of country seats, *Britannia Illustrata*, published in 1708. The best visual record of the houses and gardens of Devonshire gentlemen at the beginning of the eighteenth century is to be found instead in the portfolio of drawings executed by the amateur artist Edmund Prideaux in 1716 and 1727.[17] Allowing for a somewhat naïve technique, the drawings appear to be remarkably faithful renderings of what Prideaux saw as he visited the homes of his friends and relations. They confirm that although Devon gardens of the period were relatively small in compass and generally backward-looking, they contained some of the elements – albeit provincially interpreted – associated with much grander gardens. While

Edmund Prideaux's early eighteenth-century view of Soldon, showing (right) a small parterre in an otherwise very simple garden

The French-inspired formal garden at Forde Abbey (Edmund Prideaux, *c.* 1727)

Thuborough at Sutcombe had little more than a couple of walled enclosures (one with an orchard), Soldon near Holsworthy possessed the curlicues of a small parterre. At Lynham (Yealmpton parish) there were definite hints of axial treatment, with a broad walk bisecting a series of decoratively-walled gardens, and at Poltimore not far from Exeter there were both a parterre, and an avenue leading up to the main entrance. All of these, however, paled before the grandeur of Forde Abbey, Thorncombe, the one Devon layout depicted by Prideaux which successfully aspired to the mainstream. At Forde the sumptuous array of cascade and canal, clipped evergreens, parterre and *allées* had little of the arrogance of the grandest French gardens, at Versailles and Marly, but nevertheless was a conscious echo of them. In favouring a style that flaunted the human mastery of nature, the absolutist French monarchs demonstrated by implication the complete control they exercised over their own kingdom. Their English cousins, harbouring a similar ambition, promoted it as the court gardening style. It is, therefore, hardly surprising that one of their more prominent public servants, Francis Gwyn, should have remodelled the grounds of his country seat, Forde Abbey, after this fashion upon succeeding to the property in 1702.[18]

It is ironic that Gwyn should have been Commissioner of Trade (1711–13) and Secretary at War (1713–14). These offices symbolize the principal routes whereby Britain gained great power status at the beginning of the eighteenth century, eclipsing France in the process and consequently diminishing the reputation of French culture in the eyes of the increasingly patriotic British. According to commentators like Lord Shaftesbury, 'Princely gardens' were a mockery, not worthy of respect.[19] Rather, classically educated Britons, who regarded classical antiquity as the most glorious epoch of human existence, began to turn their attention to Italy for inspiration; not to the terraced fancies of the Renaissance, but to the suggestions of the informality of Roman gardens contained in classical literature, and to the countryside of the Roman Campagna as depicted by the much collected artists Nicholas Poussin, Salvator Rosa and Gaspar Dughet, and witnessed in person on the Grand Tour. In doing so they sought a landscape of nature in its primitive state, which contrasted favourably with the artificiality of Versailles and its confrères, and which allowed flattering parallels to be drawn with the noble British virtues of liberty and freedom. The revolution in taste was not immediate. Not until 'Capability' Brown's arrival later in the century did the concept of the proto-landscape reach its zenith. Nevertheless, the 1730s and '40s witnessed a transitional phase, during which formality and informality coexisted in an increasingly unequal relationship.

In Devon, the Prideaux drawings are again valuable for illustrating the early course of this transfiguration. At Buckland Filleigh, for example, in north-west Devon, he depicts both an orchard and walled areas in his drawing inscribed 1728. Yet in 1735, the poet Alexander Pope – in his day perhaps the foremost advocate of 'following nature' – was exhorting Buckland's owner, William Fortescue, to

. . . concert this Michaelmas some improvements of your wood &c at Buckland *factura nepotibus umbras*. But cut some walks for yourself while you yet have legs and make some plain and smooth under your trees to admit a chaise or chariot when you have none.[20]

Prideaux portrayed a parterre with topiary and statues next to the house at Heanton Satchville, no later than 1727. Twelve years later, when Badeslade and Rocque published a view of the place in *Vitruvius Britannicus*, this layout had been swept away and replaced with a featureless lawn. Small, geometrical 'boxes' remained, but well away from the house, on the other side of the entrance forecourt.[21] In 1739, at Mount Edgcumbe, Badeslade and Rocque showed not only small gardens to the east and west of the house, but down nearer the waters of Plymouth Sound a 'wilderness' of trees, highly irregular in pattern, with a small temple at its heart. None of

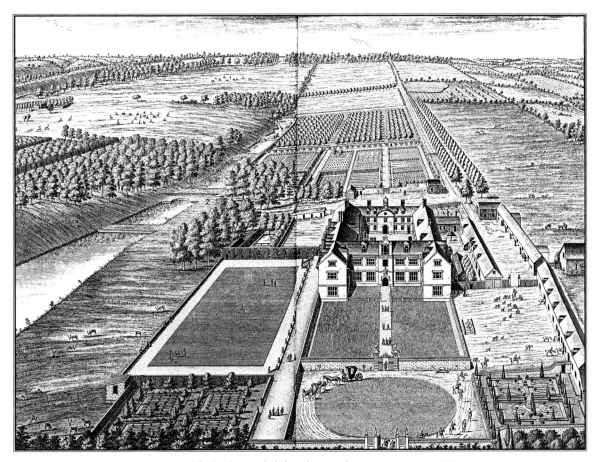

Heanton Satchville, from Badeslade and Rocque's *Britannia Illustrata* (1739)

this was apparent in the earlier Prideaux drawings of Mount Edgcumbe, so it is likely that these features were introduced in the 1730s.

It would be straining the point to claim that these gardens were of the significance of the outstanding transitional landscapes at Stowe, or Lord Burlington's Chiswick. Curiously, though, a *c.* 1730s design exists for Boringdon at Plympton which contains elements obviously derived from both.[22] Boringdon was home to the Parkers before their move to Saltram, and there is no particular evidence that they actually put the garden plan into effect before their departure. Had they done so, it would have been one of the most remarkable in Devon, with sinuous (and therefore natural) paths, and groves arranged like those at Chiswick, and a Temple of the Worthies and an Altar of the Saxon Gods clearly modelled on the Temple of the British Worthies and the Altar of the Saxon Gods at Stowe. At Stowe these buildings were calculated to provoke contemplation of the founders and defenders of British liberty and, by implication, the patriotic foundations of the new gardening style. It must have been the intention that Boringdon would have been, likewise, in part a garden of association in which the ideas and sensations provoked by an object or scene were as important as their purely visual aspects.

The designer associated with these features at Stowe and Chiswick was Lord Burlington's protégé, William Kent. Landscapist, architect and artist, Kent had trained as a painter in Italy and therefore not only produced

classical garden buildings aplenty to remind the educated observer of the ancients, but carefully composed his garden scenes to resemble a landscape picture. William Kent's personal involvement at Boringdon is unlikely. Rocque's engraving of the Chiswick plan and the local example of the Mount Edgcumbe wilderness are the probable sources of inspiration for the anonymous designer.

Kent's name has also been linked over the years, and with no greater substance in fact, to Werrington Park near Launceston and to Castle Hill at Filleigh in north Devon. At Castle Hill, it is true, Lord Burlington advised its owner Hugh, first Baron Fortescue, on the remodelling of the house in 1729. Paintings of Castle Hill by Lange (dated 1741) show an eclectic assortment of garden buildings (some of which might merely have been projected).[23] There is some suggestion, therefore, of a Kentian pictorial/associational intent. Be that as it may, there is no incontrovertible evidence of Kent's involvement. Certainly, to contemporary observers the landscape seemed to be fully in the French taste, with its grass terraces falling away from the house to a cruciform pond, and the axis prolonged across the valley with an avenue ascending to an eye-catcher (an arch) on the opposite hill. Hugh Fortescue was a frequent visitor to France, and it is to be suspected that he brought back with him an idea or two, if not a complete plan.

At the opposite end of the county, Bicton near Budleigh Salterton, formerly the seat of the Rolles, is of a strikingly similar design. The eye is led from a classical temple down over a series of grass terraces to a regular

Castle Hill, 1741. One of a pair of paintings by J. Lange, showing the axial treatment of the landscape, with eye-catching buildings scattered liberally throughout

A vista at Bicton, photographed in 1903

body of water, and then beyond that to an obelisk on a distant hill. The layout at Bicton is dated 1735 and sometimes ascribed to the great French gardener André Le Nôtre; however, Le Nôtre had by 1735 been dead for thirty-five years, so this attribution seems unlikely. A more plausible explanation for the scheme at Bicton is that the Rolles, who were major north Devon landowners, had already witnessed the probably slightly earlier development at Castle Hill and simply devised a version of the same thing for their own property. In this connection it is worth noting that a Rolle of Hudscott, a few miles from Castle Hill, was a trustee in 1732 for the new church and yard at Filleigh, built to replace those lost when Castle Hill mansion and garden were extended.[24]

The landscapes at Bicton and Castle Hill exemplify two particularly important themes in Devon garden history of this period. First, the tenacity of the formal impulse. Long after 1751, when Hugh Fortescue's half-brother and successor Matthew had begun to deformalize the layout at Castle Hill, the steward Hilliard preached caution wth regard to the grass terraces or 'slopes':

I have observed strangers who have any pretensions to taste dislike the slopes from mere motives of prejudice, and have heard them give their opinions with a promptness which seemed to betray an inconsiderable judgement. It has happened that some, upon reflection, have retracted and rather approved of what they had hastily condemned.[25]

To this day the form of the slopes survives intact to a considerable degree.

The sweeping view over the park at Mount Edgcumbe towards Plymouth (W. Finden, after J.D. Harding and Jendle, 1842)

The second theme is that of the private improver. In common with most of the rest of the country up to the mid-eighteenth century, the bulk of the gardens so far noted in Devon were almost certainly the work of amateur enthusiasts, laying out their own grounds, albeit with the published assistance of Batty Langley and others. Nor did this tendency cease. At Mount Edgcumbe, for example, successive lords Edgcumbe and earls of Mount Edgcumbe transformed the place into one of the most visited landscapes in England from the 1740s onwards. They capitalized on its natural setting to juxtapose a series of enclosed gardens and glades with boundless vistas over land and sea; these were in turn designed to arouse a series of different emotions in the visitor: of pleasure and terror, melancholy and rapture. At Nutwell Court, near Exmouth, Sir Francis Henry Drake took a very particular interest in the formal planting of his garden in the mid-1700s. Not far away, at Oxton, Kenn, the Revd John Swete brought his Picturesque eye to bear upon a garden which, upon inheriting it in 1767, he found to be old-fashioned and formal. Notwithstanding, he recognized that

> If I accomodated my plans to what nature had herself done a sweet valley would be found . . . where every object visible was not only discriminated but rural and picturesque . . .

and so from 1781 he proceeded to remodel the grounds accordingly.[26]

The impact of the amateurs, individuals of taste and learning, was profound and continuing, in Devon as elsewhere. Nevertheless, from around 1750 the professional landscape gardener gained an ever more secure

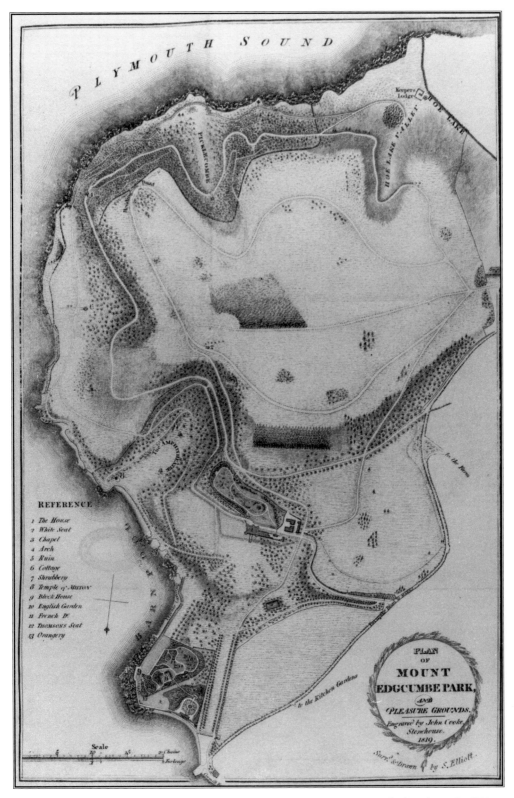

Plan of Mount Edgcumbe, 1819, by S. Elliott (from *A Walk Around Mount Edgcumbe*, 7th edn., Plymouth, 1821)

foothold. The most prominent was Lancelot Brown, nicknamed 'Capability' from his habit, when viewing the site of a new commission, of saying 'I see great capabilities of improvement here'.

As head gardener at Stowe in the 1740s he evolved a formula which he was to use throughout England in the succeeding forty years on over 200 commissions – indeed, it has been said that 'much of what we now accept as the "natural" landscape of lowland England is the work of "Capability" Brown and his followers.'[27]

Brown's most characteristic work in Devon is at Ugbrooke Park, laid out for the fourth Baron Clifford around 1770. The aim and method are clear. Brown sought to re-create a state of simple and perfect nature, such as existed in the ancient world. With this object in view, he dispensed with the embellishments and symbols of the associational garden and filled his landscape instead with the three basic elements of grass, water and wood. At Ugbrooke he arranged these in his customary fashion: a perimeter belt of woodland, encircling a park of gentle hills, with greensward running right up to the mansion; clumps of trees were scattered through this verdant setting; and – in the middle distance from the house – a sheet of water was created by damming a small stream to form three lakes.[28] Three other Devon gardens are also linked with Lancelot Brown. The earliest, dated to the 1750s, is Widdicombe House at Stokenham, owned by a Holdsworth of the Dartmouth merchant dynasty. This attribution remains unproven, as does Brown's possible involvement at Sharpham House near Totnes. There is definite evidence, however, of Brown giving advice to the third Viscount Lisburne about the repair of Mamhead House and the enhancement of its environs in 1773, this being the landscapist's last recorded venture into the county, some ten years before his death.[29]

'Capability' Brown's characteristic landscape at Ugbrooke (W. Le Petit, after T. Allom, 1832)

The park at Saltram designed by 'Capability' Brown's one-time assistant, Nathaniel Richmond (W. Angus, after Lord Duncannon, 1790)

Brown came to dominate his profession, but his brightly burning flame did not completely obscure the glow of lesser lights. Many 'followers' practised in the Brownian manner both during and after his lifetime, notably Richmond, Eames, and Woods. Of this triumvirate, Nathaniel Richmond[30] – a sometime Brown assistant – is known to have worked in Devon. He laid out the park at Saltram for John Parker, first Lord Boringdon, between 1767 and 1774, probably upon the recommendation of the Parkers' friends, the Pelhams of Stanmer in Sussex. It is worth remarking, however, that Lord Boringdon took an active and personal interest in the development of the landscape, quite apart from what Richmond had done. In late 1784, for example, 38,000 trees arrived by ship for use in his lordship's plantations,[31] and in January 1785, expressing a wish to acquire many curious plants, he enquired of his brother-in-law if he had any seeds from Spain.[32]

None the less, the figure most usually singled out as Brown's successor is Humphry Repton. Having lived the life of a political secretary, merchant and, latterly, artistically-minded country gentleman, Repton had little training in the practicalities of gardening. He sprang from the realms of the amateur improver. The story has it that he simply awoke one morning in 1788 and announced to his friends that he had become a landscape gardener. In the following thirty years he contrived to work on nearly two hundred properties. Repton himself acknowledged the inspiration of three men: Brown, Richmond (interestingly, in view of his subsequent obscurity), and Kent. The Kentian connection is especially enlightening in that it emphasizes the pictorial nature of so much of Repton's work. The late eighteenth-century Picturesque theorists, notably Richard Payne Knight and Uvedale Price, building on essentially early eighteenth-century concepts, called for a landscape of intricacy and variety to produce a scene such as only a painter could envisage. They lambasted Brown for his 'monotony and baldness'[33] and coupled Repton with him in their attack. In fact, although Repton owned that 'utility must often take the lead of beauty and convenience be preferred to Picturesque effect', he too was equally concerned to introduce the qualities of intricacy and variety into his work.

Nowhere is this more clearly seen than in the two landscapes he designed in Devon: at Luscombe Castle, Dawlish, for the banker Charles Hoare in 1799, and Endsleigh Cottage, Milton Abbot, for the sixth Duke of Bedford in 1814. In his Red Book of proposals for Luscombe, he prescribed 'a foreground of highly dressed Lawn and Pleasure Garden on which trees or shrubs may be planted to vary the surface', thus introducing resources of 'cheerfulness and intricacy'.[34] At Luscombe the differences between the techniques of Repton and of Brown are readily apparent, the former favouring moving water rather than a lake (in this case, the sea in full view), lusher planting, and the reintroduction of a flower- and shrub-bedecked terrace to distinguish the environs of the mansion house from the park. These features are equally present at Endsleigh Cottage. Repton, in what is one of his most accomplished landscapes, used to full effect the dramatic views of the River Tamar, its valley sides clothed with dense plantations. Near the house, he planned a terrace with rock plants, fruit walls and a conservatory, and a children's flower garden.[35]

It would be a mistake to assume that interest in the growing of flowers suddenly died out during the age of 'Capability' Brown, as is sometimes suggested. It is the case, however, that floriculture gained considerably in

Luscombe Castle. Humphry Repton's garden, full of Picturesque 'intricacy and variety' (W. Le Petit, after T. Allom, 1830)

popularity at the beginning of the nineteenth century. This was in part due to the increased attention given by landscape gardeners like Repton, but more particularly because nursery firms were importing and raising an ever greater number of species drawn from all over the world (many of which could only be cultivated in the heated glasshouses made possible by the technological advances of this period). Several Devon nurserymen took a leading role in this process, of whom the Veitchs of Exeter are undoubtedly the best known. The founder of the dynasty, John Veitch, came to Killerton from Scotland in 1771 at the behest of Sir Thomas Acland, the seventh baronet, to lay out the park. He became a trusted adviser and agent for the Acland estates, but also found time to create a nursery and to act as a landscape designer for other estates. The nursery moved from Budlake near Killerton to Mount Radford in Exeter in about 1830 and continued, on different sites but still under the direction of the Veitch family, until 1969. The firm employed the finest collectors, including the brothers Lobb, and Richard Pearce, and the hybridizer John Dominy, who all contributed to its worldwide reputation. The other major Exeter nurserymen, Lucombe, Pince and Company (as they became in the 1820s), were also active in this field, introducing the first English tea rose, the Devonport-raised *Rosa* 'Devoniensis', in 1841, and specializing in the hybridization of fuchsias.[36]

It was the super-energetic Scot, John Claudius Loudon, who perhaps developed Reptonian principles most successfully and in doing so laid the foundations for nineteenth-century gardening. In the *Gardener's Magazine* which he founded in 1826, and in a host of other publications, he argued that a garden was a work of art; any attempt, therefore, to create the illusion of nature merely exhibited poor taste. The growth of non-native species which could not possibly survive without assistance, and geometric layouts, were honest statements of artistic contrivance, maintaining at the same time the intricacy and variety beloved of Repton.

These well-propagated beliefs gave rise to two distinct strands of Victorian gardening, the first, the great collections of trees organized into arboreta and pineta, such as that at Bicton. Planting in the arboretum there, upon which Loudon advised, began in around 1830, and in the pinetum in 1839. When Loudon and his wife visited Bicton in 1842 he remarked that:

> One great beauty of the Bicton arboretum is, that every tree and shrub which it contains may be seen, and the name on its label read, by a person while sitting in a carriage, and driving through it along the green walk.[37]

The second strand of Victorian gardening was the expression of intricacy and variety through the re-establishement of formality and the bedding-out of exotics. When Loudon called at Kitley (Yealmpton parish) in 1842 he was shown the relatively simple symmetrical layout, reputedly designed by the sculptor Sir Francis Chantrey. This was planted with blue lobelia, *Phlox drummondii*, geraniums of various hues, petunias, verbena, white centaurea and yellow pyrethum.[38] Generally speaking, designs became increasingly complex as the century wore on, often carried out in a rather fussy Italianate style distinguished by terraces, fountains, clipped conifers, evergreens, sculpture and geometric bedding. At Powderham, the scheme developed at the time of the castle's remodelling by Charles Fowler between 1837 and 1848 centred on a terrace garden with geometrical massed bedding and columnar Irish yews. At Mamhead the plan included terraces, clipped yews, an intricate semi-circular bed and a quadripartite parterre with central fountain – a scheme which may have been devised, following the completion of the house in 1838, by W.A. Nesfield, who became one of the most prominent garden designers of the mid-Victorian period.[39]

Whereas Powderham was the seat of an earl and Mamhead of a baronet, Streatham Hall on the outskirts of Exeter was built as the residence of an East India merchant, Richard Thornton West, in 1866. Thornton West

Mamhead. The remains of the mid-nineteenth-century Italianate scheme, possibly devised by W.A. Nesfield, *c.* 1838

had inherited over a million pounds from an uncle – said to have been a blockade runner in the Napoleonic Wars – and spent a considerable amount of it on his Exeter property: some £80,000 on the house (a scaled-down Osborne) and £70,000 on laying out the estate.[40] The grounds included an arboretum, planted by Messrs Veitch with many specimens which were possibly the first of their kind in Europe; a series of elaborate terraces connected by flights of balustraded stone steps; and a group of hothouses of which the Palm House was described by *Country Life* in 1899 as

> . . . certainly one of the finest in the West of England and . . . artistically planted with ferns, palms and foliage plants tastefully disposed amongst the rockwork.[41]

The fondness for the Italianate persisted right up until the First World War. But even before 1914, the decline in income from landed property associated with the Great Agricultural Depression of the late nineteenth century served to make a style which was so expensive to create and maintain progressively less alluring. Perhaps its last great flowering in Devon was at Lindridge, Bishopsteignton, designed by Edward White of Milner White and Son for Sir Ernest Cable in 1913–14. Cable, created a peer in 1921, was another East India merchant; he did not have to rely on the precarious profits of a Devon estate to finance his ambitious garden scheme, but rather was able to devote to it the fruits of a successful career in commerce in the sub-continent. Photographs of the terraces sweeping down from the house to a domed rotunda set in the middle of a lily pond

indicate that the garden at Lindridge was impressive (or, at least, designed to impress). Be that as it may, when Christopher Hussey came to write of the property in 1938 he was critical of the design, and hinted that the entire idiom had run to seed:

> . . . the criticism may be made that, as seen from the house, it is a little lacking in strength. The general effect inclines to be spotty and the architectural features insufficiently bold in relation to the extent and dignity of the plan. . . . These blemishes (in my opinion) are largely characteristic of pre-War garden design. . . .[42]

Facets of the Italianate – conspicuously, carpet bedding – contrive to flourish to this day in the many public parks in Devon, especially on the coast. The principal alternative to the Italianate in private situations was what became known in the 1890s as 'the formal garden'. This style, however, had roots which reached back to the 1860s at least, when interest in cottage gardens increased and with it a preoccupation with the hardy flowers and herbaceous plants that they contained. This by no means betokened a widespread lurch towards wild gardening. Rather, it was believed that cottage gardens were characterized by simpler geometrical patterns, based on the regular subdivision of rectangles and circles, on straight paths, clipped yews and gardens split up into compartments by hedges and trellises.

Lindridge. The terraces and Italian garden as seen from the house in 1938

Sir Edwin Lutyens and Thomas Mawson were perhaps the leading members of this late nineteeth- and early twentieth-century school of reformed formality. Their work in Devon includes Mawson at Wood near South Tawton (1898–1905), and Hannaford Manor, Poundsgate (*c*. 1906);[43] and Lutyens at Castle Drogo, Drewsteignton (*c*. 1920), with planting by George Dillistone,[44] Mothecombe, Holbeton (1922–5), and Saunton Court near Braunton (1932). Two of Lutyens' pupils were also vigorous in this sphere. Oswald Milne is thought to have planned the architectural garden features at Coleton Fishacre (Kingswear), concurrently with the house which he produced for Rupert D'Oyly Carte in 1925–6.[45] Fred Harrild, who had been articled to Lutyens from 1907 to 1910, designed the garden at Castle Tor, Torquay, around 1928–34, based on a series of limestone terraces and highly reminiscent of his mentor. But perhaps the most influential garden of this type is Dartington Hall, the product of several rather than merely one designer: H. Avray Tipping in 1927, Beatrix Farrand in 1933 and Percy Cane from 1945.[46]

A common theme of so many of these large early twentieth-century gardens is that they were built using non-landed sources of wealth – Dorothy Elmhirst, the châtelaine of Dartington, for instance, injected her substantial resources as an American heiress into the purchase and development of the estate. Nevertheless, such layouts depended on the use of plentiful and cheap skilled labour, and when that came to an end with the Second World War so the formal garden fell out of fashion. Greater reliance was placed thenceforward on flowering shrubs in garden design, which gave all the 'variety of colour, texture and form of herbaceous plantings' but with less work.[47] This is typified by the simplification of the formalized Victorian planting at Knightshayes near Tiverton after 1950, and the extension of the garden into the woods with the introduction of bulbs and shrubs.[48]

Many notable post-war gardens derive their character from informal plantings of choice shrubs and trees which thrive in the Devon soil and climate. Marwood Hill, the Garden House (Buckland Monachorum), and Rosemoor near Great Torrington are particularly fine examples of the genre. Under the guiding hand of Lady Anne Palmer, Rosemoor developed into a plantsman's garden first and foremost, with all the freedom of structure that that implies.[49] Despite this, the Royal Horticultural Society, to whom Lady Anne presented the garden to become their western outpost, have proceeded to add new areas of quite massive geometric bedding. Although this is barely in keeping with the original, it is arguably fully in accord with the late twentieth-century trend towards the re-establishment of formality as a viable alternative style.

This new movement arises in large measure from the burgeoning awareness of the historical importance of parks and gardens. The growth of the National Trust's property holdings after 1945 and the subsequent explosion in visitor numbers contributed towards an enhanced scholarly study of country houses and their surroundings and deepening public appreciation of them. This has led some private individuals to experiment with new formal gardens of their own (greatly helped by the advent of labour-saving machinery), and institutions such as the National Trust to re-create period gardens like the highly successful 'Victorian' flower garden at Arlington Court, north Devon. More than this, many historic landscapes are now subject to thorough investigation with the aim of faithful restoration, including Castle Hill and Endsleigh. National government has conferred recognition, if not statutory protection, with the compilation of the English Heritage *Register of Parks and Gardens of Special Historic Interest,* on which thirty-six Devon gardens now figure. The local counterpart to this national initiative has been provided by the County Gardens Trusts which became a potent force in the 1980s and early '90s. The Devon Gardens Trust was founded in 1988 with the stated purposes of promoting the education of the public on matters connected with the arts and sciences of garden land, and to preserve, enhance and re-create for the education and enjoyment of the public whatever garden land may exist or have existed in and around the county of Devon. The Trust's energy in prosecuting these objectives testifies to the dynamic interest which Devonians still take in gardens and gardening.

REFERENCES

1. W.G. Hoskins, 'The Ownership and Occupation of the Land in Devonshire 1650–1800' (unpublished Ph.D. thesis, University of London, 1938), pp. 1–23.

2. A. Emery, 'Dartington Hall, Devonshire', *Archaeological Journal* CXV (1958), pp. 201–2.

3. M. Westcott, 'Katherine Courtenay, Countess of Devon, 1479–1527', in T. Gray, M. Rowe, and A. Erskine (eds), *Tudor and Stuart Devon: the Common Estate and Government* (Exeter, 1992), p. 24.

4. Westcott, 'Katherine Courtenay', p. 27.

5. H.P.R. Finberg, 'A Cellarer's Account Book' in W.G. Hoskins and H.P.R. Finberg, *Devonshire Studies* (1952), pp. 261–4; H.P.R. Finberg, *Tavistock Abbey: a Study in the Social and Economic History of Devon* (Cambridge, 1951).

6. J.A. Youings, (ed.), *Devon Monastic Lands: Particulars for Grants, 1536–55,* DCRS, New Series, 1 (1955), pp. 18–19.

7. Youings, *Devon Monastic Lands*, p. 19.

8. Youings, *Devon Monastic Lands*, p. 13.

9. W.G. Hoskins, *Devon* (2nd edn., Tiverton, 1992), p. 94.

10. W.J. Blake, (ed.), 'Hooker's Synopsis Chorographical of Devonshire', in *Devonshire Association Transactions* 47 (1915), pp. 337, 334.

11. W(est) D(evon) R(ecord) O(ffice), Yonge 107/65, Lease, 2 March 1640/1.

12. J. Prince, *The Worthies of Devon* (1810 edn), p. 649.

13. Prince, *Worthies*, pp. 485–6.

14. M. Binney, 'Sharpham House, Devon', *Country Life*, cxlv (1969), p. 955.

15. D(evon) R(ecord) O(ffice), Acland 1148M/add/10/5/1.

16. T. Risdon, *Survey of the County of Devon* (1810 edn.), pp. 6–7.

17. J. Harris, 'The Prideaux Drawings', *Architectural History*, 7 (1964).

18. J. Cornforth, 'Forde Abbey, Dorset', *Country Life* cxxxiii (1963), pp. 540–3, 595–9, 656–9, 714–7.

19. Anthony Ashley Cooper, third Earl of Shaftesbury, *The Moralists* (1709).

20. R. Polwhele, *History of Devonshire* (3 Vols, 1793–1806), vol. 1, p. 325, Pope to William Fortescue, 3 September 1737.

21. T. Badeslade, and J. Rocque, *Vitruvius Britannicus*, vol. IV (1739), plates 73–4.

22. J. Cornforth, 'The Making of the Saltram Landscape', *Country Life*, cxli (1967), pp. 594–7.

23. J. Harris, *The Artist and the Country House* (1979), Nos. 186 and 186b.

24. Filleigh Church Records, transferred to Chittlehampton. Deed, 1732.

25. DRO Fortescue 1262M/E29–17. Hilliard to Fortescue, 23 June 1771.

26. DRO 564/M, F2. J. Swete, *Devon Tour*, vol. 2 (1792).

27. R. Bisgrove, *The English Garden* (1990), p. 99.

28. A. Rowan, 'The Landscape at Ugbrooke, Devon', *Country Life*, cxli (1967), pp. 790–3.

29. D. Stroud, *Capability Brown* (new edn. 1975) and R. Turner, *Capability Brown* (1985).

30. D. Brown, 'Nathaniel Richmond (1724–1784) – a Research Note' in *Garden History Society Newsletter*, 36 (Autumn 1992), pp. 22–3.

31. WDRO Parker of Saltram 1259/3/57. Letter from Anne Robinson to Frederick Robinson, 20 December 1784.

32. WDRO Parker of Saltram 1259/3/58. Letter from Anne Robinson to Frederick Robinson, 18 January 1785.

33. U. Price, *Three Essays on the Picturesque*, I (1810), pp. 50–1.

34. C. Hussey, 'Luscombe Castle, Devon', *Country Life,* cxix (1956), pp. 248–1, 292–5, 336–9.

35. C. Hussey, 'Endsleigh, Devon', *Country Life*, cxxx (1961), pp. 246–9, 296–9; H. Repton, *Fragments on the Theory and Practise of Landscape Gardening* (1816), Fragment xxxiv, pp. 213–26.

36. C. Rogers, 'The Historical Background' in the National Council for the Conservation of Plants and Gardens – Devon Group, *The Magic Tree* (Exeter, 1989), pp. 16–28.

37. P. Boniface, (ed.), *In Search of English Gardens: The Travels of John Claudius Loudon and his Wife Jane* (1987), p. 246.

38. WDRO Kitley 74/540/14/5; Boniface, *Loudon Tour*, p. 242.

39. S. Evans, 'Talented Twice Over', *Country Life*, clxxxvii (1993), pp. 64–6.

40. J. Caldwell et al., *The Grounds and Gardens of the University of Exeter* (Exeter, 1969), pp. 5–28.

41. 'Streatham Hall, Exeter', *Country Life*, v (1899), pp. 496–500.

42. C. Hussey, 'Lindridge, Devon', *Country Life,* lxxxiv (1938), p. 360.

43. T.H. Mawson, *The Art and Craft of Garden-Making* (5th edn., 1926).

44. J. Sales, 'Where Jekyll Would Not Do', *Country Life,* clxxvii (1985), pp. 60–2.

45. H. Hellyer, 'A Doyly Carte Garden Rediscovered', *Country Life,* clxxxi (1987), pp. 78–80.

46. R. Snell, *From the Bare Stem: Making Dorothy Elmhirst's Garden at Dartington Hall* (Exeter, 1989).

47. R. Page, 'English Gardens from 1900 to the Present Day', in J. Harris (ed.), *The Garden* (1979), p. 72.

48. H. Meller, *Knighthayes Court* (National Trust, 1984), pp. 35–9.

49. H. Hellyer, 'Rare Plants in a Composed Setting', *Country Life,* clxxix (1986), pp. 982–4.

Chapter Two

THE MEDIEVAL, TUDOR AND STUART PARKS OF DEVON

ROBERT ILES

The earliest parks in Devon were created as medieval hunting reserves. They were similar to later landscape parks in only two respects: first, they were large open areas while at the same time enclosed and separate from agricultural land; secondly, in their time, they were large and ostentatious status symbols of the wealthy and powerful.

It has been estimated that over 1,900 parks were created in medieval England[1] and that figure is likely to be a considerable underestimate. Although not all were in use at the same time, parkland must have been a fairly common feature of the landscape. Devon had fewer medieval parks than counties to the east, although probably more than has been generally appreciated. Nevertheless, there are at least forty-five references to parks in Devon between 1086 and 1500 and a further fourteen possible ones on the basis of later field name evidence.

The owners of these parks ranged from the Crown down to the level of a lord, who might have a few manors. The king, of course, also had exclusive rights of hunting in the Royal Forests of Dartmoor and Exmoor.[2] An eminent family might aspire to own a number of parks scattered on its major landholdings, frequently close to where it had a castle. For instance, the Courtenays had parks at Chulmleigh, Colyton, Norton, Okehampton and Tiverton. Even the more important ecclesiastical landlords aspired to their own parks; the bishops of Exeter had parks at Crediton, Morchard Bishop and Paignton. William Talbot is an example of a lesser lord who had his own park. In the late thirteenth century he held three manors, on one of which, Spreyton, he had what was described as a little park.

Medieval parks varied widely in size, which in part reflected the wealth and status of their owners. Most parks, though, were between 100 and 200 acres in extent. Two fairly typical parks were Dartington and Berry Pomeroy, which were described as being 100 acres in the early fourteenth century. At Uffculme, Richard Coggan was given a licence to enclose the wood of Uffculme and 300 acres in 1336. Undoubtedly the size of the parks changed over time, many of them becoming larger, although some did shrink. Dartington, for example, ended up at 66 acres.

It is often assumed that it was necessary to get a royal licence to enclose a park, but I have found only eight documented examples in Devon. The earliest licence found is for Berry Pomeroy Park in 1207. Four licences date from the fourteenth century including one, at Weycroft, for 800 acres. Even towards the end of the seventeenth century, landowners still occasionally obtained licences from the Crown, as happened for Ugbrook Park (1673) and Boringdon Park (1699).

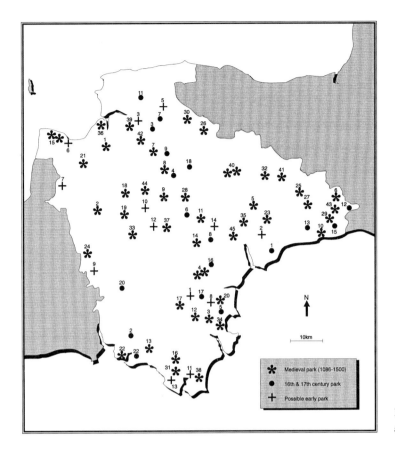

Distribution of early parks in Devon (see appendix, p. 27)

The commonest documentary references to early parks result from the activities of poachers, which not only provided good game and venison but were also a means of cocking a snook at the local lord. In one example, at Morchard Bishop Park in 1334, a large group of poachers were mainly members of just three families. The price for getting caught was high, so this activity could lead to some violent incidents. A group of poachers at Langdon Park in 1345 took some deer and then assaulted the owner's servants, incapacitating many of them for a long time.

Sometimes poachers came from sections of society that might not normally be expected to engage in such activities. In a case of poaching at North Molton Park in 1339 one of the accused was T. Fleming, the parson of South Molton. In another case in 1265 at the Bishop of Exeter's park at Paignton, Henry de Pomeroy admitted climbing over and damaging the park ditches and killing a number of deer. In recompense he agreed to replace the dead beasts (presumably from his own park at nearby Berry Pomeroy), repair the damaged ditches and give a guarantee of 100 marks.

The main purpose of a medieval park was to keep and hunt deer. Some parks were really too small to hunt in and would have been little more than a sort of larder for fresh venison. The deer and the maintenance of the park would have been the responsibility of a paid official, the park keeper or parker. One is referred to in the eleventh-century Winkleigh Park. When Thomas Courtenay forfeited his lands to the king in 1469, the king appointed Richard Milton to be his parker for the Assheley and Guddesber parks in the manor of Tiverton. He received sixpence a day as wages for this office. The two parks in one ownership at Tiverton was not a common occurrence, but there are other documented examples at Bovey Tracey and Hartland. It may have resulted from keeping different types of deer – fallow and red deer – in separate but adjoining parks.

While venison was highly prized, the keeping of deer could not be justified economically. Frequently the land in parks was put to additional uses, some of which were economic and others more associated with lordly whims and privileges. An example of the latter was the establishment of part of the park for use as a warren or the creation of fish-ponds; the park boundary provided them with extra security. A value was often given for the pasture or wood within a park. An inquisition post-mortem in 1314 for Gilbert de Clare included a reference to his park at Chittlehamholt, which was 800 acres and had herbage, pannage and loppings worth 20s. a year.

Early parks usually had circular or elliptical boundaries without projections or indentations. This was deliberate, because the major cost of creating and maintaining a park was its long boundaries. Parks were normally created out of woodland and waste beyond the cultivated land. Okehampton Park was laid out in about 1300 partly over a number of demesne farms and fields, but the circumstances are unusual and these farms appear to have been in existence for only about one hundred years, on land that is marginal.[3]

The actual boundary of an early park was usually a hedge or paling on top of a bank with an internal ditch. Where stone was readily available the park might be enclosed by a stone wall. The remains of substantial stone park walls can still be seen around sections of the parks of Berry Pomeroy, Dartington and Chagford. Much more common, though, was the paling fence, which is invariably shown demarcating parks on the county maps of Saxton and Speede (see overleaf). Some parks also utilized watercourses for boundaries. More than half of Okehampton Park was bounded by watercourses.

Internal ditches were often present to make it more difficult for deer to leap out, although they might be able to jump in from outside. Some parks also had a special device known as a deerleap, which was created specially to allow deer in but not out again. West Ogwell seems to have had two deerleaps. In 1306 a piece of land was purchased on the east side of Okehampton Park to make a deerleap.

As mentioned earlier, deer parks often possessed fish-ponds and warrens, the latter being as much of an attraction as the deer for poachers. In 1363 some men broke into the Bishop of Salisbury's park at Chardstock and took deer from the park and hares, rabbits, pheasants and partridges from the warren. It is likely that remains of warrens within parks take the form of boundary walls or long low mounds, called pillow mounds by archaeologists. The outline of two fish-ponds can still be seen in Berry Pomeroy Park, in the valley just to the north of the castle; there also seems to have been a water-mill there.

Lodges were the only buildings to be found in medieval parks. They were built either as houses for the park keeper or, more grandly, to be used by a lord on hunting trips. The remains of a lodge are to be found in the centre of Dartington Park. Perhaps Berry Pomeroy Castle, which was in the centre of a medieval park, was established originally as a park lodge by the Pomeroys. Likewise, the Courtenays may have refurbished and rebuilt the domestic apartments at Okehampton Castle because of its proximity to the good hunting grounds of Okehampton Park. It has also been suggested that one of the earthwork remains in the centre of Okehampton Park may have served as a park lodge.

Woodland was an important element in medieval parks, providing cover and forage for deer. A fifteenth-century licence to impark Hatch Park in Loddiswell specifically referred to its including two areas of woodland, one of 60 acres and the other of 40 acres. The distribution of medieval parks in Devon is very similar to that of woodland recorded in Domesday.[4] The areas with the least or no woodland, such as the high moors and north-western Devon, are the areas that had very few parks. The culm measures belt across the centre of the county had the most woodland and the greatest density of parks.

Most medieval parks in Devon were created in the thirteenth and fourteenth centuries. New parks continued to be made between the fifteenth and seventeenth centuries, although not in such numbers. These later parks

Part of Speede's map of Devon (1610) showing several deer parks

The ruins of Okehampton Castle. The Courtenays may have favoured residence here as it was adjacent to the good hunting grounds of Okehampton Park (S. Alken, after the Revd T. Rackett, 1797)

were different in character: they could no longer be carved out of the waste on the fringe of farmland. They were also more likely to have irregular boundaries. From the late medieval period onwards they began to be valued for amenity; grand houses were built in them, but they would still have had deer and might have been used for hunting. For instance, Bicton Park and House date from the sixteenth century and there were deer in the park until 1946.

Many parks were disparked in the late medieval and early post-medieval period as there was pressure to make more economic use of the land by dividing it up into fields. The medieval parks of Weycroft, Coldridge and Dartington all seem to have been disparked by the early seventeenth century. Other parks survived, perhaps changing in size, into fairly recent times. Dunsford Park, dating from the fifteenth century, was only disparked and divided into separate farms in 1860. A good number of older parks have even survived to the present day, although their boundaries may have been altered several times.

Comparatively little research has been done on medieval parks in Devon. The only park that has been looked at in detail is Okehampton Park, the medieval and later landscape of which has been the subject of a great deal of scrutiny.[5] In many ways Okehampton Park is not typical. It is believed to have occupied more than 1,600 acres and was built right alongside Okehampton Castle. Interestingly, excavations in the castle have produced evidence of two different sorts of deer bones: native red deer, presumably hunted in the forest

Bicton Park and House, dating from the sixteenth century (J. Walker and J. Greig, after Miss Rolle, 1800)

of Dartmoor; and, from the 1300s, fallow deer, which were probably specially introduced into the deer park.[6]

This brief survey of early parks in Devon has been based on limited research, mainly using general accounts,[7] the Devon Sites and Monuments Record, notes made by L. Gallant (held with the Sites and Monuments Record), and Public Record Office calendars. There remains great scope for identifying further documented medieval parks and for filling in this skeletal outline by the study of individual parks. The main sources are documentary references, place and field names and the actual evidence on the ground for park boundaries and associated features.

If there has been little research on early parks in Devon, there has been virtually none on early gardens. Manor houses, later medieval castles and monasteries would all have had small enclosed gardens, and it should be possible to locate them. In the sixteenth and early seventeenth centuries gardens were still formal and enclosed but became much more extensive, and considerable evidence of them should still be visible.

The best evidence often survives where an important house was abandoned at an early date. One particularly noteworthy example is the garden remains at Oldstone, Blackawton, where the Royal Commission on The Historical Monuments of England has recently noted and then surveyed the surviving earthworks and garden structures over a large area. Curiously, other places to look for Tudor and Stuart gardens are monastic sites occupied after the Dissolution by grand houses.[8] There must be many more early remains like those of Oldstone waiting to be discovered in Devon.

APPENDIX

Medieval Parks

1   Annery, Monkleigh 1420
2   Beaworthy 1366
3   Berry Pomeroy 1303
4   Bovey Tracey 1388
5   Bradninch 1271
6   Chardstock 1273
7   Chittlehamholt 1375
8   Chulmleigh 1302
9   Coldridge 1317
10 Colyton 1292
11 Crediton 1303
12 Dartington 1326
13 Ermington 1305
14 Great Fulford 1462
15 Hartland 1299

16 Hatch, Loddiswell 1462
17 Holne 1326
18 Iddesleigh 1278
19 Inwardleigh *c.* 1300
20 Kingskerswell *c.* 1300
21 Kismeldon Bridge 1343
22 Langdon, Wembury 1346
23 Larkbeare, Talaton 1467
24 Lifton 1271
25 Mohuns Ottery, Luppitt 1303
26 Molland
27 Monkton 1298
28 Morchard Bishop 1334
29 Newenham 1255
30 North Molton 1339

31 Norton 1346
32 Oburnford, Halberton 1348
33 Okehampton *c.* 1300
34 Paignton 1265
35 Poltimore 1286
36 Raleigh, Northam 1379
37 Spreyton 1287
38 Stokenham 1329
39 Tawstock 1379
40 Tiverton 1469
41 Uffculme 1336
42 Umberleigh, Atherington 1313
43 Weycroft 1427
44 Winkleigh 1086
45 Wonford, Exeter 1292

Sixteenth- and Seventeenth-century Parks

1   Bicton, sixteenth century
2   Boringdon 1699
3   Brightley, sixteenth century
4   Chawleigh, sixteenth century
5   Cockington 1659
6   Copplestone, Colebrook
7   Castle Hill, Filleigh 1630

8   Holcombe 1610
9   Kings Nympton, sixteenth century
10 Merton 1575
11 Shirwell 1575
12 Shute *c.* 1540
13 South Leigh *c.* 1540
14 Stevenstone *c.* 1600

15 Trill 1540
16 Ugbrook, Chudleigh 1673
17 West Ogwell *c.* 1600
18 West Worlington *c.* 1540
19 Whiddon, Chagford, sixteenth century
20 Whitchurch *c.* 1540
21 Wolleigh, Beaford 1610
22 Yealmpton 1575

Possible Early Parks (based on field name evidence only)

1   Ashburton
2   Aylesbeare
3   Bishops Tawton
4   Brendon
5   Charles

6   Clovelly
7   Holsworthy Hamlets
8   Ipplepen
9   Milton Abbot
10 Sampford Courtenay

11 Sherford
12 South Tawton
13 West Alvington
14 Whitestone

REFERENCES

1. L. Cantor, *The Medieval Parks of England: A Gazetteer* (Loughborough, 1983), p. 3.
2. F. Barlow, 'Hunting in the Middle Ages', *D(evonshire) A(ssociation) T(ransactions)* 113 (1981), pp. 1–11.
3. D. Austin, R.H. Daggart and M.J.C. Walker, 'Farms and Fields in Okehampton Park, Devon: The Problems of Studying Medieval Landscapes', *Landscape History* 2 (1980), pp. 39–58.
4. H.C. Darby and R.W. Finn (eds), *The Domesday Geography of South West England* (1967), pp. 256–60.
5. RCHME, *Survey of West Park, Okehampton Park, Okehampton Hamlets, Devon* (1992), Austin, et al., 'Okehampton Park'.
6. R.A. Higham, J.P. Allen and S.R. Blaycock, 'Excavations at Okehampton Castle: the Bailey', *DAT* 40 (1981), pp. 19–152.
7. E.P. Shirley, *Some Account of English Deer Parks* (1867); Cantor, *Medieval Parks*.
8. D.R. Wilson, 'Old Gardens From the Air', in A.E. Brown (ed.), *Garden Archaeology* (1991).

Chapter Three

'THEIR IDOLS OF WORSHIP': FRUIT TREES AND THE WALLED GARDEN IN EARLY MODERN DEVON

TODD GRAY

In 1669 John Flavell, the Rector of Dartmouth, demonstrated in his *Husbandry Spiritualized or the Hevenly use of Earthly Things* a diverse personal knowledge of gardening, including such areas as the growing of tulips in knot gardens and the care needed to protect frost-tender plants. He also drew the example of a gentlewoman who undertakes to remodel her own garden after seeing a neighbour's 'curious and neat garden'. He wrote that 'not a weed or stone is suffered in it, but all must lie in exquisite order, and whatever ornament she had observed in her neighbour's [garden] she is now restless till she see it in her own.' In all his examples Flavell draws a spiritual lesson, and this may be one on the dangers of envy.[1] But along with Flavell's knowledge of the spiritual lives of his parishioners there must have been familiarity with their gardening interests, and when writing he may well have had in mind a particular lady who was an enthusiastic gardener. Little is generally known of the local interest in gardening and yet the city of Exeter, which was the cultural, political and religious centre of Devon, made an early effort to provide civic garden amenities: in 1612 'a pleasant walk' in Northernhay was laid out and, later, wooden benches were set out for the residents' use. In 1633 new gravelled walks were made for 'citizens and others that walk for their recreations that way'.[2] Certainly, the South West was generally known for its undertakings in agrarian 'improvement' and it must be assumed that its gentry shared the national fascination with husbandry, which resulted in an outpouring of literature on agrarian topics. In the sixteenth century John Hooker, alias Vowell, the illustrious Chamberlain of the City of Exeter, revealed in his *Synopsis Corographical* an impressive familiarity with the most influential Italian herbal of his time, Pierandrea Mattioli's *Commentarii in Sex Libros Pedacii Dioscoridis*. This vast work, in which Mattioli reinforced the importance of the writings of the first-century Greek scholar Pedianos Dioscorides, was never translated into English. Hooker read, and may well have owned, one of the Latin editions. Perhaps he first became acquainted with Mattioli's work during the 1540s, when he was resident in Cologne and later Strasbourg.[3] A listing of the books in one large late seventeenth-century library included several concerned with botany, horticulture or husbandry. Richard Coffin of Portledge in north-west Devon read, or at least owned, John Worlidge's *Vinetum Britannicum*

or a Discourse of Cidar, as well as John Gerard's *The Herball or Generall History of Plants.* In Coffin's library there was also:

> The French Gardiner: A Choice Garden of all sort of rarest flowers alsoe a kitchin-garden furnished with all manner of herbs, rootes and fruites for meal or sawce used with others. With the art of planting an orchard of all sorts of fruit bearing trees and shrubs showing the nature of grafting, inoculating and pruning of them together with the right ordering, planting and preserving of them with their select virtues by John Parkinson, Apothecary of London and the King's Herbarist.[4]

The eighteenth-century library of Francis Kirkham of Pinhoe near Exeter included John Evelyn's book on fruit trees (1670) and Thomas Hale's *A Compleat Body of Husbandry* (1756). Kirkham also owned Philip Miller's *Gardener's Dictionary* (1754),[5] which in 1756 the owner of the garden at Nutwell Court near Exeter insisted his estate manager consult when gardening.[6] Likewise, in 1768 the library of Thomas Binford of Exeter included a copy of Miller's *Dictionary*, Gerard's *Herball* and several other titles on horticulture and husbandry.[7] It must be assumed that other Devon gentlemen owned similar books.

While it may be argued that relatively little is known about the gentry's interest in gardening in Devon in the early modern period, even less has been written about the types of plants grown in their gardens. Presumably the county's seafarers returned home with plant specimens from their overseas voyages. Were there corners of the gardens at the home of Sir Francis Drake of Buckland Abbey that were used for African, Asian or American plants, even if only for the potato? Notwithstanding this possibility, there was evidently something of a preoccupation with fruit-growing in the county. At the end of the eighteenth century one visitor, William Marshall, wrote that 'Their Orchards might well be styled their Temples and Apple Trees their Idols of Worship'.[8] Such, indeed, was the case throughout the early modern period.

The garden at Nutwell Court, located on the east bank of the River Exe between Exeter and Exmouth, was an enterprise of great interest to its owner, Sir Francis Henry Drake, although he was resident in either Hampshire or London for most of the year. He was said to have been a very shy man. Revd John Swete later claimed that Drake knew few of the county's gentlemen and once his duties were over at Court, Drake would seclude himself in his garden. Drake's heir was even more private: Swete was unable to persuade the 'Dragon portress at the lodge' and noted that 'no Spanish don could be more jealous of his fair spouse or contrive more sedulously to keep her from the contaminating eye of man, than has been done by Lord Heathfield in regard to his grounds!'[9] Drake was well informed of developments through regular reports from his estate manager, Nicholas Rowe, whose letters from 1749 to the late 1760s survive. Drake was rebuilding Nutwell Court, and much of the correspondence involved instructions regarding that work — such as when a brick summer-house was built in 1757. Drake also received detailed, not to say tedious, information on local weather conditions. Rowe wrote of the difficulties that the weather presented to him (for the task in hand it was often too wet or dry, if not too cold or hot) and also of the garden's destruction by wild creatures. Among the latter were rabbits that ate the flowers, birds that consumed the cherries, wasps that attacked the plums and figs, and rats that were 'like the plague to Egypt' and caused widespread damage throughout the garden. Finally, Rowe even suspected 'nasty great' earthworms of eating the roots of the apple trees.[10]

Many workers were needed to tend the garden. From 1754, Rowe passed on Drake's orders to a principal gardener and to one Solomon Northmore, who seems to have been responsible for the manual labour. Occasionally there were difficulties in obtaining wage labourers for tending the garden as well as for general work on the estate. In March 1755, for example, local men disappeared because there was a naval pressman

Nutwell Court (Ackermann, after J. Gendall, *c.* 1824)

searching for able-bodied men.[11] Rowe appears not to have had good relations with his fellow employees; at least, he often found withering comments to make on them. Solomon was called a drunkard, a local woman who was employed chiefly in weeding was dubbed 'Dame Crabb', and he regarded another servant as being not only 'nasty beyond expression' but also 'a miserable nasty creature'. Because the latter woman was ill when she was sent to Buckland, and died there shortly afterwards, there was a scandal among the local people in nearby Lympstone. Only then did Rowe write of her in a compassionate manner.[12] Finally, and not surprisingly, when the gardener was replaced Rowe wrote that he was to be 'married to the wench . . . [which will] fix both in misery'.[13]

Rowe repeatedly wrote that he had little knowledge of gardening, but this does not explain his clumsiness when he once fell into the orchard's water tank and required pulling out from the mud. However, a letter written in December 1759 may indicate some personal knowledge, or at least suspicions, concerning the introduction of new gardening techniques. At that date the kitchen garden was in need of being dug over, and Rowe urged Drake to 'be particular in your orders about trench-plowing which is not understood here.' As he had earlier explained, 'for my part I am only a looker on, admiring the wisdom of the present generation, though I don't understand it.' Nevertheless, he was certainly being dry when he wrote, 'I wish I had Solomon's skill of plants (not our Solomon) how happy I should be in your correspondence but I am a stranger to everything but the shrub, an emblem of your humble servant who dwindles daily.'[14]

Drake was greatly concerned with introducing a large variety of plants at Nutwell. Rowe's letters mention fig trees in 1752 (there was a white fig in 1762), cedars were planted in 1754, and in 1755 he was planting laurels and evergreen oaks. By 1756 he had grape vines, a raspberry tree, a strawberry tree, a weeping willow, plane trees, cypresses, tuberose roots, Newfoundland firs, larch trees and a cistus.[15] In 1758 he had black poplars and

well-established apricot trees, in 1759 barberries, and in 1760 two orange trees from Dartmouth. Also that year he had a capsia and artichokes. By 1761 there were Weymouth pines, by 1763 myrtle, in 1765 Scotch pines and in 1766 phillyreas and lagerstroemias.[16] Clearly he had limited familiarity with some plants, and he had apprehensions about the suitability of others to the climate. This was most likely to have been the case with some magnolias that were planted by 1759. In October of that year he instructed Rowe to cover the plants with mats, but in the following January Rowe wrote back that neither Sir William Courtenay, at Powderham just across the river, nor one Mr Hall protected their magnolias.[17] Drake was probably concerned because he knew that a severe frost in the winter of 1739/40 had destroyed many magnolias. Sir John Colleton has been credited with introducing *Magnolia grandiflora* 'Exmouth' into England from South Carolina. Possibly, as will be discussed later, Drake's magnolias were from Colleton's garden, which was located only a few miles down the estuary in Exmouth.[18]

Drake obtained his plants from various sources. Some he raised himself at his own nursery and others were bought in Exeter. He also acquired plants from two notable local gardens. In 1755 he sent his gardener across the River Exe to Mamhead, the former residence of Sir Peter Ball, Recorder of Exeter and Attorney General to

View of Mamhead from Exmouth (after W.H., 1790)

Queen Henrietta Maria. Drake was informed that the subsequent owner of Mamhead, Wilmot Vaughan, the first Earl of Lisburne, had instructed his servants to supply Drake's own gardener with plants. However, the operation was only partly successful: that year some pine cones were acquired, which were used for seeding, but the former gardener there had largely destroyed the flowering shrubs. Nevertheless, some other seeds were rescued as well as laurel, mountain ash and white elder.[19] Drake may have hoped to plunder Mamhead of plants established there through Richard Bradley, the plant collector and author of such books as *New Improvements of Planting and Gardening* (1717–18), *A General Treatise of Husbandry and Gardening* (1721) and *Dictionarium Botanicum* (1728). One of Bradley's patrons was Robert Balle, the fifth son of Sir Peter Ball, who was probably responsible for introducing Bradley to Mamhead. Bradley's familiarity with the garden there is evident from his writings, and he most likely gave practical advice while visiting. It is also possible that Robert Balle acquired plants for Mamhead while resident in Livorno in Italy.[20] By the middle of the eighteenth century the gardens may have become neglected but in 1778 a visitor noted their beauty and wrote that they were being replanted.[21] Not long after this date John Swete noted that when Lord Lisburne inherited Mamhead it was:

> a good house and surrounding plantations which for their scarcity and variety were not be matched in any part of the kingdom. These were introduced by Mr Balle, from Italy, and are now one of the chief ornaments of the place, the Cork tree, the Ilex, the Wainscot oak, the Acasia, the Spanish chestnut, several sorts of firs, and above all the cedar are here seen thriving as in their native soil, and seeming as it were indigenous.

Robert Balle may have brought these plants from Italy or obtained them from other family members who were in Sicily.[22] Acquiring plants from other local gardens must have been widespread. In 1756 Rowe wrote to Drake that 'Mr Hall's gardener has sent to know if you want anything out of Sir John Colloton's garden, I suppose by his master's direction.'[23] Colleton had died only a few years earlier, in 1754, and Mr Hall must have been his successor at Exmouth.[24] Probably this is where, and how, Drake obtained his magnolias by 1759. Drake also had many plants brought down from London, such as 4 cherry, 6 plum and 10 pear trees in 1751.[25]

In Rowe's letters the growing of fruit trees features prominently. Among those Drake cultivated were apples, peaches, pears, nectarines, apricots, cherries and quinces. Drake had a practical use for his fruit, in that not only was Nutwell itself provisioned but when in London he regularly had fruit sent up to him, such as apples, pears and peaches, and he even used his cherries for making cherry brandy.[26] He also owned Buckland Abbey, where his mother was resident, and hired a gardener to prune the fruit trees there. Cider was regularly produced there.[27] The fruit trees were sufficiently well known for William Marshall to note in 1796 that:

> One of the orchards of Buckland priory is said to be the oldest in the country, and this is spoken of as being about two hundred years old. Nevertheless, this orchard is still fully stocked and in full bearing.[28]

The importance of fruit-growing can also be seen in the earlier gardens of the Reynell family, resident near Newton Abbot. In 1587 they were living at East Ogwell, when their herb garden was walled in. In the following year a grander house was built at West Ogwell and it took Richard Reynell many years to establish the gardens. In 1591 a pear garden was planted, a wall was made 'round about the house' and a row of elms was planted, as was a 'thorn' hedge. In April 1596 a wall was made around the courtyard as well as another garden, and ash trees were planted 'for walks'. The following year an apple orchard was planted in front of the house. A survey undertaken in the early seventeenth century noted that there were 'gardens and orchards furnished with all

Buckland Abbey. Buckland and Nutwell were the principal seats of the Drake family (Buck, 1734)

kinds of fruit'. However, in 1751, when the building was reconstructed, the garden was also redesigned: in order to create a new and larger garden a part of the Great Orchard, as well as 'the large garden house and my Lady's Garden', were destroyed.[29]

Likewise, the garden at Shute, near Colyton, was an important part of the estate to its owner, Sir Courtenay Pole, and fruit was prominent. Shute was a considerable building, particularly so for Devon; it was assessed as having twenty-nine hearths for the Hearth Tax in 1670 (the owner's enthusiasm for the tax in Parliament earned him the nickname Sir 'Chimney' Pole).[30] The continual references in Pole's account books to work in the garden provide glimpses of its character. In 1657 he had seventy elms and thirty-five sycamores transplanted in order to create some 'large walks'. In 1668 Pole had a summer-house built, and thinned some woodland with a view to leaving some oaks for 'ornament and shade'. The following year he ordered thirty cypress trees from 'John Totie the Salisbury gardener' and had some plum and apricot trees sent down from London. He also acquired some apple, medlar and French walnut trees in 1669. But throughout he maintained a nursery garden at nearby Colcombe.[31]

Many of the gardening entries in Pole's account books are concerned with the kitchen garden; it was continually being expanded or reshaped. Thus, for example, in 1668 almost four thousand whitethorn and privet plants were used to create a hedge for the garden. In 1671 Pole instructed his gardener to plant cabbages, raspberries, gooseberries, currants and strawberries in a new lower kitchen garden. He also planted fruit trees in the kitchen garden. In 1658 he bought bricks from a local brickmaker, and it is possible that these were used for the kitchen garden walls.[32]

Prominent in the accounts is the planting of fruit trees. In 1668 Pole noted the planting of two hundred Gilliflower (apple) trees, but in earlier accounts he recorded several other purchases of fruit trees that must have represented an enormous personal enterprise. In 1658 he had a 'very, very great apple' and also a 'Gersie' apple

Shute House, the seat of Sir Courtenay Pole. Note the espaliered fruit trees on the wall to the right

which was 'very red both within and without' from one Captain Slade of Axminster.[33] He also had apple trees from several other sources. In 1663 he had 144 'fair handsome' trees from his cousin Nathaniel Pole at Escot in nearby Talaton parish, of which seventeen were 'an apple full of red streaks called a French long stay'. The young trees were part payment for the 'head' rent of Talaton farm. From 27 to 31 October eight horses brought the trees the 12 miles or so to the new orchard at Shute. Two days later the same eight horses began bringing another sixty-four trees. The trees were purchased from one John Wickes, possibly a nurseryman, of Larkbeare in Talaton. In addition, in 1671 Pole bought thirty young apple trees from the son of 'old Mr Paulmer'. He also planted trees raised from his own nursery at Colcombe.[34]

As well as the 1663 acquisitions described above, Pole acquired yet more fruit stock in the autumn of that year. These trees arrived on 10 and 11 November, probably on the same eight horses. In all, sixty-seven pear trees were bought from the son of John Pincent, the former Rector of Talaton. Pole noted that the fruit trees 'were the labours of his father during the time of his persecution and sequestration in the late wars and it is told to me he was very choice and curious to get the best fruit'.[35] Pincent senior had married the widow of the previous rector, Thomas Flavell, and curiously it was another Flavell, the previously-mentioned John, at about this time the Rector of Dartmouth,[36] who revealed in his *Husbandry Spiritualized* a detailed knowledge of the grafting of fruit trees.[37] In 1714 Dr John Walker noted in his *Sufferings of the Clergy* that Pincent had been deprived of his living in 1645, but held a small manor in his own right throughout the Interregnum.[38] It was there presumably that he developed his nursery. A glebe terrier of Talaton of about 1680 noted that there were two orchards of about one-and-half acres and also a small nursery. Pincent must already have had a strong interest in fruit there before the Civil War, and appears to have been unusual among Devon's clergy during the

Commonwealth for his interest in husbandry.[39] Certainly fruit-growing was practised in the parish, because his immediate predecessor disputed the amount of tithes on the apples grown on fruit trees with several of his parishioners.[40] In 1672 Pole glumly noted that although the pear trees from Talaton had cost him 5s., they had yet to yield him that much in fruit during the nine years he had had them.

However, Pole's greatest endeavour was connected with London. On 16 April 1658 his father died in Bromley-St-Leonards, where it appears the family had a home. But just before this Pole obtained some fruit stock from his father at 'Bromeley Garden', which was also referred to as Bromeley near 'Bowl'. This was not Bromley in Kent but that near Stratford-Le-Bow in east London. On 7 and 8 April Pole, together with one 'Hurle' who was presumably his gardener, grafted the fruit stocks onto trees in the Great Orchard at Shute. The trees were set out in at least twelve rows with up to fourteen trees per row. A great number of the grafts were apples, including those varieties he noted as being known as the Spanish Pippin, Russetting, Old Wife, Golden Rennett, Apple Dainty, Codling, Gilliflower and the Summer Apple.

Two years later Pole acquired other fruit trees from London, including quinces and a fig, and he had others of which he was very specific regarding the varieties: in 1660 he noted that he had brought down from London apricots (some of which were an early variety), pears (both Bergamot and summer Bon Chrétien), peaches (Newington, Nutmeg, Double Blossom and Carnation), nectarines (Roman, Red and Green), plums (Queen Mother and Grass), cherries (Duke and May) and three 'malligottoones' (presumably a melocoton, which was a peach grafted onto a quince stock). Altogether there were thirty-two fruit trees, which cost him £4 5s.

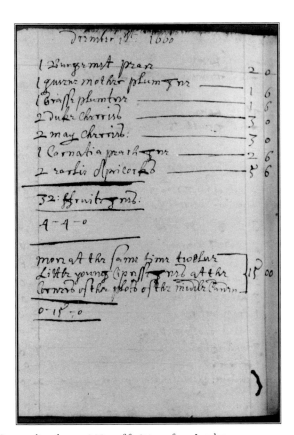

Entries from Sir Courtenay Pole's account book for 1660, recording the acquisition of fruit trees from London

Pole was personally interested in grafting and appears to have been slightly competitive with his gardener. He was also experimental: on one of his existing trees in the kitchen garden, possibly an apple, he grafted two types of stock. One of these was a medlar and the other was Captain Slade's 'very, very great apple'. He noted in his accounts that he did this 'to try a conclusion'. He also grafted two stocks on a different tree in the walled orchard.[41]

As stated earlier, throughout this period there was a great interest among the gentry in general in husbandry and agricultural 'improvement'.[42] One of the fundamental interests was the introduction of new varieties of fruit. Nevertheless, Pole's recording of fruit varieties is unusual for Devon. Surprisingly, neither of Devon's two early Stuart topographical writers, Tristram Risdon and Thomas Westcote, were very informative about fruit-growing, although the latter wrote that 'We are also furnished with great variety of fruits, and of most of them sundry choice of species.'[43] At Tiverton Castle during the Christmas season of 1523, Katherine Courtenay, 'daughter, sister and aunt of Kings', bought Warden pears for her household use.[44] Fortunately, John Hooker noted of Devon in the late sixteenth century that:

> for frute trees greate changes as the aple and peares wch in the pticulers be hardely to be named but yet of many theise few be most in use, as of aples the pepyn the renate Cowicke quarenden, Comewater, pomewater, bellebone, portegue, Tretegolde Churnepyne the soure aple the sweete aple the Crabbe tree the syder frute. And of peares the Sowton peare the peare mayne the bishops peare the Genet ['the Kathergt peare' crossed through] the Grace peare the Katheren peare the warden and many others not to be named.

An early twentieth-century photograph of Shute House. Much of the right-hand portion shown in the earlier drawing was demolished when the eighteenth-century mansion was constructed

He also noted cherry, mazard (a wild or black cherry), plum, medlar and mulberry trees.[45] The reference to mulberry trees predates the 8,500 trees sent in 1609 to some of the Devon justices at the invitation of James I. The trees were part of a national endeavour to produce silk in England.[46] In an Exeter garden in 1637 six varieties of apples (Rennet, Pearmain, Pippin, Quarrendon, Stubbard and a 'Green Henning') were growing, as well as a cherry and an apricot tree.[47] In 1676 John Worlidge noted in his *Vinetum Britannicum* that the 'Bitter-scale' was the popular cider-apple in Devon.[48]

Some of the varieties in use in the eighteenth century are also known. There were several kinds of pears and apples grafted at Nutwell Court between 1754 and 1761; these included the Buree de Roy, Bloiskind, Worcestershire, Windsor, Bergamot, White Stire, Red Stire, Fox Whelp and Red-Streak.[49] In 1729 Batty Langley included in his *Pomona or the Fruit Garden Illustrated* a 'Curious Account of the Most Valuable Cyder Fruit of Devonshire' written by Hugh Stafford of Pynes near Exeter in 1727. It was about this time that Langley surveyed Stafford's grand mansion in Upton Pyne.[50] Stafford's account was later reprinted posthumously, with additions, as his *Dissertation on Cyder and Cyder Fruit* in 1755. In it he wrote that there were three apple varieties 'which do as yet bear the greatest reputation for cider' in Devon. In about 1711 an apple tree was discovered growing in a quillet, possibly land that was part of Cleve, belonging to Mr Francis Oliver in St Thomas parish near Exeter on the road to Okehampton. Stafford thought that the tree might have been seventy years old in 1727. Robert Woolcombe, the Rector of Whitestone, discovered that the apple produced superior cider. He named it the Royal Wilding but it was also known as the Red-Hill Crab, after the area of St Thomas in which it was originally discovered. Stafford credited Woolcombe with first grafting the Royal Wilding in his own nursery in Whitestone. A terrier of the glebe lands of the parish in 1745 recorded two orchards as well as 'the Red-Streak Nursery'. The Whitesour was a popular variety in the South Hams. It was thought to have first been propagated in Modbury. There were three varieties, the best of which was the 'Panerg'. There was also the Meadyate, named because it was originally found near a meadow gate in Ermington near Plymouth. Its cider 'in Devon is called Hewbramble or Bramble cider alluding to its roughness, which causes a sensation, as if a bramble had been thrust down the throat and suddenly snatched back again'. Finally, there was also an Irish variety, the Cockagee. It was also referred to as the Irish Crab but in Ireland it was known, perhaps for its colour, as the 'Gooseturd'. It was first brought into Devon in about 1720 but had been previously introduced and cultivated near Minehead in about 1700 by 'Councillor' Pynes.[51] William Pynes, of Newcastle in County Limerick, leased the tenement of Canus and Ballyregan from Sir William Courtenay of Powderham. In 1748 the orchard there was not noted for the excellence of its trees.[52]

There were also other apple varieties, including the Backamore which was named after Baccamoor, a farm in Plympton St Mary, and a crab apple named after two trees that grew by Cowley Bridge near Exeter.[53] In 1748 the principal varieties were noted by William Ellis in *The Compleate Cyderman*. He was informed by an unnamed inhabitant of Plymtree in east Devon that the chief varieties were the Gold[en] Pippin, Deux-Ann, Jersey, French Long-Tail, Royal Wilding, Cullvering, Russett, Holland Pippin and Cowley Crab.[54] Later the Revd Thomas Putt of Gittisham in east Devon developed an apple, which he named after himself, that was used both for the table and for the making of cider.[55] In 1796 Marshall noted that Devon did not then have as many apple varieties as Herefordshire but that they were still numerous. The Golden Pippin was becoming less common.[56]

Finally, the accounts of the Powderham kitchen garden from 1810 to 1812, and again from 1819 to 1822, mention many fruit varieties. The two books note apples simply described as 'common' and dessert, as well as such specific varieties as the Nonpareil, Dutch Codling, Hubbard, Red Quarrendon, Royal Pearmain, Loan Pearmain, Nonsuch and Norfolk Beefing. There were also five kinds of pippins (Ribston, Golden, New Town, Taunton and Chiswick). The gardener also had at least ten varieties of pear trees, including Jayond, Catern,

Cattron, Worcester, Gansel's Bergamot, Shumontle, Brown Bury, Cole Man, Largonel and Swans Egg. He had five types of cherries (Kentish, Duke, White Hart, Morello and 'Bigroom')[57] and besides the damsons and greengages he also had six kinds of plums (Violet, Orlean, Red Imperial, Magnobonum, Imperative and Blue Perdyon). There were also peaches, apricots, nectarines and mulberries, and a considerable number of pineapples were grown.[58]

Names appear to have been applied to varieties of fruit in an irregular fashion. John Hooker notes in his *Synopsis Corographical* that Pierandrea Mattioli wrote in his Italian herbal of the sixteenth century that:

> they have borrowed various appelations either from the men who first received them for use as food, or from the places from which they came, or from marks which they will bear having received them from some [?other] fruits or from their own colour or from the time.[59]

Not surprisingly, some of the names Hooker notes as varieties support Mattioli's statement: the Peppin and the Pomewater are just two of the several varieties that were nationally well known and were probably grown and sold as those varieties; the Cowick Quarrendon and the Sowton Pear may have been named after those places near Exeter, which Hooker himself must have been acquainted with; and the Sour apple and the Sweet apple most probably derived their names from their taste. Nevertheless, Hooker himself may not have been a reliable recorder of fruit: the Pearmain is more generally known as a variety of apple than pear,[60] and could his 'portegue' apple be the Portuguese quince? Several generations after Hooker and Mattioli, the haphazard fashion of naming fruit trees continued. Pole noted that among his grafts from Bromley Garden were a number of 'Bromleys', of which he wrote, 'I call it so because upon that bundle there was no name fixed on it as on the rest.'[61] Finally, in the early eighteenth century, Hugh Stafford of Pynes wrote that he contemplated naming a tree he raised from a Red-Streak kernel the 'Pyne-Apple'.[62]

Hooker's list demonstrates that there had been a long-standing tradition of fruit-growing in Devon, and this was of course not limited to the gentry. Tithe disputes in the early seventeenth century show the range of fruit grown throughout the county. For example, in the parish of West Worlington there were cherry, plum and pear trees, and in Colaton Raleigh there were mulberry trees.[63] Moreover, in 1601 Christopher Upton of Totnes grew apples, pears, plums, walnuts, medlars, damsons, cherries, mazards, mulberries and services. There are few other references to the growing of service trees in the county. Upton also grew soft fruit such as gooseberries and raspberries.[64] Occasionally there were bumper years, such as 1590, when it was noted that in North Devon there was a very good harvest of cherries and mazards.[65] The value of fruit trees is indicated by a court case of February 1637 in which two men were accused of stealing sixteen apple trees out of a nursery in Whitchurch parish near Tavistock.[66]

The Customs accounts of the sixteenth and seventeenth centuries show a considerable importation of such continental fruit as prunes, figs, raisins, currants, almonds, oranges and lemons. Such Mediterranean fruit had first been imported into England in the medieval period. But there are only occasional references to apples, one rare example being a February 1615 reference to one hundred bushels of apples being brought into Dartmouth from Dunkirk.[67] Perhaps these apples were the famous French Longstays, which were finding a market in Dartmouth among ships' victuallers. The lack of many references to apple imports must indicate that Devon was generally self-sufficient. This could explain why an unusual apple was marketable, and may indicate that the Longstays were not commonly produced in south Devon.

Much of the fruit was for home consumption (such apples were put in the 'hoard') and some fruit was sold locally. Some of the varieties were known for their cooking qualities, such as the Codling and the Warden, and

others as 'dessert' apples, such as the Devonshire Quarrendon.[68] But one of the chief reasons for the interest in new varieties of apples was the production of cider, and to some extent new kinds of pears for the making of perry. Many of the varieties noted by Hooker, Drake and Pole were used for cider-making. Hooker noted that a considerable amount of cider was made in Elizabethan Devon, a great quantity being sold for victualling ships. It was thought that cider had qualities that made it a particularly useful drink on voyages to warmer climates. Hooker also noted that a significant amount of cider was produced for household and local consumption.[69] Risdon went so far as to claim that there was so much produced that 'many copy-holders may pay their Lord's rent with their cider only'.[70]

The introduction of new varieties had a great impact on the flavour of Devon cider. Although it was noted in 1750 that 'They have an apple called the Bitter-sweet, which gives a fine flavour to the cider . . .', it was also claimed that the Herefordshire Red-Streak had improved local cider-making. However, the new Hereford apple was not universally welcomed. Philip Luckombe wrote that the South Hams was 'famous for that noble rough cider, which is generally preferred to the soft, sickly Hereford redstreak; and so near wine in taste, that it has tempted some vintners and coopers in London, as well as in other cities and towns, to mix it with their port wines.'[71] Both Hereford and Devon, among other counties, were noted for their cider, but the long public enquiry into the connection between Devon cider and the 'Devonshire Colic' did not enhance the beverage's national reputation.[72] Nevertheless, it was Devon's distinction in fruit-growing that prompted a request from Hertfordshire in 1748 for sixteen cider-apple trees of the best Devon varieties.[73]

Clearly there was a broad interest in fruit-growing in early modern Devon. Some Devonians planted fruit trees for decorative purposes, often as ornamental features in walled gardens. Others no doubt grew certain fruit, such as peaches, figs or apricots, because they were novelties or luxuries. Some must also have been interested in new varieties because of their sheer pleasure in gardening, and for others there was an interest in beating fellow gardeners. But many were interested in fruit, particularly apples, for more commercial reasons. The making of cider, and also perry, has been a traditional endeavour in the county. Irrespective of their motives, Devonians were especially interested in new varieties. Throughout the early modern period new sorts of fruit were introduced from other parts of England and the continent. Many new varieties were also discovered and developed in Devon. Some, like the Cowick Quarrendon and the Sowton pear, have disappeared, while other early types, like Tom Putt, are still to be found in Devon gardens and orchards. Fruit trees may no longer be considered 'idols of worship' in Devon, but the evidence of the former interest in them survives.

ACKNOWLEDGEMENT

I would like to thank Dr Jonathon Barry and Mrs Ann Cronne for their help with an early draft of this paper.

REFERENCES

1. John Flavell, *Husbandry Spiritualized or the Hevenly use of Earthly Things* (1669, edn. of 1968), vi, pp. 256–9.
2. Samuel Izacke, *Remarkable Antiquities of the City of Exeter* (1723), p. 145; D(evon) R(ecord) O(ffice), ECA, Act Book 7, pp. 92, 96, 107, 836; D. Portman, *Exeter Houses, 1400–1700* (Exeter, 1966), p. 52.
3. DRO, Z19/18/9, p. 12; Wilfrid Blunt and Sandra Raphael, *The Illustrated Herbal* (1979), pp. 132–6, 14–16.
4. DRO, Z19/8/5. This may have been the 1656 edition of Parkinson's *Paradisi in Sole, Paradisus Terrestris*. There was also 'A Discourse of Tobacco by Dr Everard'.
5. DRO, 312add7M/F2/11a.

6. DRO, 346M/F340.

7. DRO, 4508M/F49. He also owned *Gardeners' Calendar* and *Maw's Gardener*.

8. William Marshall, *Rural Economy of the West of England* (1796), i, p. 237.

9. Elizabeth Drake, *The Family and Heirs of Sir Francis Drake* (1911), i; DRO, 564M, vol. 16, p. 70.

10. DRO, F484, F231, F419, F471, F410.

11. DRO, 346M, F310, F311, F314.

12. DRO, 346M, F332, F475, F444, F446, F447.

13. DRO, 346M, F333.

14. DRO, 346M, F354, F393, F221, F277.

15. DRO, 346M, F224, F456, F272, F314, F302, F342, F339, F346.

16. DRO, 346M, F371, F378, F393, F420, F405, F411, F433, F462, F471, F476.

17. DRO, 346M, F392, F400. The other neighbour was one Mr Hall, who was probably of Exmouth.

18. National Council for the Conservation of Plants and Gardens – Devon Group, *The Magic Tree* (Exeter, 1989), p. 69.

19. DRO, 346M, F286, F309, F310, F311, F326, F333, F371, F372.

20. Blanche Henrey, *British Botanical and Horticultural Literature Before 1800* (Oxford, 1975), ii, pp. 425, 427, 431, 437, 439–40, 451, 455.

21. Norfolk Record Office, Rolfe (add), PR/DM, GUN127, 'Tour into Devonshire 1778'. He wrote: 'Mamhead the seat of Lord Lisburne . . . is a most beautiful spot and in a few years will be more so, as great improvements are begun both in the walks as well as the house.' He also noted that 'Mr Parker's house and shrubbery at Saltram is well worth seeing. . . . It will take about two hours to see the whole.'

22. DRO, 564M, vol. 2, p. 16; 484M/F5, will of John Ball.

23. DRO, 346M, F326.

24. William Webb, *Memorials of Exmouth* (1872), pp. 21–2; Eric R. Delderfield, *Exmouth Milestones* (Exmouth, 1948), pp. 35–6.

25. DRO, 346M, F222.

26. DRO, 346M, F231, F242.

27. DRO, 346M, F224, F242, F247, F298, F299, F300, F301, F302, F341, F344, F394, F416, F428, F446, F461.

28. Marshall, *Rural Economy*, i, pp. 213–14.

29. DRO, 4652M, F5/1.

30. DRO, 235M, E3, fol. 75: the receipt for the tax is enclosed with his account for that year; Steven Pugsley, 'Landed Society and the Emergence of the Country House in Tudor and Early Stuart Devon' in Todd Gray, Margery Rowe and Audrey Erskine (eds), *Tudor and Stuart Devon: the Common Estate and Government* (Exeter, 1992), p. 97; M.F. Bridie, *The Story of Shute* (Axminster, 1955), pp. 108–34.

31. DRO, 235M, E3, fol. 57 & fol. 68, E2, fol. 38, fol. 40, fol. 58, E3, fol. 36.

32. DRO, 235M, E2, fos 1–10; E3, fol. 310; E1, fol. 210.

33. DRO, 235M, E2, fol. 38. This was probably the Jersey apple, which was still grown in Devon in 1748. This may have been the same Slade of Axminster for whom he bought a fowling gun which Slade had pawned at an alehouse: 235M, E3, fol. 257.

34. DRO, 235M, E1, fos 211–12 & E3, fol. 250.

35. DRO, 235M, E1, final pages (not numbered).

36. Percy Russell, *Dartmouth* (1950), pp. 119–20.

37. Flavell, *Husbandry Spiritualized*, p. 180.

38. F.C. Hingeston-Randolph (ed.), *Sufferings of the Clergy* (Plymouth, 1908 edn.), pp. 148–9.

39. Gowers, 200–25.

40. For example, DRO, CC5/239.

41. DRO, 235M, E1, final pages.

42. Joan Thirsk, 'The Farming Regions of England' in *The Agrarian History of England and Wales* (Cambridge, 1967), IV, p. 74; Joan Thirsk, 'Making a Fresh Start: Sixteenth-century Agriculture and the Classical Inspiration' and Andrew McRae, 'Husbandry Manuals and the Language of Agrarian Improvement' in Michael Leslie and Timothy Raylor (eds), *Culture and Cultivation in Early Modern England* (Leicester, 1992).

43. Thomas Westcote, *A View of Devonshire in 1630* (Exeter, 1845), p. 38.

44. Margaret Westcott, 'Katherine Courtenay, Countess of Devon, 1479–1527' in Gray, Rowe and Erskine (eds), *Tudor and Stuart Devon*, pp. 23, 28.

45. DRO, Z19/18/9, 12. Original spelling and punctuation retained.

46. DRO, DQS, OB 1/3, fol. 31.

47. D. Portman, *Exeter Houses*, p. 52; DRO, ECA/ED/FC/69.

48. John Worlidge, *Vinetum Britannicum* (1676), p. 163.

49. DRO, 346M, F229, F363, F417, F433, F374.

50. Batty Langley, *Pomona or the Fruit Garden Illustrated* (1729); Bridget Cherry and Nikolaus Pevsner (eds), *The Buildings of England: Devon* (1989), p. 885.

51. E.V.M. Whiteway, *Whiteway's Cyder* (Newton Abbot, 1990), pp. 14–15; unknown, *A Treatise on Cyder Making . . . to which is prefixed a dissertation on cyder and cyder fruit, the second edition with additions by Hugh Stafford* (1755), pp. 1–2, 7, 11–13, 15, 21–5; DRO, St Thomas Church Rate, 1686, fol. 2; DRO, 1508M/Irish leases, pp. 3–5.

52. DRO, 1508M/Devon/Irish Rentals/3.

53. *A Treatise on Cyder Making*, pp. 21–3.

54. William Ellis, *The Compleate Cyderman* (1754), pp. 79–83, 43, 54.

55. W.G. Hoskins, *Devon* (Newton Abbot, 1972 edn.), p. 401.

56. Marshall, *Rural Economy*, i, pp. 226–7.

57. Possibly the Bigarreau.

58. DRO, 1508M Devon/Accounts/Volumes 19 & 40.

59. DRO, Z19/18/9, pp. 12–13. I would like to thank Mrs Margery Rowe and Mr John Draisey for their translation.

60. Teresa McLean, *Medieval English Gardens* (1989), p. 227.

61. DRO, 235M, E1, final pages.

62. *A Treatise on Cyder Making*, p. 13.

63. DRO, CC19a/122, CC20b/89.

64. DRO, CC15/212; for more on service trees see Francesca Greenoak, *Forgotten Fruit* (1983), pp. 13–14.

65. J.R. Chanter (ed.), *Sketches on Some Striking Incidents in the History of Barnstaple* (Barnstaple, 1865), p. 95.

66. DRO, DQS, Bundle Box Epiphany 1637, examinations of Richard May, Nicholas Aishe and Edward Aishe.

67. Duchy of Cornwall Office, Dartmouth Petty Customs Accounts, Michaelmas 1614–1615.

68. H.V. Taylor, *The Apples of England* (1947), p. 102.

69. DRO, Z19/18/9, 27.

70. Tristram Risdon, *The Chorographical Description or Survey of the County of Devon* (1811), p. 7.

71. Dr Richard Pococke, 'Travels through England' (1750), in R. Pearse Chope (ed.), *Early Tours in Devon and Cornwall* (Newton Abbot, 1967 edn.), pp. 215, 146 n. 2.

72. George Baker, *An Essay concerning the cause of the Endemial Colic of Devonshire* (1767); Thomas Alcock, *Some Observations on Dr Baker's Essay on the Endemial Colic of Devonshire* (1767); Thomas Alcock, *The Endemial Colic of Devon* (1769); *A Candid Examination of what has been advanced on The Colic of Poitou and Devonshire* (1778); R.M.S. McConaghey, 'Sir George Baker and the Devonshire Colic', *Medical History*, 11, 4 (1967), pp. 345–60.

73. Ellis, *The Complete Cyderman*, p. 43.

Chapter Four

CASTLE HILL: THE FORMAL AND TRANSITIONAL GARDEN

ROBIN FAUSSET

'This is allowed to be one of the most beautiful places in the country', wrote Bishop Pococke of Castle Hill during the course of a long inspection and tour of gardens in the west of England in the year 1764.[1] If we return to 1764, we find England at the height of its powers. Beau Nash had died two years earlier in Bath, having instilled into country squires the rules of polite society and banished the sword as an obligatory part of dress. The learned were writing in English instead of Latin. Continental links had become stronger. 'Le Grand Newton' was admired as much in Paris as in London and Edinburgh. It had become necessary for young gentlemen to be shown the glories of classical Rome by their tutors, and to return home laden with drawings and tales of their reception at foreign courts. True, although Wedgwood was making pots, and the spinning jenny had just been invented, neither Birmingham nor Manchester was represented in Parliament. Admiral Byng had been shot on his own quarterdeck *pour encourager les autres*. But Clive had swept through India, and Wolfe's capture of Quebec had caused the French to leave America, and Fort Duquesne to be renamed Pittsburgh.

Forty years earlier, Robert Walpole had ruled as Prime Minister, had hunted his beagles in Richmond Park, and is said to have opened his gamekeeper's letters before any others. At about this time – having succeeded to his family estates near South Molton in 1719 – Hugh Fortescue started to build his new mansion of Castle Hill and create its garden, most of which survives today in the full maturity of two hundred and fifty years.

THE FIRST PHASE: HUGH, FIRST LORD FORTESCUE, 1719–51

It is to Hugh, first Lord Fortescue, that the design of the garden at Castle Hill as we see it today must be primarily attributed. There is no evidence that the designers of the day (for example, Kent, Bridgeman or Gibbs) had any hand in it. Therefore a few words must be said about his life, although virtually nothing is known about his character. At the age of twenty-four he was appointed Lord Lieutenant of Devon; four years later, he became Lord of the Bedchamber to the Prince of Wales, the future George II. He had already claimed through his mother the barony of Clinton and in 1746, at the age of fifty-one, he was created Earl Clinton and first Baron Fortescue. But long before this time he had abandoned the court and government, the hurly-burly of the political scene, and like so many disillusioned noblemen, particularly in France, retired to his country estate.

We are told that he was employed on various mysterious missions in France. We know also that he spent two years in Istanbul. These events must have had an influence on what he did at Castle Hill.

On leaving London, his first step was to redesign both his house and garden. We can conjecture that the old manor house of the Fortescues was a typical stone and cob barton, possibly with a thatched roof, of which there are so many still extant in Devon. He decided to rebuild the house and move the church, which then stood next door to the house.[2]

The first documented date is on a contract of 22 February 1723 with Roger Morris, the architect, for the Portland stone exterior of the house 'which shall be as my Lord Burlington and Lord Herbert shall direct'.[3] The second date is 7 January 1730, for the building of a new church in the neighbouring village of Filleigh, half a mile away from the house. The instruction to Roger Morris to abide by the advice of Burlington and Herbert is important, because they were in the van of the movement to bring the Palladian style to England. Burlington, who was the patron of William Kent, had already built the exquisite Chiswick House in London where so many artists and dilettantes gathered, and was laying out at Chiswick a classical garden complete with exedra, *patte d'oie* and temples. It was natural that Hugh Fortescue should follow Burlington's example and become one of the 'gardening earls', as the old sage Horace Walpole called them.

Like so many Devon houses, Castle Hill is finely sited on a shelf protected from the north by a hill and overlooking a wide valley. Werrington Park near Launceston and Creedy Park near Crediton are other West

Castle Hill. Prospect to the north, engraved for the *Universal Magazine*, 1749. Possibly derived from John Wootton's painting of *c.* 1735–40, it similarly depicts a (probably conjectural) rotunda on the hill behind the house, where the Gothic castle was ultimately sited

Country examples. The opportunity for dramatic layout was immense, and Hugh Fortescue took full advantage of it.

Behind the house, on the hill immediately to the north, is the gothick castle after which the house was named. There is a slight mystery here because in an oil painting of the house executed by John Wootton sometime in the 1730s a domed temple is shown on the hill, not a castle. Possibly the temple was a conjecture on the part of the artist, or suggested to him by the owner so that he could visualize the effect. At all events, there is no evidence that it was ever built. But the castle was, and is, imposing. It was of course a mock-gothic fortification with blind round and quatrefoil windows, crenellations, and pointed entrance arches. Ruinous today, it probably conveys more exactly now than then 'the true rust of the baron's wars', as Horace Walpole described the larger Gothic castle in Hagley Park, Worcestershire, designed by Sanderson Miller for Lord Lyttleton, who married Hugh Fortescue's half-sister Lucy.

Bishop Pococke says that the castle was 'lined with old wainscot and there are ancient carv'd settees and tables'.[4] It was for a hundred years a source of pride to the family, who used to picnic there and view the estate. The word 'picnic', incidentally, began to enter the language in about the year 1785, but there is no certainty as to its origin. The castle was on a mound on the hill, surrounded by a lower outer wall with eleven small towers on bastions. There were twelve swivel guns and a flagstaff. 'The guns are to be sealed and painted', ordered Hugh's half-brother Matthew, second Lord Fortescue, 'and care taken that their tompions are always kept in'.[5] Below the castle lay the bowling green with Bowling House. An instruction in 1752

The Gothic castle from which the house takes its name

The triumphal arch, closely modelled on the Arch of Constantine

orders that 'the nine pin alley must be weeded and kept clean and also the Turkey sopha with its cushions wiped and cleaned as they need.'[6] One suspects that the 'Turkey sopha' was a memento of Hugh Fortescue's two-year stay in Istanbul.

From the mansion a main axis descends down the slope, across a cruciform pond, over the Filleigh hamlet road, and up the hill opposite to culminate in a triumphal arch on the horizon. This was very much an interpretation of French axial garden planning. Trees were planted on each side of this axis so that the eye was compelled to follow the route from house to triumphal arch. At the same time a drive was laid from and to the road through the trees in a sweeping crescent, with the house at its apex. At this point, in front of the main entrance of the house, was a stretch of gravel that was known as the viewing platform. At each end of the crescent was a colonnaded lodge and an obelisk, visually marking the beginning and end of the drive.

The triumphal arch with its large centre arch and smaller side arches is closely modelled on the Arch of Constantine in Rome but without any of the latter's carvings of triumphal events. In fact, the Castle Hill arch is perfectly plain. Other classical allusions took shape. In the valley to the west of the house a temple with four simple Doric pillars and a plain pediment was erected next to the stream and called Satyr's Temple. Opposite, on the other side of the stream, a grotto was dug in the hillside and christened Sybil's Cave in honour of the legendary Sibyl of Cumae, south of Naples.

The story of this sibyl and her encounter with Tarquin, King of Rome, is worth repeating. She offered to Tarquin nine books of prophetic utterances at a vast sum. Tarquin laughed at the offer and the sibyl burnt three

An early photograph of Sybil's Cave (right) and Ugly Bridge (centre), in the valley to the west of the house

of the books. She then returned and offered Tarquin the six remaining books at the same price. Again Tarquin refused and sent her away. The sibyl burnt three more books and returned to Tarquin and offered the three remaining books but still at the original price. Tarquin was so surprised that he doubted the wisdom of his earlier rejections and bought the three books. The sibyl vanished but the books were kept in the Temple of Jupiter in Rome where they were used to interpret omens of doubt until fire destroyed the Temple and the books in 82 BC.

Above Sybil's Cave was the Chinese Temple, an open-fronted lath-and-plaster building, understandably known as the bandstand, which disintegrated in the 1960s; in 1987 its position at the confluence of five paths was taken by a lead statue of Pan bought from Halswell House, Somerset.

The estate forge on the road was given a classical façade and called Vulcan's Temple. Between it and the house was the stud, perhaps called the Indian Temple, but dignified architecturally by a classical portico. Above, on the hillside called Oxford Down, were the kennels designed 'in the gothick taste'. Further south was the British Spa House, ornamented by Doric pillars and a pediment, where the chalybeate spring water could be drunk. Bishop Pococke remarked that 'this is esteemed good for the gout'.[7] Opinions today on the taste of the iron-rich water vary, but to some it is not displeasing. Finally, in this perambulation of the landscape, to the west of the triumphal arch were the new church and also the Temple of Venus, tucked high into the hillside a few hundred yards from the arch. In front of the temple was a lawn flanked by trees. No

a

b

c

d

e

Engravings from Dr James Fortescue's *Dissertations* of 1759:
(a) the castle; (b) the Palladian villa at Clatworthy; (c) Filleigh church, designed to serve as an eye-catcher from the house;
(d) the Hermitage; (e) the avenue leading to the triumphal arch

trace of the temple remains today, but a painting of 1741 by the little-known artist Lange suggests it was a rotunda.

A mile to the east, between the old deer park wall and the river, the Hermitage was built. A hermitage was a traditional feature of an estate like Castle Hill, with a rustic outlook, a Greek cross over the entrance and a tiny garden. Often the walls were fancifully decorated and sometimes the floor was made of sheep or deer bones, as at Bicton House, east Devon, which is a very late example dated 1839. Only a few shards and tiles remain of the Castle Hill hermitage on the edge of the river, but in its day it was impressive, and a perfect place for a rendezvous or picnic. Whether a hermit with bible and lanthorn was ever installed is not known. Paid hermits were difficult to find and almost impossible to keep. The customary requirement not to cut nails or hair and to be ready for visitors to espy, studiously bent over a book, proved more than the wage was worth.

Bishop Pococke says of the Hermitage that:

it is covered inside and out with wood of different colours which resemble trees; in the middle room is an altar in a niche, made of the root of a tree, with a crucifix on it. On one side is the kitchen, on the other the bedroom with all the proper apparatus.[8]

Also to the west of the arch, but on the far side of the river, was a Palladian villa, called Clatworthy but sometimes misnamed either Nazareth or the Menagerie, with 'three office rooms below and three little rooms above. It is built with a false loggia of the Ionic order.' Finally, at a time when many great landowners were

The view to the south, across the valley, to the triumphal arch on the horizon

forcibly removing villages that spoilt views, Hugh, Lord Fortescue built Shamtown, a model village with a mock church tower grafted onto one house; this may be compared with the crenellated farmhouse at Stowe, which was deliberately intended to catch the eye and interest the spectator. Time after time the Castle Hill correspondence (preserved at the Devon Record Office), particularly between Matthew, second Lord Fortescue, and his agent Mr Hilliard, talks about how passers-by on the road will enliven the scene. Obviously the isolation of Castle Hill, in an underpopulated part of Devon, made busy human activity desirable. Today the reverse is true.

All of these buildings could be seen from the viewing platform immediately in front of the main door of the house where the two hemispherical arms of the drive converged. This stretch of grass and gravel, enclosed by a balustrade ornamented by urns, was the pivot of the garden. Behind lay the house, ahead a walk, bounded by lead lions and sphinxes, which led down to the great pond, which covered approximately 1½ acres. Thence, as we have seen, the grand walk led up the opposite hill to the triumphal arch. An unusual feature below the balustrade is the sculptured terracing of the slopes. Such turf treatment may be seen at Moor Park, Hertfordshire; Farley Hill, Berkshire; and Lainston House, Hampshire. The treatment is depicted in A.J. Dezallier d'Argenville's *La Théorie et la Pratique du Jardinage*, published in 1709.

Other influences were at work apart from Burlington and Herbert. The Duke of Newcastle was building Claremont with the help of William Kent; more importantly, Lord Cobham was creating Stowe. Both, like Hugh, Lord Fortescue, were Whigs. More particularly, Cobham was at the centre of an extensive network of relations that included the Lyttletons of Hagley and Fortescue at its periphery: Fortescue followed him into opposition in 1733. But it is impossible not to guess that Hugh Fortescue's 'mysterious visits to France' showed him garden treatments of the formal order to copy. The great lake at Chantilly, with its axial arms, is like a grander version of Castle Hill's cruciform pond. The descent from the house across water, up a grand walk, tightly bounded by trees, and then up to the horizon, is almost identical to the garden layouts of the châteaux of Marly and Sceaux. Most design is derivative and often duplicates.

HOW DID PEOPLE VIEW CASTLE HILL?

Bishop Pococke, as we have seen, was an enthusiast: 'the house is most happy in the ground and the command of water'. Dr James Fortescue, a distant cousin, wrote in a poem published in 1759,

> These lawns, these groves, these vista wide which vie,
> If not in pomp yet elegance of taste,
> With those of Stowe, of Marli or Versailles[9]

But not all were of the same opinion. It was remarked of Lord Cobham, with his endless flow of building at Stowe, 'well is his name Temple'. And William Gilpin, who was to be such a major influence on English garden theory with his interpretation of the picturesque, wrote that the Fortescues had been guilty of overbuilding their improvements:

From one stand we counted eight or nine buildings. The lofty castle might be object sufficient from almost every part of his improvements. This is the common error of improvers. It is a much easier matter to erect a temple or a Palladian bridge, than to improve a piece of ground with simplicity and beauty, and give it the air of nature.[10]

But that was 1798, when a new order was affecting garden design.

NATURALIZING THE LANDSCAPE AND ALTERING 'THAT FALSE FRENCH TASTE'

Before he died in 1751, Hugh Fortescue was beginning to doubt his own judgement and the landscape he had created. His half-brother Matthew, who succeeded him as the second Lord Fortescue, had already discussed the subject with him and, before he died, Hugh Fortescue had drawn a sketch of how the pond might be altered. Upon inheriting, Matthew seems to have determined to act upon his half-brother's intentions by deformalizing the landscape at Castle Hill. Mr Hilliard, the devoted and imaginative agent who contributed so much to the planning, said tactfully of Hugh Fortescue that 'the only mistake he seems to have been guilty of is sacrificing his happy genius to the test of his time.' (Letter, Christmas Day, 1770.)

On taking over the estate Matthew Fortescue issued these instructions 'for keeping the walks and other pleasurable places for a year':

1. For mowing and carrying the grass off the walk from the western iron gate to the end of long fir walk four times a year.
2. For raking leaves and cutting the bushments against the walk in Addabeer road as often as they need.
3. For mowing the platform before the Spa Bath House six times.
4. For mowing the Platform, cutting Yews, turning of borders before House.
5. For cutting the thorn hedges each side of the fir walk three times and keeping the fence.
6. For planting trees in room of them that are dead.
7. Keeping the clumps of firs on the Oxford Down.
8. Cutting the shady walk from Squire's house to the church and the evergreens the backside of the church as often as they want.
9. Cutting the hedge in Barnstaple road six times a year.
10. Cutting the thorn hedges round the Paddock six times a year.
11. Keeping a good fence round the paddock.
12. Weeding and keeping the black gravel walks and platform before the great house in good order.
13. Mowing, sweeping and carrying the grass round the paddock walks twelve times a year.
14. Keeping of grass and the bushments cut and carried away in the walks of both paddock roads.
15. Weeding and keeping the nine pin alley and before Turkey sopha clean, and the cushions wiped and aired as they need.
16. Mowing and carrying the grass, raking and cleaning the trees in the green plot by the little serpentine river paddock.
17. Cutting the yews and that part of the paddock road that overdrapes the yews and turning the borders of the yews all round.
18. Propping up trees that shall be pruned or thrown down.
19. Opening and cleaning all drains that shall choke.
20. Carrying in and out the urns.
21. Cutting the rushes in the paddock and great walk to the Arch as they appear in sight of the Hall Door.
22. Keeping all the edges of the serpentine rivers and canals.
23. Keeping all the vistas cut that point to the buildings.
24. Cutting the grass three times each side of the serpentine river in Dark Lane Wood and carrying it away.

25. Mowing the walks and cutting the slopes in Dark Lane Wood twelve times a year and carrying the grass away.

26. Cutting the grass under the trees twice a year and carrying it away and cleaning the trees from twigs and annual shoots as often as they shall want in Dark Lane Wood.

27. Cutting the yews, turning the borders round the Chinese Temple.

28. Cutting the bushments, keeping the walks clean from the Chinese Temple down to Sybil's Cave. Weeding of rockwork and walls for the Cave and Satyr's Temple.

29. Mowing the walk from the Chinese Temple to the north park through Mr Burgess' ground six times a year.

30. Cutting the grass on the Castle Green twelve times a year.

31. Cutting the hedges to the park gate from the house twelve times a year and keeping it in repair.

32. Mowing, carrying the grass away, raking leaves, carrying them away, six times a year in Clatworthy Wood.

33. For keeping the hoops in the paddock as usual.

34. Repairing all the cascades and sluices.

35. For a boy to roll before the house and other walks.

36. Raking the leaves in the park twice a year, carrying them away, mowing the walks all round the park three times a year and before the Hermitage four times, cleaning out and looking after the cascades in the park and taking away such trees as are dead and planting others in their place and carrying off the stocks and limbs where they fall.[12]

Prospect to the north by W. Watts, after Feary, 1785. Matthew Fortescue's deformalized landscape, with a serpentine river in place of the cruciform pond

But he had more things in mind than just the maintenance of his brother's garden. New prophets had appeared in the land. 'At that moment appeared Kent', said Horace Walpole, 'painter enough to taste the charms of landscape and opinionated enough to dare and to dictate. He leapt the fence and saw all nature was a garden. He felt the delicious contrast of hill and valley changing inperceptibly into each other, tasted the beauty of the gentle swell, or concave scoop, and remarked how loose groves crowned an easy eminence with happy ornament.'[13]

Alexander Pope, who valued his garden more than his poetry, sneered at the old formality where 'each alley has a brother and half the garden just reflects the other' and advised people to 'consult the genius of the place in all'.[14] Horace Walpole, writing in 1770, said: 'In Kip's views of the seats of our nobility and gentry, we see the same tiresome and returning uniformity.' William Kent was designing (1730) Rousham, which is probably still the most sublime garden in the country, and 'Capability' Brown had begun work at Stowe in 1741. The word 'serpentine' was coming into fashion to describe a new look in paths and rivers; no longer were they allowed to be geometric. Sir Thomas Robinson praised the practice of laying out gardens 'without level or line'.

So on 25 October 1769 Matthew Fortescue issued further instructions through Mr Hilliard:

1. The banks of the new sheet of water to be completed and closed up to the weir.
2. The spot of land under the bank, beyond the weir, to be planted with willows and other aquatic plants, the same behind the bank in the meadow belonging Town House Barton.
3. The bank of earth on the Bray side, under the copse, to be removed, and all the hedgerow rooted up from the corner of Bray Copse to the upper end of the meadow as far as the hedge is cut down.
4. The upper end of the meadow to be laid down to water, and the soil which is carried off to be laid in Holwell Meadow to prevent it being flooded but disposed as to lead the eye to the water and not to have any appearance of a bank.
5. The deception of a port to be favoured as much as possible; some of the trees by the side of the river, below the sheet of water, shredded and formed into masts in order to trace the entrance into the port.
6. The copse in Holwell to be cleared and the path made wider.
7. The path from the Meadow Park Wood to be made wider, and the borders planted with roses, woodbines etc. A list of the sorts is given to the gardener by his Lordship.
8. The roots on the side of the hill to be stacked up and the ground cleared to make a verdure.
9. The new pleasure ground in Holwell to be fenced in, and the Ha-Ha in the Meadow Park filled up.
10. The appearance of a rustic bridge to be made by the side of the Tucking Mill Road in the Wheat Park.
11. A hedge of Mr Locke's near Clatworthy which obstructs a view to be plashed.
12. The Pyramid to be drawn in masonry.
13. The schooner to be built, for which a contract is made with Henry Cross but I am to find all materials as well as the rigging of the vessel.
14. The Hot House to be altered agreeable to the contract.
15. A Tower or Temple to be built in Holwell according to the design which his Lordship has fixed upon, the whole of the expense not to exceed one hundred pounds.
16. A battlement to be put upon the ruin of the old lime kiln.
17. The wood belonging to Town House to be examined and, if felling of it will disfigure the landscape, to let it stand.

18. All the buildings to be put into thorough repair before the frost sets in.

19. The fences to all the pleasure grounds to be thoroughly secured so that no cattle can break into the walks.

20. The balustrade around the platform to be repaired, painted and sanded and the vases which are in decay repaired with heart of oak.

21. Ducks to be reared to stock the ponds.[15]

These matters were soon put in hand. The plan that Hilliard had drawn up for reshaping the river was rejected as still too formal. A series of minor projects were begun. A pyramid in the style of the one to Sestrius in Rome was erected in memory of a travelling companion of Hugh Fortescue. The old lime kiln was crenellated and a portcullis fitted. An ice-house was built and laurels planted around it to keep it cool. An octagonal menagerie was built, where Lady Fortescue kept her chickens and made a garden. T. Knott was paid a shilling a day for three days' work in filling the ice-house and foddering the deer; Grace Hunt was paid two shillings a week to clean and maintain the menagerie. Planting trees (particularly beech), cleaning ditches, turf-cutting, raking gravel, 'general weeding', gathering moss (for the Hermitage), planting ivy, filled in 1761 the normal week of nine people employed on the Pleasure Garden. But there were two major projects.

First, Matthew was determined to redesign the waters. The minds of 'men of taste' were full of the Claudean scene where a winding river lingered between high hills, crowned by classical ruins; where banditti played and an air of romantic dalliance epitomized the pastoral scene. This was the picturesque conception, where the land was required to conform to the picture, not the other way round. In theory, Castle Hill was ideal for this treatment and the river ripe for serpentining.

But the construction proved much less simple than the idea. The cruciform pond, covering between three-quarters and one-and-a-half acres, had to be filled, and a juncture forged with the new sheet of water planned below the projected temple of Holwell. There were problems of levels and volume. Hilliard wrote: 'You will be pleased to recollect that the water which runs from the west is very small and cannot, except in floods, cover any considerable length of weir to form a cascade.'[16] The ground was very hard to dig. Six carts with nine labourers were employed from seven o'clock in the morning until five in the afternoon. By May 1775, 12,000 cartloads had been excavated, quite apart from what was carried on the back. In the end the depth of the water varied from 4 ft at the lower end to 10 to 20 in at the higher. The basic problem was the declivity of the ground. Water could not, regettably, be made to run uphill, and the result was that it was difficult to see it from the viewing platform in front of the house. Also, it was not easy to connect the stretch of water from the Satyr's Temple in the west with the new water in the east under the Holwell Temple. This problem was more or less solved by concealing the juncture in the woods next to the lodge entrances. As for the visibility from the viewing platform, no solution was found, and the problem remains today. Hilliard propounded that 'by making the level of the banks easy and laying the turfs down to the low water mark the canal will appear full from the platform in the dry season.'[17] But, because of the steep descent from the platform, this helped only slightly. Only a much greater width of river would allow the water to be seen. And the willows that pierced the river banks were difficult to control.

The work was hard. Hilliard reported to Fortescue:

The weather though exceptionally cold has been favourable to the work in the paddock and considerable progress has been made this week but I found some difficulty yesterday morning to prevail upon the labourers to face the easterly wind. The most powerful argument was a glass of Cherry Brandy which I provided the last summer for these exigencies with common spirits. It is extremely cold with hurricanes

of snow but one of these days is equal to two in the business. The horses do their work more easily and expeditiously, the ground being hard and the labourers must plough their shovels briskly or starve.[18]

Lord Fortescue's reply sums up the easy relationship between the two men:

Your letter dated of the 17th instant is now before me, in which you seem most thoroughly to enter into the true spirit of the intended plan for the water as I have the ground quite perfect in my mind . . . but, without any compliment to you, you enter so thoroughly into the true spirit of the beauty of the place that I suspect myself of being in the wrong whenever I differ in the least from your plans.[19]

Hilliard enjoyed it all and occasionally philosophized:

Your Lordship's idea of planting clumps to take off the formality of the slopes in the paddocks may have a pleasing effect but I beg the favour to make some reflections before answering the question. The rectilineal form of the scene, though it may not please the casual spectator, yet when considered as an outline to the necessary regularity of the house and platform has some propriety in it though not conformable to present taste. This age seems to have run unto a contrary extreme to the last and has confounded all order and regularity indiscriminately. The palace and mansion house are levelled with the lodge or mere hunting seat. The latter is certain in taste if left to nature with the herds grazing at the door. But I humbly conceive the magnificence and elegance of the former not only justifies but demands some appearance of regularity.[20]

Castle Hill today. The south front from the triumphal arch

54

The second major project arose from Matthew Fortescue's decision to erect an elaborate new temple at Holwell Wood in honour of his late half-brother Hugh. He chose a superb position on the extremity of a bluff outlined against the sky with a valley below and the Holwell wood on one side. Its situation was remarkably similar to the Temple of Theseus, which his brother-in-law Lord Lyttleton was erecting at Hagley Park. To add to the drama of the scene, the meadows below were flooded and the trees shredded 'to favour the deception of a port'. Originally intended to cost no more than £100, the eventual cost was £700 because of constant difficulties in design, construction and materials. The final plan showed a square of 23 ft with the upper storey thrown into an octagon. The design was strictly classical. Four Corinthian pillars fronted a portico with a dentil-corniced pediment and six niches in the entrance wall behind. Pilasters carried round the cornice on each side. Hilliard suggested an abbey window from a Batty Langley textbook, but Matthew Fortescue did not care for the idea. He felt there was too much Gothic already on the estate. He ordered nine large urns instead, to grace the three fronts. His brother-in-law and constant adviser Lord Lyttleton supplied a recipe for stuccoing the bust of Hugh Fortescue which occupied the most prominent niche. By August 1772 the temple was complete, rising dramatically above a sheet of water in the flooded meadows below, with a small portable temple nestling just above the water. Around the frieze ran the inscription: ERECTED BY MATTHEW LORD FORTESCUE IN GRATEFUL REMEMBERANCE OF HIS BROTHER HUGH EARL CLINTON MDCCLXXII. But with this, Matthew Fortescue had had enough. As he told Hilliard:

> I would have all improvements stopped. The expense of the temple should in some measure be made to correspond with the great obligation I owe to my brother's memory – not only to this Temple but by hiding as much of that false French taste which in those days generally prevailed.[21]

He was content now to complete the details. A Thames skiff was ordered, and altered to resemble a gondola. A schooner was constructed to sail on the new sheet of water. It flew three flags, its figurehead being the Fortescue greyhound. To close the view of the river on the east a Chinese bridge with a false side (possibly similar to the one at Kenwood standing today) was constructed, but removed after a few years.

Hilliard reported:

> The improvement of many years reflection have been accomplished in a great measure, and must of necessity be more immediately felt in your Lordship's revenue than if gradually carried on but, as your Lordship will have the immediate enjoyment, I hope it will compensate for it.[22]

CONSOLIDATION 1785–1991

Possibly the most surprising aspect of Castle Hill is how little the gardens have changed in the last two hundred years. After Matthew, second Lord Fortescue, died he was succeeded by his son Hugh, created first Earl Fortescue. He lived almost all his life at Castle Hill, devoting himself to improving the park and estate around the garden. This was a wider aspect of gardening, so thoroughly endorsed by Humphrey Repton.

The deer park was extended east; Shamtown was made habitable and the parsonage was moved nearer the church; woods were planted throughout the estate, and it was reckoned by 1839 that a million trees had been introduced. Two new temples were built from demolished buildings: Sunrise Temple, also called Shrubbery Temple, was erected east of the house below the castle; Sunset Temple was built in the lee of the Castle hill. Here the first earl could view the sea off the north Devon coast as far as Lundy Island. Continuous problems

The two early nineteenth-century temples erected by Hugh, first Earl Fortescue: (left) Sunset Temple; (right) Sunrise (or Shrubbery) Temple

with the lake dam underneath the Holwell Temple resulted in the dam being demolished and the marsh land returned to pasture.

Sir John Soane carried out major alterations to the house at the end of the eighteenth century. Then in 1842, when the second Earl Fortescue had succeeded to the estate, the mansion was remodelled by Blore. Rubble from the rebuilding was used to fill in holes below the viewing platform, form a terrace walk, and repair the old road below the terrace to enable easier access from east to west. Significant changes were made externally and internally to the church so that the interior assumed a high Victorian feeling, with an elaborate monument to Georgina, Countess Fortescue, and rich foliage painting on the wagon roofs, the chancel roof being painted by Lady Susan Fortescue. But the most important alteration was the re-routing of the entrance drive, which was taken away from the front of the house and led to the back. This enabled much easier access to the stable court, and allowed the house and viewing platform to preside over the terraces and river uninterrupted by coach and wagon traffic.

Accident and nature have inevitably taken their toll. In 1934 a fire destroyed a large part of the house. Lord Gerald Wellesley and Trenwith Wills were employed as architects to rebuild it. Severe storms in 1982, and especially in 1990, caused grave damage to the house, woods and arboretum. But many of the finest trees survived, including the largest Sitka spruce in the country, nicknamed the Cathedral because of the way branches have layered and become trees in their own right. Finally, the destructive hand of man was only stayed in 1988 when a thoughtful planning inspector ruled that it would be sacrilege to run the North Devon Link Road in front of the house. But it was a close-run thing.

Ugly Bridge today

Satyr's Temple

During the Second World War Hugh Peter, Viscount Ebrington, only son of the fifth Earl Fortescue, was killed in action while serving with the Royal Scots Greys at El Alamein. On the death of the fifth Earl in 1958 ownership of Castle Hill passed to his daughter Lady Margaret Fortescue, who set about an extensive restoration of the entire estate. This included rebuilding the triumphal arch, Ugly Bridge and Satyr's Temple and also opening Sybil's Cave, which had been closed during the war for fear of injury to schoolchildren evacuated to the house. She has now built a tower at Shamtown in memory of her brother. In 1990 Lady Margaret transferred the estate to her daughter, the Countess of Arran, who currently lives at Castle Hill and is intent on continuing to keep it 'one of the most beautiful places in the country'.

REFERENCES

1. Dr Richard Pococke, 'Travels of Dr Richard Pococke Bishop of Osary in 1764', 1, British Museum Add. MS. fols 78–81.
2. Hugh, second Earl Fortescue, 'Castle Hill. Begun in 1854', Unpublished MS. Castle Hill Papers.
3. D(evon) R(ecord) O(ffice) 1262 M/E1/93.
4. Pococke, 'Travels in 1764'.
5. DRO 1262 M/E1/95.
6. DRO 1262 M/13 October 1752, Instructions.
7. Pococke, 'Travels in 1764'.
8. Ibid.
9. James Fortescue, *Dissertations, Essays and Discourses*, 2 vols (Oxford, 1759), I, p. ii.
10. W. Gilpin, *Observations on the Western Parts of England* (1798), pp. 174–5.
11. DRO 1262M/E29/17.
12. DRO 1262M/13 October 1752, Instructions.
13. H. Walpole, *Essay on Modern Gardening* (1785), p. 55.
14. A. Pope, *Epistle to Lord Burlington* (1731).
15. DRO 1262M/25 October, Instructions.
16. DRO 1262M/E29/17.
17. DRO 1262M/E29/18.
18. DRO 1262M/E29/17.
19. DRO 1262M/E29/17.
20. DRO 1262M/E29/17.
21. DRO 1262M/E29/18.
22. DRO 1262M/E29/17.

Castle Tor, Torquay. A design by one of Lutyens' pupils, Fred Harrild, dating from the late 1920s

The formal garden at Bicton, dating from around 1735

The rose garden at Castle Drogo, planned by Sir Edwin Lutyens to be seen in a deliberate sequence from bottom to top. The sunken rose beds are flanked by herbaceous borders and framed within yew hedges

The Garden House, Buckland Monachorum

The terraced garden at Arlington Court. After many years of simplification, the National Trust has returned to it some of the complexity of its Victo

Runnymede Gardens and Southern Slopes, Ilfracombe. The recently constructed bandstand marks the welcome revival of a tradition much threatened elsewhere

Wood. The prospect over the carriage court to the croquet lawn

Edward Kemp, a pupil of Joseph Paxton, laid out the bowling green at Knightshayes in the 1870s. Seventy years later Sir John and Lady Heathcoat-Amory excavated it to form the lily pond, one of the most tranquil features to be found in any of England's gardens

The terrace and formal borders at Killerton were designed by William Robinson around 1900. His original planting of roses was replaced by herbaceous plants and dwarf shrubs in 1957

An informal area at Coleton Fishacre. The main path through the gardens follows the line of the stream, which supplies this and one other pool on its descent from the rill garden to the sea

Chapter Five

JOHN SWETE AND THE PICTURESQUE

PETER HUNT

The Revd John Swete died in 1821 at the age of sixty-nine. The memorial in the Oxton pew at Kenton church relates that he had been a prebendary of Exeter Cathedral with a relish for liberal and elegant studies, courteous and humane, who lived and died in the bosom of his family. He lived an untroubled life in a troubled world. The American War of Independence took place, wars with France were fought and the French Revolution overthrew tradition. In England, the Industrial Revolution developed and agrarian change included the enclosure of two million acres of land between 1790 and 1810. Travel and transportation became easier with the completion of toll roads and canals. Radicalism and reform were beginning to change society, while the romantic movement – stimulating revolt against the formal orderliness of the eighteenth century – encouraged the educated with literary inclinations in their appreciation of unspoilt nature (particularly in its wildest form).

The surviving volumes of John Swete's diary present a revealing picture of Devon between 1789 and 1801, when he traversed the county, and these are illustrated with over six hundred of his own watercolours.[1] Description of some outstanding landscape or feature is often spiced with incidental comment on contemporary affairs. He refers, for example, to the purchase of Werrington, near Launceston, by the Duke of Northumberland for £60,000, together with Launceston and St Stephens, which returned two members each: 'Thus we are represented', he comments drily.

His own good fortune arose from a gift of the Oxton and other estates by his cousin Esther Swete of Trayne, Modbury, on condition that he change his name. His father was Nicholas Tripe, the Vicar of Ashburton, whose wife was one of the wealthy Martyn family and related to the Swetes. John Swete was brought up in Devon, schooled at Eton and went to University College, Oxford, before becoming curate at Kenn, a few miles from Exeter and close to his Oxton property.

Serving at Kenn between 1775 and 1782, he whiled away his leisure hours meditating like 'a Gray or Thompson whilst sitting in an arbour formed on the trunk a few feet from the ground' of a fine yew. The red sandstone church is largely unaltered, and the dreaming curate would still find his favourite tree (if a little mutilated). Here he became a friend of the neighbouring curate Polwhele, a keen historian, and together with their wives and other friends they formed a literary circle in Exeter where archaeology and the history of county families were discussed.

Towards the end of Swete's time at Kenn, the Revd William Gilpin (1724–1804), the pioneer of the picturesque movement, began to produce *Observations* on his journeys. Gilpin was much given – in an age of improving road systems – to travelling the British countryside in search of picturesque scenery. His tours of

Oxton House. The old Elizabethan mansion, inherited by John Tripe from a cousin, on the condition that he changed his surname to Swete (Swete, 1781)

the River Wye, the Lake District and the Highlands were published between 1782 and 1800 and inspired many of taste to follow his example. It is clear that the aesthetic principles that guided Swete were essentially those of the picturesque and, indeed, the parallels between Gilpin and Swete are obvious. Gilpin defined the picturesque as 'precisely nothing more than such ideas as can be formed into a picture'. He expressed a modicum of approval for 'Capability' Brown's landscape improvements, but a characteristic of Brown's work was beauty associated with smoothness; to be truly picturesque, a scene must contain elements of roughness. Objects in nature are naturally rough, but 'Nature . . . seldom passes abruptly from one mode of scenery to another', which suggests the desirability of concord between the individual elements of a view.[2] Gilpin's judgements are strikingly echoed by Swete, who, when contemplating the ruins of Newenham Abbey near Axminster, wrote:

There is confessedly a beauty which displays itself in elegant buildings, in many lawns, smooth and firm, which have not an ingredient of the picturesque and on the other hand, scenes may often be met with bordering on the romantic, rough and uncouth, which though they are strikingly picturesque have nothing of the beautiful. In contradistinction then to this sort of picturesque there

may be conceived to be another, whose characteristic trait may be that of beauty, where there is a harmony of pleasing objects – rough features softened, trees, buildings, rocks, roads, bridges, water – so charmingly intermingled as to present to the eye no discordant points . . . well adapted to the pencil.

Prosperity in the latter part of the eighteenth century allowed old houses to be altered or rebuilt and whole landscapes to be changed, often combining elegance and efficiency, landscaping and productivity. Estates were laid out with 'the hand of taste'.

The mixture of practical provision, picturesque outlook and landscaping technique was well expressed at Oxton, where Swete spent £6,000 on building a new house and laying out the grounds. The work was begun in 1781, the year he became a prebendary of Exeter Cathedral, and he admitted to having no regrets ten years later with the task still unfinished. The house was built on the site of an Elizabethan mansion, on a hillside looking across a valley to the south, and eastwards along it towards the Exe. The simple Georgian house was spacious, with detached servants' quarters and offices on the north side, with a courtyard between. The walled garden and a cottage were a short way from the house. The old mansion had been surrounded by garden walls and had an artificial terrace, where ancient yews formed an avenue of pyramids and where there were orchards and hedges. These were swept away to provide a lawn and open grass of a 'sweet valley descending between old woods of oak, through which a rivulet crept and where every object was not only discriminated but rural and picturesque'.

The new house and landscape at Oxton, created by John Swete after 1781 (T.H. Shepherd, after R. Brown, 1832)

The Gothic summer-house at Oxton, as reproduced in the *Gentleman's Magazine*, July 1793, wherein it was described as an
'elegant little house . . . lately built by Mr Swete'

The lawn was spotted with ash, oak, elm, lime and sycamore, and shadowing elms followed the stream along the valley while a series of glades within the surrounding oak woodlands aroused sombre thoughts. Swete built a summer-house with painted Gothic windows, thatched roof, and a neat pyramoidal chimney of Babbacombe stone. It had a small kitchen and bedroom beneath the stairs for elderly servants, and an upper room with a coved ceiling. Much altered, surrounded by trees, it still stands today, although it is no longer picturesque. He also built himself a Gothic gazebo beneath a group of ash trees to the south-east of the house, and this has now become an ivy-clad ruin within woodland that restricts views from the formerly exposed spot.

A red gravel path took Swete along the hilltops where he could enjoy the views, and at the Kenton entrance he built a 'ruined gateway', which through the bloody-mindedness, or perhaps stupidity, of his workmen, was pulled down twice before he had the ruin he wanted. 'It now stands a monument of taste or folly according to the humour, the caprice or sentiment of the spectator.' A lodge was built beside the gateway after Oxton was sold to Edward Studd in 1850, and in recent times the arch has been removed to allow access for farm machinery.

The 'ruined gateway' at Oxton, which had to be pulled
down and rebuilt twice before Swete had achieved the
desired effect (T.H. Williams, 1804)

The adjacent 40 ft high quarry was as beautiful as those at Exminster or Peamore. It still has tree roots
dangling down its face and old trees above – holly, mountain ash and oak, with luxuriant fern, ivy and
honeysuckle, mosses and lichens adding white, yellow and orange tints – 'So as to give the whole a delightful
effect.' He opened out the quarry by shaving down the edges, and may have created the small cave with a
curiously shaped entrance, perhaps for a hermit, after 1801.

There was a waterfall by the quarry and a lake near the entrance, and water flowed beneath an arch that
extended the ruined gateway: to give the little stream more importance, Swete raised the roadway 8 or 9 ft.
The gateway could be seen from the house, and of his sketch of the quarry and lake Swete comments: 'I have by
way of ornament, as well as to signify there are fish in the stream, introduced a man on the rock drawing a net,
but I might with equal propriety have placed a shepherd under the trees that overhang it, and, laying by his pipe,
have thereby illustrated the melody of the falling waters.'

The portrayal of rural activity coupled a suggestion of the simplicity of rustic life with picturesque
incident: stage-coaches, panniered horses, folk going about their business or merely chatting by the roadside.
Swete's painting style was not dissimilar to that of William Payne, the celebrated Plymouth artist, who in
turn visited Oxton and depicted Swete's landscape. Neighbouring properties gave Swete ample opportunity
to exercise his picturesque eye and record the scene in watercolour – Powderham, for instance, dominated by
the irregularities of the castle with its Gothic windows and doorway, pinnacled turrets and battlements, its
beauties often hidden against groves of elm and oak. He rather scornfully objects to the removal of the
shrubbery and old elms that wrapped the 'shabby front' in becoming obscurity, all because it had been found

Powderham Castle. Swete was able to exercise his watercolour technique by recording the appearance of neighbouring properties

that the servants' quarters were dingy; now 'the sun at the hour of dinner smiles cheerily on the table in the servants hall!!' There had been other 'disastrous' alterations by the late Lord Courtenay: the chapel had become a library, and he had used straight drainage channels to improve marshland instead of converting the winding River Kenn for this purpose. Newly planted clumps of fir were contrary to picturesque maxims; to have landscaped properly (he comments) would have needed a long purse and advice from a master in the art of landscaping.

All the rivers and estuaries of Devon provided wild and beautiful places as well as bearing much of the trade and prosperity of the county. The Exe was no exception, until the coming of the railways in the mid-nineteenth century. Gentlemen's homes speckled the hillsides on either bank, beyond the marshes, and merchantmen discharged their cargoes at Topsham or up the canal on Exeter's quays. Taking a boat from Powderham with his servant and two boatman, one elderly and knowledgeable and the other, one-eyed, for charity, Swete records unforgettable scenes. Encouraged by a large jug of porter bought from the Courtenay Arms at Starcross, they gently glided out past Cockwood Sod, where cottages peeped between the trees and the grandeur of Mamhead gave the hillside dignity. Two picturesque lime kilns with round towers and attendant sheds and buttresses were near the road and little river that were fringed with thorns and furze. At spring floods the little river running through a reedy valley widened into a lake that reflected them with even greater beauty.

Dr Drury, master of Harrow School, had a house on the hill beyond the village, where he had laid out his grounds with taste and cultivation, and placed a pleasure-house on top of the hill for the views. The loss of the wild for the cultivated landscape, resulting from this development, caused Swete to comment:

> I speak now as a rational member of society, who prefers the utile to the dulce and not the enthusiasm of a painter, who beholds the enroachment of art on nature with a jealous eye and who had rather cast the eye over tangled forests, gnarled oaks, and deep rutted lanes, than over the richest of pastures, the straightest and most luxuriant trees, and roads which for smoothness of surface might vie with a gravel walk.

He welcomed marshland being drained and an acre worth £3 per year rather than £1 as a consequence, but since then, Exmouth, Starcross, Topsham and Lympstone have grown, and the countryside has changed with them. Their setting is still superb, if less wild. We can still enjoy 'darling rock' and the red cliffs of Lympstone, where among the fishing huts on the Strand were two lime kilns and beautiful elm hedges behind. The kite and white stork no longer haunt the river and wildfowl have decreased with the marshes and mud flats. However, it is still possibly to enjoy a mud bank 'literally whitened by immense flocks of aquatic birds', the most attractive of which Swete felt were seagulls, best seen rising against a darkened sky heightening the contrast.

Not everything on the Exe was pleasing. He felt Ebford House, belonging to Mr Lee and built of brick, would have been better white – 'No landscape painter would ever introduce a red building into his piece!' – as invariably a white object at a distance is preferable. He may be referring to Whitestone church when he comments 'how beautiful is that white church tower embosomed in the groves of old elms have I oft exclaimed.' He evidently liked buildings with the simple roughcast of the country, with all its variations, but expressed reservations about the newly rebuilt Nutwell Court with its patent tiles, which were a little too yellow for them to be imagined Portland stone.

Swete found just as much beauty on the Rivers Tamar and Tavy. Following the Tamar southward from Greystone Bridge to Plymouth Sound he witnessed, he believed, some of the most beautiful scenery of the county, with a river winding beneath timbered cliffs. Country houses drew his attention. The groves of Mr Foot's country seat at Harewood gave the church perched above it charm, equalled by historic Cotehele and Pentillie Castle set in treed grandeur, and beautiful Budshead, the seat of the Trelawny family.

Best of all was Mount Edgcumbe, overlooking Plymouth Sound. From its terraces the wandering cleric had the most glorious views in Devon. The site, he opined, was almost too good for the house. Unbounded estuarine views included the peninsular grounds of Saltram, St Nicholas Island, the entrance to the Sound and Mount Batten, and the Citadel, bastions and town of Plymouth. Then came East Stonehouse with the finest marine barracks in the world, the Tamar, and the Dock with its arsenal, stores, forts and villas. Even more imposing were the men-of-war, 'the sure defence and vaunted glory of Great Britain'.

In the grounds 'the arbutus, the myrtle and the orange tree appear indigenous', beech, plane, chestnut and every species of forest tree flourished. Climbing the park on the northern side were extensive woods and 'here and there into the scenes of a few patches of open ground we can see the conical hill crowned with clumps of fir.'

On the far side of the Sound, Pomflet Creek was 'highly romantic', with lime kilns like round castellated towers, while Oreston had a 'delightful rural' aspect. There was a disagreeable muddy walk along the shore at Radford before arriving at a mill. He anticipated that it would be a picturesque object when reached, and was enthralled by a 'foamy waterfall gushing in the most luminous manner through the gloomy thicket'.

Saltram enjoyed tremendous views across the River Plym and the Upper Laira. The house has remained much

Saltram, painted by Swete in 1794

the same over the years, except for the enlargement of the library and the addition of a porch by Foulston in 1820. The inside was modernized by Robert Adam before 1782. When Swete visited it he records that it had 'a handsome room which for its size, elegance and expensiveness of its furniture is not surpassed by many in the Kingdom'. He also remarked on the fine collection of paintings there by Joshua Reynolds, who came from nearby Plympton. The landscape gardener Nathaniel Richmond had laid out the grounds in the 1770s, sweeping away some of the earlier features and exploiting the views. Magnificent drifts of hardwood were planted on the ridges and hilltops of the surrounding parkland. Until the freezing winter of 1797 deer were kept, but after this cattle contentedly chewed the cud amid the sylvan beauty, up to the house.

While staying with the Revd John Furneaux at Swilly, Swete painted scenes around a number of creeks, especially lime kilns. Painting rocks and quarries at Stonehouse ended abruptly when he found some men, close by, dragging a mutilated corpse from the water. It was from the thirty-two gun ship *Amphion* that had exploded and sunk a few days before. Ignoring clerical duties, he swiftly left.

Reality was introduced to the romantic Swete less gruesomely when he chatted to a miller close to Clifford Bridge on the Teign. The old mill and little wooden bridge seemed remarkably picturesque, he told the miller, who replied:

Lord Sir, for my part I can't see where the beauty you talk of lies. I thinks of how 'tis a cruel wished place; and as for the house 'tis in a most ruinous condition, I fears every hard wind 'twill tumble over my ears. Pray Sir if I may be so bold, as I see you be taking a plan on't be you going to buy it?

He replied that he only wished to draw it to remind him of this charming spot. 'The poor fellow grinned and shook his head as though he meant to say "Quod cumque ostendis nihi sic, incredulus!".'

After leaving Oxton on his old roan to explore the Teign, and before reaching Clifford Bridge, Swete sketched the ruins of Ashton House and its garden wall with a tower in the background, commenting that churches and towers were rarely beautiful. A number of his paintings belie this and, understandably, both Crediton and Cullompton churches were greatly praised, while the castellated Haldon Belvedere is repeatedly included in distant scenes. Spara Bridge at Ashton, with ivy growing over its old grey masonry, was drawn with the weir of tumbled stones serving a grist mill, like many others on the river. This and a ford close to Doddiscombleigh were delights in an enchanting landscape.

He did not follow the river slavishly, but visited Heltor and speculated about the various tumuli he found nearby, and ancient Britons. He then went on to Blackingstone Rock – 'The most curious collection of rocks I have ever met with' – and considered that the Druids might have scooped out the basins on the top, where rainwater tumbled from one to another. As an amateur archaeologist, Swete painted these rugged scenes and speculated about Spinster's Rock at Drewsteignton and the circles and standing stones of Torch Moor, where among the 'rude monuments of Ancient superstition' he describes an 8 ft stone with other smaller ones in a south-easterly line from it. He acknowledged the atmospheric contribution they made to the Moor, but concluded that they were not things of beauty.

By contrast Fingle Bridge, its surrounding hills clothed in oak, ash and sycamore with the fast-flowing Teign widening somewhat and becoming less dashing as it rolled toward Rushford Mill (which itself was splendidly sited), was remarkably picturesque. Chagford he found to be a mean and irregular place, except the parsonage owned by the Revd John Hayter, nephew of the Bishop of London. From here he was going to Prince Hall, Judge Buller's home, and set out with some trepidation north-west towards Gidleigh. Guided only by Donn's Map of the county, his trips were sometimes enlivened by losing his way. In the South Hams, for instance, he mistook his route when the signpost merely had initials for Start Point and Salcombe, while in mid-Devon, between Woolfardisworthy and Eggesford, there seemed to be nothing but a maze of roads through bleak countryside, connecting scattered farms; without the help of the local clergy he could not have crossed it. On this occasion he was fearful of being caught on Dartmoor at night (a lunacy that even locals avoided), so having taken a mutton chop and fed his horses he hurried on before darkness fell.

Mead's Warren was a wild and rugged place and 'the horizontal line of every quarter was formed by the hills and tors of Dartmoor, a wide waste where the eye found not a point to rest on.' He didn't find it romantic or picturesque, although he did find things to commend in Prince Hall. The grounds planted with beech had views of the West Dart, which could perhaps have been given more prominence, and thus, 'without violating the wild genius of the spot, give life and animation, which one seeks for in vain among the dreary hills that rise in a succession of heights beyond'. There was the romantic wildness of the West Dart and Cowsick at Two Bridges, the thundering tumblings of the Walkham River and the attractions of Sherberton, Huccaby and Brimpts, farms set in oak and pine woodlands. At Sherberton, above the valley, were ash and sycamore plantations. Beyond, thriving plantations of fir softened the scenery and made it smooth and picturesque, blending with the wild and romantic.

His view of the high moor was modified a little by the example of Dunabridge farm near Prince Hall, which a labourer earning only 4d. per day had saved to buy for £400, so becoming Farmer Leman. Thereafter, perseverance, keenness and understanding had increased its value threefold. Progress was possible, and the Moor had nothing on a mean or narrow scale. 'The great picturesque theorists, the enthusiasts who would

With Price and Knight grounds by neglect improve
And banish use for naked Nature's love

find it impossible to deteriorate the surface of the country so that it might assume a more rugged aspect.'

Swete's liking for clapper bridges probably had as much to do with their prehistoric associations (when nature was at its least trammelled) as with water crashing over boulders in romantically foaming torrents. Off the Moor, the scenery around Holne bridge and onwards to Ashburton was a delight for the painter of wild nature. Swete was even driven to wonder whether his enjoyment of Buckland Beacon and Ausewell, which with a little mist might look like castles, was that they were as a pleasure compared with the even wilder moorland.

Dartmoor's timelessness contrasted with Torbay's more recent development. For the diarist, Torquay was delightful, with pleasing and romantic scenery, rocks, woods, houses, villas and the sea, all of which were harmoniously mingled with vessels whose masts and rigging glimpsed amid the trees pleasantly enhanced the scenery. Staying at Shiphay manor, he was impressed with how the Revd T. Kitson had removed walls and opened the house to a most extensive and fertile meadow with hedgerows and an avenue of unpruned elms. The view of the bay was an added bonus.

Already, however, one of Devon's finest sights had been sown with the seeds of destruction, in the form of new villas and other building. Partly because of the sandy shores and holiday trade, and also because the fleet anchored there and obtained water from Brixham, which in turn attracted sightseers and publicized it, it rapidly grew into one of the biggest urban centres in the South West.

Approaching Torre Abbey, the home of the Carys, 'the grand display of nature was shifted to works of art, and the romantic was exchanged for the picturesque.' Swete walked through an avenue of ancient oaks with entangled branches forming an arch. The whole of the grounds and the house and old gateway were most elegant. The rooms of the family were on the first floor, and from them the impressive view sometimes included the British fleet riding at anchor.

Swete heard that that the Spanish Barn nearby was where Armada marauders – apprehended by English sailors, arriving inconveniently as the plunderers were about to start work – were driven and where they perished. Like all travellers of this time he enjoyed being awed and a little horrified, and this tale was no exception. To the rear of the house was a productive walled garden, and although Swete would have removed hedges and ditches and done away with nearby sandy lanes, he found the place attractive.

Historic ecclesiastical ruins could always be counted on for a picturesque scene, although the remaining stones at Torre Abbey were not impressive. Dunkeswell was more rewarding, as were the ivy-covered walls of Frithelstock, Polsloe and Canonsleigh (although the modern house built close to the latter and the nearby farm buildings did nothing for its setting). At Paignton, the red stone of the episcopal palace with its battlements and ivied walls and the trees around it, were a striking image. The remains of Lydwell chapel, not far from Oxton, were humbler.

Swete's relatives, the Martyns, had once been Lords of Barnstaple and Dartington and possessed Combe Martin, Martinhoe and Cockington. The old manor at Cockington with its nearby church and family associations was found by Swete to be particularly picturesque, in the days before the encroachment of Torquay. Similarly attractive was Compton Castle, a few miles away at Marldon, a baronial mansion with towers, gateway and machicolations, with its western tower covered in ivy, and its buttresses and arches striking objects. The Gilbert family owned it but had moved to Greenway on the Dart, leaving a farmer in the eastern end. At that

Swete's view of the gateway at Torre Abbey; historic ecclesiastical ruins could always be relied upon for a picturesque scene

time it was becoming derelict, but today it stands well restored and in the care of the National Trust, to whom it has been passed by the Gilberts.

To the west of Torbay, passing Brixham, which was full of bustle and had fishermen's cottages raised above each other on the hillside and where there were all kinds of 'blackguards', he reached Lupton. This was Sir Francis Buller's new house, and he approached it through newly planted grounds with a road winding pleasantly through a most luxuriant flowering shrubbery dispensing gales of fragrance, well sheltered by forest trees and a hill. In front of the house was a lawn, and already the hilltops had been extensively planted. The hill to the east was to be scooped into order like the others. The three-storey house 'has little projections, airy windows, balustrades and other harmonious decorations'.

At Dartmouth he stopped at a hotel whose landlady, Mrs Pentecost, was 'a flaunting dame and fair'. Dartmouth, with its coastal defences and a ruined chapel and a woodland walk, provided plenty to enjoy and paint, but it was the Dart and its river scenery that excited his keenest interest.

Towards Totnes the fine grounds of Sandridge, which was rebuilt in 1805 by John Nash, and Sharpham nearby, were noted for their charm and style. Lord Ashburton owned Sandridge but lived at Parke near Widecombe because it was wild and romantic, although perversely, the diarist records, he helped to soften the landscape by removing boulders and planting the hills. At Totnes, Swete stopped at the Seven Stars Hotel and explored the castle ruins:

Lupton. Swete recorded that the house 'has little projections, airy windows, balustrades and other harmonious decorations'

The distant appearance of the castle groves and the fine tower was a rich and pleasing background, whilst in the front nothing could be happier circumstanced than the old lime kiln and its natural accompaniments. The scenery at this point of the town, when the Dart was full, was of the most beautiful nature, the passing vessels and boats gave animation to the landscape on its banks which in whatever point it was viewed was of that cast with which a Swanevelt or a Vandermeer would have been delighted.

Also in the South Hams, his visits to Puslinch and Kitley were highlights. At Puslinch, the Revd James Yonge's house stood on a hillside, a 'credit to the hand of taste'. Although of red brick, the use of stone with it was a redeeming feature. A boat trip along the coast left him delighted with the beauty of the Yealm, although on his return he was critical of the barns at the Puslinch home farm, which had been crenellated. He felt that, as with the lime kiln built with turrets near the bridge at Aveton Gifford, the use of the building should be shown in its construction.

If the glories of Puslinch and the picturesque bridge at its entrance were great, then the situation of Kitley (home of John Bastard) between two arms of the sea was better. The River Silver had been dammed to form a lake, and an open lawn had been made; and in spite of its formality, the ancient avenue to the house was appealing.

North Devon, like the south, was prized by Swete and his contemporaries for its scenic qualities. For Swete, the Valley of Rocks near Lynton was wild and rugged and the daunting piles of stone and rural scenery beyond his ability as a painter to record:

The west view of Kitley. A Swete watercolour of 1794

The variety of their stupendous rugged forms, together with those rocky fragments which, broken from their shivered bases, had, during a succession of ages, rolled into a narrow plain, struck me with amazement.

Ilfracombe presented a somewhat kinder visage, 'the lighthouse, the harbour, and the wild mountainous rocks, which environ it, forming an uncommonly eccentric and romantic scenery'. Swete needed directions for his trip through Martinhoe and Trentishoe across wild and hazardous downland. But he enjoyed fine views from Buzzacot, which was newly built, of Combe Martin with deep glens, woods, hills and verdant pastures with towering hedgerow elms. Barnstaple, the principal town of north Devon, he found to be lacking in ancient buildings; the rest, he felt, 'in general seem of modern date and possess a neat and handsome appearance'. On the banks of the Taw he beheld an 'exceeding pleasant terrace walk' which, whatever its charms, was neglected by the ladies of the town in favour of a promenade on the bridge that provided a popular but rather perilous walk. Barnstaple had, like Totnes, a castle mound with remains of the fort and 'a noble prospect'.

Approaching Bideford he stopped at the old windmill at Instow (which is now only a stump) just above the church. His view of the confluence of the Taw and Torridge and all manner of craft using them, from boat and barge to merchantman, was one of the best to be found. He passed along the edge of Tapeley's grounds, the seat of the Clevelands, and found lime kilns which were supplied from Wales. The view from the old Bideford

bridge towards Instow which Swete found incredibly beautiful has been spoilt by an enormous modern crossing, but the outlook towards Torrington was equally irresistible and has changed less. There was an

> . . . assemblage of objects that harmonise vastly well with one another – the cliff fringed with ivy and old stumps and branches of trees, an ancient building beyond which were a few green enclosures with a wood rising in the highest style of placid beauty, which thrusting itself into the river helped . . . contract its width . . . one of the best exemplifications of the word picturesque.

Along the coast he viewed Lundy, admirably suited for pirates, although two or three families lived there. The 'hanging gardens' of Clovelly and the houses clinging to the cliffs created an impressive spot. The rocks here had a beautiful variety of colours, red, light brown, purple, all intermingled with a profusion of ivy and underwood which he felt produced a charming and romantic effect. Together the town and the cliffs presented 'a singular scene'.

Hartland Abbey had been altered by John Meadows on behalf of the owner, Paul Orchard, in 1779, and Swete found the grounds laid out in a superior manner. Nearby he came upon a mill set amid beautiful scenery by a little gurgling trout stream. The abbey was elegant and had a magnificent appearance in the Gothic style. The scenic glories were exceptional and included a variety of rural objects that harmonized perfectly, not least the little bridge, which he painted.

Leaving the noble parish church of St Nectan, and the attractions of the neighbourhood, he made his way across the largely unenclosed wastes to Torrington. Set on a hillside, the town has views of the Torridge winding below through rich farmland. New Bridge and Taddiport Bridge were attractive places, although the remains of the castle and town walls were a disappointment to Parson Swete. Nevertheless, from a hill opposite, 'Torrington full in view, exhibits a conspicuous and romantic object'. Close at hand was Beam, the splendid home of Dennis Rolle, 'a most lovely and sequestered spot, protected on every side by the richest woods of the finest amphi-theatrical form, the roots of which were washed by the river.'

While in north Devon Swete visited two other major houses. At Tawstock he saw Sir Bouchier Wrey's seat under construction, opposite the village, in a Gothic style very similar to Hartland Abbey; Swete thought that it would in time become one of the finest houses in the county. Surrounded by trees, it dominated the hillside that ran down to St Peter's church. It was conspicuously sited and, unlike Castle Hill at Filleigh which he also visited, he felt that the grounds had considerable beauty.

Walking through the grounds of Castle Hill, he probably accepted that the imposing Palladian mansion might have been attractive had the grounds been laid out with more taste. He disliked the terrace and its balustrade, and 'having hinted my ideas on the deformity of the Appearance I was pleased with the information that this old stile was to be abolished, and that the lawn was to ascend gradually with Nature's best embellishment to the front door.' He was similarly caustic about the feature of a dog kennel in the middle of a field. These defects were offset by the castellated gazebo that stands above the house on the hill ridge, and the River Bray flowing through the grounds. The straight avenues of trees were not to his taste, although the mature trees and a temple dedicated to Hugh, first Lord Fortescue in 1772, were.

He found a hermitage, built with taste and propriety, of tree roots, crooked branches and mosses of different colours, with three cells, the middle one an oratory with crucifix, the right a dormitory with straw couch and seat, and the left a sitting-room with a stool, old table and chimney. In Mr Seal's woods at Dartmouth was a hermitage built of the same materials, acting as the focal point of a walk. To Swete's surprise he found therein a 'ruddy faced damsel' ensconced, with a modern parlour and a kitchen more adapted to cooking a dinner for the corporation of Dartmouth than for an abstemious hermit. There was no scrumpy girl at Castle Hill.

Tawstock Court, near Barnstaple. Swete saw the house under construction and thought that it would in time become one of the finest houses in the county (*Gentleman's Magazine*, 1817)

East Devon had the same profusion of the picturesque as other parts of Devon, and among the scenes Swete described were the Otter valley and Cadhay at Ottery St Mary, Metcombe in the well-treed hills overlooking the marshlands of the Axe, and the glorious countryside around Honiton, which offered magnificent views of prosperous well-wooded hills with fine country houses like Wolford Lodge, Tracey and Buckerell.

Escot was a splendid house (which, he ventured, would have been better if rendered) with an oval pond in front, set finely among mature trees. All that it needed to make it inconceivably picturesque was for the water to be expanded by damming the valley. In fact, this had at one time been done, and a yacht had been moored before the house and a cannon fired to mark the start and finish of the working day. Unfortunately, after torrential rain the dam had burst and two or three cottages had been washed away.

At Combe House, Gittisham, the home of the Putts, Swete found hills sweeping up behind the house, covered with oak, and lower down elms, with a stream running through a valley. It seemed such a magnificent spot that with only minor changes it could have become 'grand! beautiful! romantic! and uncommonly picturesque'. Civilized scenes like this presented a contrast to some parts, like the flat land between Aylesbeare and Straightway Head near Whimple which was still unenclosed and scrubby, although agricultural improvements were being made. This had its disadvantages, and near Culmstock he found that beech trees at Maiden Down he had admired for thirty-five years had been felled. He was mollified by finding the wild unproductive common enclosed, with productive fields and new plantations.

There were modern seats, like Bridwell at Uffculme, with 'the embellished lawn, the grove, the plantations, the rivulet and the sheet of water, . . . possessed of those elegant beauties of rural nature of which our forefathers knew little or nothing'. The combination of architecture and landscape seemed to Swete to embody an elegance and refinement unknown outside England, where it had been brought to perfection.

On the way to Bampton there were equally fine sights. Bickleigh Castle, seen across a flat valley grazed by cattle, had become an ivy-clad ruin inhabited by a farmer while Collipriest, overlooking the Exe, was more impressive, 'seated in a hollow between two hills, clad with wood, and had a pleasing appearance'. At Bampton he admired the natural beauties of a quarry face that rose steeply beside the river. The church and the countryside around were just as attractive, but the kilns and the carters who used the quarry appealed even more. He noted that a hogshead of lime cost 13s. 10d., or 13d. more than in Westleigh, because of labour costs and type of material.

The rugged scenery at Chudleigh aroused similar sensations. The woods, rocks and waterfalls around Chudleigh were sufficiently romantic for him to compose a sonnet and to record his awe of the 120 ft high rock face, where two or three people had been killed.

The beauty of waterfalls often caught Swete's attention but he was careful to point out that Chudleigh, Lydford, Becky, Canonteign and Brent were all attractively different. Passing through Lydford Gorge, he drew the cascade and reaped a little horror from the story of a suicide that had occurred at Lydford bridge. The gorge

Oxton, John Swete's greatest love and pride. 'All together were in harmony, and were accommodated to the building, and character of the place' (Stewart and Burnet, after Revd J. Swete, 1808)

'was highly picturesque and in particular at the point where the stream rushing from the cascade formed a conflux with the Lyd'. It depended almost entirely on the variety of the woods and the light and shade, but the cheerful song of a woodcutter carting away timber made it the more romantic – 'it was the very woodman that Virgil has portrayed.'

Swete's descriptions of his travels are complemented by his paintings. Both, it must be said, are 'general views'. Detail is lacking, by and large. Rarely, for example, does he mention in depth the cultivation of flowers, despite his consuming interest in landscape. Only at the Abbey Farm in Exeter, once the Priory of St James, does he do so. Widow Templar used a stone coffin for growing flowers: 'the dead body of a monk had been supplanted by a little parterre of flowers, which gave a decoration, beautiful at least, if not appropriate' of hyacinths and polyanthus.

> Where the dead monk intumulated lay
> Sweet flowers arise to scent the breath of May.

Swete's travels were interspersed with intellectual homilies, and in truth only really come to life with accounts of the wealthy and their works, and once or twice with those of humble folk of no consequence, who were the essential warp in the fabric of country life. He displayed the greatest affection for his home county and its countryside, but his greatest love and pride was Oxton. There, as at neighbouring Trehill, Bickham, Mamhead and Powderham, the grounds had been improved, keeping ancient groves and providing gravel walks winding through them, or verdant lawns. 'All together were in harmony, and were accommodated to the building, and character of the place.'

REFERENCES

1. 'The Picturesque Sketches of Devon' by the Revd John Swete originally ran to twenty volumes. Volumes 3, 5 and 19 were destroyed during the Second World War; volumes 2 and 11 were damaged to an extent that renders them unfit for production now. The remainder, from which the material for this study has been drawn, are available at the Devon Record Office (DRO 564/M).

2. M. Batey, 'The New Forest and the Picturesque' in G. Hedley and A. Rance (eds), *Pleasure Grounds* (Horndean, 1987); D. Jaques, *Georgian Gardens: The Reign of Nature* (1983).

Chapter Six

The Creation of Endsleigh: A Regency Picturesque Masterpiece

Richard Stone

Endsleigh has been described as 'A uniquely complete example of the Picturesque taste' by Christopher Hussey, the leading authority on the subject and author of *The Picturesque*, the pioneering study, published over fifty years ago, of the aesthetic movement of the late eighteenth century and early nineteenth century, applied to art, architecture and landscape design.

The inspiration behind the creation of Endsleigh was Georgiana, Duchess to the sixth Duke of Bedford. An inscribed stone tablet set above the fountain in the stable courtyard at Endsleigh records:

> Endsleigh Cottage was built and a residence created in this sequestered valley by John, Duke of Bedford, the spot having previously been chosen for the natural and picturesque beauties which surround it by Georgiana, Duchess of Bedford. The first stone of the building was laid by her four eldest sons . . . September 7, 1810.

The picturesque masterpiece was the result of a Regency collaboration between the Duke and Duchess of Bedford, their architect Jeffry Wyatt (later Sir Jeffry Wyatville) and Humphry Repton, landscape gardener. Wyatt designed the house, stables and other picturesque buildings about the estate and Repton advised on the gardens and wider landscape setting.

Wyatt was a prominent Regency architect with a reputation for period restorations and additions to historic mansions. He came from a family reputed to have produced 25 architects, 11 surveyors, 8 builders, 5 sculptors and 3 painters. He was the nephew of James and Samuel Wyatt, two of the leading English architects of the time. His masterpiece was the romantic remodelling of Windsor Castle for George IV, earning him the distinctive suffix 'ville', and for which he was given a knighthood in 1828.

By the time Endsleigh was under consideration, Repton had established himself as the leading English landscape gardener of the period, taking over this mantle from his great mentor Lancelot 'Capability' Brown (1716–83). Repton's success was largely due to the persuasive way his proposals were presented to his clients, using his famous Red Books, so-called because of the colour of the leather bindings. These cunningly attractive

The Tamar Valley setting of Endsleigh Cottage (F.C. Lewis, *c.* 1840)

devices took the form of a manuscript text interspersed with drawings, often with moveable flaps showing the grounds before and after improvement.

The land at Endsleigh was originally owned by the Abbots of Tavistock, to whom it was granted by the Edgcumbes, whose seat was nearby. After the Dissolution of the Monasteries, the entire 15,000 acre estate was granted in 1540 to John, Lord Russell, first Earl of Bedford, at the same time as Woburn Abbey. Although the Russells were a West Country family, originating in Dorset, none made a permanent residence on the estate until the sixth Duke decided to do so at the start of the nineteenth century. The site selected for the house by Georgiana was remote. A pencil sketch by Wyatt shows a small thatched building there. Repton confirms this, and wrote in his Red Book: '. . . an irregular Farm-house, little better than a Cottage, backed by a hill and a beautiful groupe of Trees'. He considered it impossible even to wish it to be replaced by an abbey, castle or palace, 'not one of which could have been so convenient and so applicable to the scenery, as this cottage or rather "groupe of Rural buildings".'

Repton had been consulted by the duke since at least 1804, and produced the Red Book for Woburn Abbey, his Bedfordshire estate, early in the following year. Family letters tell us that Repton was in contact

intermittently thereafter, probably supervising work at Woburn and eventually discussing developments at Endsleigh.

At first Repton and his two architect sons, John Adey and George Stanley, were consulted on the siting and layout of the proposed house at Endsleigh, which was to serve as an occasional sporting retreat for the Duke and his family. Naturally, landscape considerations came to the fore when determining the style of architecture for the retreat. Prompted by the existing farmhouse in the heavily wooded dell site, the Reptons considered the style 'most applicable to the scenery' to be *cottage orné*. Their proposals for the house were presented to the duchess in the form of a plan and three watercolour perspectives, all of which are signed and dated 'H. Repton and Sons 1809'. Although both of Repton's sons were included in the credit for the designs, it is most probable that John Adey made the biggest contribution to the work. It was always his father's intention that John should assist in, and eventually take over, his practice; George Stanley, the second son, also trained as an architect, but pursued a career largely outside the family practice, whereas John was meticulously groomed to follow his father. Furthermore, the Tudoresque lodge at Woburn had been built (1804) to a design by John, so it was perhaps inevitable that he would work in partnership with his father on the proposals for the house at Endsleigh.

To avoid the incongruity in the landscape of a single large structure simply dressed in the style of a cottage, the problem of housing the duke and duchess and their extensive retinue was to be avoided by planning a group of individual thatched cottages, arranged picturesquely, and linked by covered walkways. The Reptons' plan for the house is captioned:

Ground Plan of a Cottage for Her Grace the Duchess of Bedford serving to show the proposed sites of the several detached parts – which may be more extended or compressed on the Plain – the buildings two stories high are distinguished by blacker colour, the others being only one storey high or walks and corridors and thus any quantity of low building may be added and concealed by the corridor without altering the design for the flatter site near Tavistock . . .

The flexibility described in the caption for the house plan allowed the layout to be adjusted to suit either of the two alternative sites proposed. The envisaged effect is illustrated in three beautifully executed watercolour perpectives accompanying the plan. One of these, captioned 'Effect of a cottage proposed for the site in the field near Tavistock', depicts the cottage as if it were built in accordance with the plan and equates approximately with the eventual siting of the house. The other two perspectives show the effect of the cottage as if built on the alternative 'Dell' site, which can be identified as being located on the western slopes of the steep-sided valley west of the present house. The overall impression given by the three watercolours is of a picturesque hamlet rather than of a single dwelling with offices attached.

The Reptons' proposals for the cottage were evidently rejected by the duke and duchess, in favour of a rather more lavish and substantial *cottage orné*, with associated stables and offices, designed by Jeffry Wyatt. Although Wyatt was a prominent and fashionable architect at the turn of the century, it is puzzling that he should have been chosen as the architect to build in the *cottage orné* style at Endsleigh, especially as most of his prior commissions were for Classical or Neo-Gothic/Tudor mansions. Nevertheless, Wyatt's design for the house clearly demonstrates his appreciation of the natural advantages of the magnificent site. In planning the layout of the house, his primary consideration was aspect rather than symmetry; accordingly, the wings were angled to exploit the glorious views to the east, south and west that the site afforded.

Although Repton and his sons presented a design for a *cottage orné*, the commission ultimately went to Jeffry Wyatt. The south elevation of Endsleigh Cottage as built (E. Byrne, after J.P. Neale, 1818)

While Repton would have been disappointed at not being commissioned to build the house, he at least had the consolation of knowing that his recommendations concerning its style and siting were ultimately adopted by Wyatt. Repton and Wyatt had worked together at Longleat, but it is unlikely, in view of the competition for the house commission, that their working relationship at Endsleigh was entirely harmonious. Of the house, Repton wrote:

> With respect to the manner in which the design has been executed, I shall only say, it is such as will do credit to the *name of Wyatt* when time shall have harmonized the raw tints of new materials. The design and outline are so truly picturesque that I must regret my inability to do them justice.

Derek Linstrum, in his biography of Wyatt, regards Repton's comment as 'unusually cool for a writer who was almost as obsequious in his attitude to the architects associated with him as to his employers', and believes 'the raw tints were not entirely pleasing to Repton's perceptive Eye of Taste.'

In 1814, some four years after the foundation stone had been laid for the house, Repton was eventually commissioned to advise on its garden setting and also to make proposals for the improvement of the surrounding grounds. Endsleigh came about when Repton was approaching the end of his celebrated career, throughout which his theory and practice were continuously evolving, and at a time when he was confined to a

wheelchair, as a result of a carriage accident in 1811. In the introduction to the Endsleigh Red Book, Repton greatly regretted the fact

> . . . that the most picturesque site to which I have been professionally consulted should have been reserved to so late a period of my life, that I could only become acquainted with its recondite beauties, by being carried to places otherwise inaccessible to a cripple.

By the turn of the century Repton had moved away from the precepts of 'Capability' Brown with his sinuous lines, great sheets of water and classical mansions set, sculpture-like, on shaven lawns, sweeping up to and surrounding the house. Instead, his essentially pictorial conception led him to consider the house as an integral part of the landscape. He also reacted against the 'bare and bald appearance' of Brown's work around the house, and in response at Woburn, from 1804, he was creating a series of linked specialist gardens close to the house. This 'gardenesque' concept was to be taken much further by Repton; by 1813, at Ashridge, Hertfordshire, he was proposing many different styles of garden close to the house.

Perhaps such close attention to the immediate vicinity of the residence was evolutionarily inevitable in view of the creative influences that were beginning to have their effect on garden design at the turn of the century. It is also likely that his concentration on such specialized and revivalist details was encouraged by Repton's diminished mobility after his crippling accident.

Repton was evidently anxious about access at Endsleigh, and a letter he wrote dated 14 July 1814 records that his daughter would be in attendance as his nursemaid during his visit. He also had to rely on the services of John Hutchins, a local land surveyor, to prepare the necessary survey plan for the Endsleigh Red Book, which was presented to the duke only three years before Repton's death. Letters Repton wrote at the time indicate that he made only one visit, lasting four days, in connection with the preparation of the Endsleigh Red Book. He arrived 'on the spot' on 8 August 1814. What he found can be interpreted from various contemporary reports and letters written by himself and others, and also from the contents of his Red Book (prepared afterwards), particularly the text, survey plan and watercolour perspectives showing views of the grounds as he found them.

Having entered past the existing lodge, Repton would have seen 4 acres of new planting to the north side of the coach drive to Endsleigh Cottage and a further 8 acres to the south, either under preparation or actually planted. He would have seen the Cottage in an advanced state of construction, and while the Dairy was yet to be started, a 4 acre plantation had been made west of the house in 1812, with a further ½ acre above the house. Four acres more were planted to cover the Kitchen Court in the year of his visit, and a large nursery had been established by the autumn of 1814, by which time no fewer than 240,000 plants in about twenty-five varieties were said to have been set out there.

Repton had been directed to pay special attention to the sloping area of grassland that fell away from the south front of the house down to the Tamar – crucial to the whole landscape potential of this remarkable site. Work was already proceeding here when he arrived. About halfway down the gradient a curious double ha-ha-like earthwork was being formed and retained by a stone wall and bastion.

Looking south-east from the dining-room ran a long broad terrace, unfenced along its cliff face fronting the river, and with an ornamentally planted bank, partly walled, running the full length of this grassed walk. Near the Cottage, a small pathway led north from the terrace, presumably, as now, to an upper broad, gravelled path running parallel with the former, to terminate by an old quarry. In Repton's *Fragments* (1816) he shows in the

Repton's panoramic 'before' view from the dining-room at Endsleigh (from *Fragments on the Theory and Practice of Landscape Gardening*, 1816)

The 'after' view, showing Repton's proposed conservatory, the pierced wall on the left-hand side, and the cottage by the bend in the Tamar with a smoking chimney to 'enliven the scene' (*Fragments*, 1816)

panoramic 'before' and 'after' views a classical temple poised above the final visible bend of the Tamar, seemingly more distant and on a lower level than the extant shell house. The published panoramic view, in fact, compresses the sweeping Red Book original laterally, reducing considerably the angle of vision yet retaining all essential features.

Repton records that eastward beyond the terrace, two drives diverged — one onto the upper slope, the other down to the Tamar flood plain. Some of the existing drives in Leigh Wood were rather terrifyingly steep, 'sublime' experiences to be mastered, rather than aesthetically picturesque scenes to be enjoyed. Other drives were screened by trees to the exclusion of delicious views, and promising rock faces were obscured totally by brushwood.

The dingle (later Dairy Dell), west of the house, had to wait for Wyatt's dairy, but some work had already been done to harness the copious natural water supply to good effect. Two leats had been cut along the contours of this valley: one, towards the top of the Dell, flowed out to adjacent meadows and the other, on the east side, supplied water to the house. Land on the Cornish side of the Tamar, beyond and below the bastion, had apparently only recently been annexed to the house grounds, but there was no crossing-point for the river.

The question arises as to who was responsible for the earlier landscape work at Endsleigh, before the house had been completed. At Woburn Abbey an important employee about the estate was Repton's 'ingenious friend', Mr Salmon. Buildings there are still named after him, and his name is mentioned by Repton in connection with the very steep drives at Endsleigh. What has been deduced of these early works gives the impression of an amateur hand directing operations. Yet there was an underlying appreciation of the site's potential, if not the vision and skill to master its subtleties.

It is almost certain that it was Wyatt who was responsible for the design of the terraces and bastion walls under construction at the time of Repton's visit, and subsequently described and illustrated in the Red Book. It is evident from the clear and careful drawings made by Wyatt for Ashridge in Hertfordshire that he was an architect who was prepared to take great pains with garden details, and he most likely produced similar drawings for the earlier landscape works at Endsleigh; later detailed drawings for garden features certainly suggest this to be the case.

Like Wyatt, Repton was also consulted by the Earl of Bridgwater at Ashridge, and presented his Red Book in the latter part of 1813. The earl wanted gardens immediately around his new house, and Repton planned a collection of no fewer than fifteen 'gardens of different styles, dates, characters and dimensions' associated with the house at Ashridge. No doubt this close attention to the detail of the gardens around the house influenced Repton's thinking at Endsleigh; just as at Endsleigh, he was unable to supervise the garden at Ashridge, and it was left to Jeffry Wyatt to execute his proposals.

Repton devoted a section of the Endsleigh Red Book to a discussion 'of the Picturesque'. In the text he defines 'picturesque circumstances in real Landscape' under three headings: 'Steepness of Ground', 'Abrupt Rocks' and 'Water in rapid motion'. All of these qualities he recognized as being present at Endsleigh, and advised that they should be revealed to view:

In the Drives through Leigh Wood — some advantage has been taken of the Steepness — but it should be shown as an object of beauty from the precipitous side of the Road, and not as an object of terror by making Roads too steep. There are many places in which romantic Rocks are now totally hid by brushwood, these doubtless require to be brought into view — but of all picturesque subjects there is none so interesting as Water in rapid motion — and it is the duty of Art to avail itself of every opportunity to force it into notice, since in a mountainous Country, there hardly exists a dell or dingle in which some stream does not steal off imperceptibly under long grass or foliage or brushwood, which might be drawn forth to form a more conspicuous part in the Picturesque Landscape.

What Repton proposed at Endsleigh is graphically explained and illustrated in his Red Book, and also in a series of letters and a report leading up to its production. The extent to which his proposals were implemented may be judged from the evidence on the ground, and also from various archival sources post-dating his visit. A most outstanding illustrative record of the implemented proposals is provided by a beautifully executed series of watercolours painted by John Cook Bourne, dated 1841. These paintings show, in the most exquisite detail, views of the gardens not long after their completion; they provide a unique record of this picturesque creation.

Repton was quick to appreciate the enormous potential of the site. Almost immediately, and certainly within a day of his arrival, he had drafted a report recording the proceedings of the day spent on site with William Adam, the duke's agent. Repton evidently ran out of paper, which suggests that the report (written in pencil) was prepared either at Endsleigh or in his lodgings in Tavistock: he would hardly have run out of paper in his office at home. In the introduction he points out that the Brownian approach would not be appropriate for Endsleigh:

> The character of it – totally different from all others and requires a kind of treatment accordingly – I suppose Convenience, Comfort and Picturesque effect to be the first consideration – equally distinct from the gardens of the palace – or the shaven lawns and serpentine lines of Brown's School – The dressed ground in front of the house being fenced at a considerable distance – it may perhaps be too late to say – I should have preferred it only being the width of an ample terrace – but now I have marked such patches for flowers or shrubs as will take off that bare and bald appearance so justly condemned by Brown's opponents – the bastion in the front will be improved by steps at the angles and indeed where such a wall circumscribes the house lawn it is highly advisable to make as many outlets as may be convenient to give that freedom which is always sacrified by a ha!ha! – This pleasure ground is proposed to be connected with Leigh Wood by a walk described to the gardener and marked on the spot but it should also connect with the dell to the west and also the ground to the north.

It was in this report that Repton first advanced his proposal for the walled kitchen garden, the siting of which he regarded as crucial for 'much of the habitable enjoyment of the place'. He went to great pains to promote the

The dressed ground in front of the house (W. Deeble, after W.H. Bartlett and H. Worsley, 1831)

idea of bringing the kitchen garden close to the house to take advantage of 'dry walks along a sheltering wall, which in summer may produce fruit and in winter yield comfort and protection'. In choosing the steeply sloping ground to the north of the house (immediately adjacent to the stables), Repton concluded that 'there cannot be a better situation for the three purposes of orchard, nursery and succulents than the fields which hang towards the south and will not be visible from the approach when the plantation grows up. I should therefore advise the fruit walls be collected together in hanging terraces in the concave hollow.'

To protect against the exposure to south-westerly winds, to which the gardener at first objected, Repton proposed that 'the sweeping winds from the valley would be checked partly by the house and conservatory – and also by the terrace or espalier walks for apples, pears and filberts, the two end walls dropping down the hill would give new aspects and tend to shelter the garden.' A plan and section showing the effect of the kitchen garden demonstrate that Repton proposed to link it to the house by a bridge over the coach road and connecting to a trellis-work conservatory contiguous with the house.

In summing up his first report, Repton wrote:

Three general hints has occurred to me relating to such situations at Endsleigh – viz
first – to let no water to escape invisibly
second – to show rocks where they are hid by brushwood
thirdly – to make no roads or walks too steep.

Repton found that there were three major landscape components to exploit and articulate with the Cottage, and the whole of this contrived area to consider in relation to the given remarkable natural features of the broader scene, namely:

(i) the sloping ground and panoramic view south of the house,
(ii) the terraces extending south-east, the sweep of the Tamar beyond and the rising ground to the north-east, and
(iii) the dingle, later Dairy Dell, with its waterways, to the west of the residential buildings.

In seeking to exploit the first of these landscape components, lying to the south of the house, Repton sought to take full advantage of 'that line of River which constitutes the leading feature of the Place by an interrupted continuity of glitter . . .'. When he attempted to mark out the positions of 'flower patches on the naked lawn' sloping from the house to the valley, he found it 'impossible to site a single rose bush without hiding the line of the Tamar'. Evidently the duke was dissatisfied with the work already in progress south of the house, presumably under the direction of Wyatt, because Repton was instructed to direct particular attention to 'the fence and line of Demarcation, betwixt the Lawn to be fed and that to be mown and dressed as Pleasure Ground . . .'.

Repton wanted the incomplete high wall forming the 'fence' between the gardens and pasture beyond to be removed immediately, arguing that 'the present fence is dreadfully dangerous for the Children without a Check Rail – and that would cut the line of water in the views from the window.' He proposed that the fence be brought much nearer to the house and a grass terrace formed, 25 ft wide, in front of and extending to the east of the house. A central stonework bastion, like that which had been built on the slope south of the house, would, Repton advised, 'easily be converted into a hillock on which Groupes of Cows would often assemble and enliven the foreground of a Landscape which would otherwise want animation'. He intended that these

remedies would allow plants to flourish on the exposed terrace, and full visual value to be gained from the pasture and river beyond, both of which would be brought fully into view. Thus the dressed lawn and grazing would visually unite, cattle would gather on the mound 'to animate the Landscape, and by their perspective effects, to show the distance betwixt the house and fed Lawn'. He also suggested that part of the land on the opposite side of the river might also be converted to pasture to improve the view. Although Repton was unable to supervise the work, most of his recommendations concerning work already in progress to the front of the house appear to have been implemented. Perhaps realizing that his deteriorating health might prevent him from returning to Endsleigh, Repton took the precaution of staking out his proposals with Mr Forrest, who appears to have been superintending the work.

With the annexation to Endsleigh of the woods on the opposite side of the Tamar, the need for a bridge to provide access became a matter for discussion. A substantial structure was evidently being considered, and the great bridge-builder John Rennie had already been consulted. Repton advised that such a bridge:

> would present an object totally at variance with that calm sequestered Retreat, which forms the striking Characteristic of Endsleigh, since a great bridge announces a great Road, and a great Road destroys all Solitude both real and imaginary.

He also objected to the proposal to site the bridge downstream from the house, explaining:

> The part of the Tamar forming the chief view from the house is so nearly a straight line that it would more resemble an Artificial Canal than a natural River, if the extremity now forming a graceful curvature were to be terminated by a Bridge, and especially one so large as to rob the River of all its importance.

In place of the bridge downstream, Repton proposed crossing the river immediately opposite the house by means of a weir, constructed with flat stones set about 18 in below the usual summer water level, and thus making it a safe ford for carriages. Large blocks of stone were also to be inserted into the river bed, to act as piers for a simple wood or cast-iron bridge for horses and foot passengers. On the opposite bank he proposed a picturesque thatched corn mill, with a water wheel driven by a stream brought through the woods from sufficiently high a level up river to enable a cascade to be formed over the rocks on the hillside opposite the house. The cascade was to be topped by a rustic covered seat within the woods. He makes his usual plea that the scene should be 'enlivened by the smoke of a Cottage on the opposite side of the Water', adding that if the Cottage were a mill, 'the occasional traffic and busy motion of persons crossing the Tamar would add to the picturesque effect of a Landscape which at present wants a little more animation.'

The duke evidently heeded Repton's advice not to build the substantial bridge, and instead a ford was built, as suggested, opposite the house. The proposed mill, cottage, cascade and rustic covered seat were not implemented. Instead, a boatman's cottage and associated ferry crossing were built; Repton had at one point envisaged a small boat with a rope and a winch. However, the surviving remnants of these features are located well upstream from the point suggested by Repton, and apart from the convenience the river-crossing afforded, and the required chimney smoke to give a vapoury repose upon the scene of a summer's evening, it appears that the *raison d'être* was missing by placing the building here.

The second major landscape component that Repton sought to exploit at Endsleigh lay generally to the east of the house. It comprised the terraces extending south-eastwards, the sweep of the Tamar beyond, and the rising ground to the north-east. His Red Book illustration, taken from the dining-room window, shows the

Repton's view of Endsleigh Cottage from the opposite bank of the Tamar. The rustic corridor, conservatory and fruit garden above, shown to the right of the house, were never built (*Fragments*, 1816)

terrace already under construction – presumably in accordance with plans prepared by Wyatt – with a partly built wall retaining the sloping bank on the side of the terrace away from the river. Repton proposed replacing this wall with a 'pierced' wall, the top of which was to be planted with rock plants to bring them close to the eye. For the unprotected side of the grass terrace, overlooking the river, he proposed a second retaining wall surmounted by a low fence with adjacent planting that would break, but not obliterate, the choice views of the river below. At the end of this terrace a bastion was proposed to provide a lookout from which to view the river.

Repton's proposals for the steeply sloping bank overlooking the grass terrace were intricate and highly contrived. They were intended as a foil, to 'act like a frame for the natural landscape'. The Red Book shows how he intended to articulate the house, terraces, and fruit garden by way of a conservatory at the east end of the house, a rustic corridor (like one he had successfully designed for Woburn Abbey), and a bridge leading north over the carriage drive. It appears that none of these luxuries was constructed. After the great care exercised by Repton in designing and promoting his hanging, terraced walled garden, he would have been doubly frustrated to find that the kitchen garden was built by the entrance lodge, far too distant to transport back the prize fruit he had envisaged. Moreover, people in the house were deprived of the delightful dry, warm and sheltered winter walks adjacent to the house that he had ingeniously designed on paper – and it was particularly during the shooting season and in winter that this rural retreat was likely to be most frequently used by the family.

Running along the top of the 'pierced' wall Repton proposed a gravelled terrace (for further dry walks near the house in winter) leading to a quarry, which he suggested 'might be converted into a Grotto-like receptacle for specimens of the fossils and Ores abounding in the neighbouring mountains'. A flight of rock steps in the quarry led to the bastion proposed at the end of the terrace. From this bastion, two diverging paths were proposed: one towards an upper drive in Leigh Wood, by way of a viaduct he proposed across an existing ravine, the other descending via the meadow to a lower drive in Leigh Wood. The Red Book visualization shows that Repton intended to create the illusion of an ancient aqueduct crossing the River Tamar. To make the structure appear larger than it actually was, he suggested it should be 'constructed using small flat fragments in preference to large blocks'. The precise siting of the viaduct was crucial to achieving the required illusion because, Repton realized, 'there is one point of view, in the road to the house, from which this Viaduct will have a singular effect, the Tamar appearing to come towards it in a perpendicular line and then pass under it.' No doubt Repton included this bridge in his proposals as compensation for the bridge he was trying to discourage the duke from building across the Tamar. In the end, the viaduct was not built either, although there appears to have been a floating bridge built across the river at one time.

The third and final component of the landscape that Repton wanted to exploit in his proposals was the steep-sided dingle (Dairy Dell) lying west of the house. This valley was visible from the western side of the house and is shown in the background of the Red Book watercolour depicting the children's garden. Although Repton illustrates the children's garden, it is evident from Wyatt's drawings that he was in fact the designer responsible. He wanted the terrace to act as a link between the principal part of the house and the small western wing – built specifically for the duke's young family – and orientated to take advantage of the views of the Tamar upstream and also of the dingle.

Evidently, Repton also wanted to change the arrangement of the fountain forming the point of egress for the water flowing along the stone coping to the parapet wall. This proposal was not adopted, and the simple trickle emanating from the stone mask into the stone basin below remains as designed by Wyatt, serving well enough for this clear-cut and precise feature.

In the dingle itself, two channels had already been dug to capture a water supply from the existing, rushing stream: one, along the west side, to irrigate the adjacent meadows; the other, on the east side, to convey water to the house and water features about the gardens. Repton was a master at handling small-scale water works to advantage, without recourse to artifical pumps. All he needed was a copious supply of water to enliven ingeniously even a relatively level site. He soon realized that the dingle at Endsleigh was something of a gift, and during his visit he had an experimental channel dug on the west side of the valley. The position of this channel can be precisely located from the Red Book watercolour, because Repton shows himself pointing at a rock, which still exists, over which he was directing the water to flow. Although a cascade does exist in this area, it appears not to be in the position indicated by Repton; instead it is further up the valley, to the north of the dairy.

Two watercolours (with characteristic flaps) and a detailed plan in the Red Book convey vividly what Repton found on arrival 'on the spot', and what he intended. The sequence of small-scale pools, trickles, falls and channels he proposed were broadly created, and have survived. He also advised that after the water works were laid out, 'walks should be so contrived as to show them to the greatest advantage'. The intricate network of footpaths in the Dairy Dell shows that his advice was adhered to in laying out this part of the garden. Repton's proposals for Dairy Dell related to the lower half of the valley, below the catch-pit that supplies the two channels. Subsequently, garden development in this valley more than doubled as a result of the laying out of the arboretum in its upper half, together with the large Edgecumbe pond and associated waterfall.

The vista westwards towards the site of the Dairy Dell (Le Petit, after T. Allom, 1830)

Repton completed the Endsleigh Red Book just three years before his death in 1818. There is no record of his having made any further visits to the site after August 1814; in any case, his declining health would have undermined any intentions he might have had to supervise so distant an undertaking. Nevertheless, in spite of his absence and the effect of the other creative influence, a surprising proportion of his proposals were eventually adopted as part of the development of the gardens and surrounding grounds, in spirit at least if not in fine detail.

Just as had happened at Ashridge, where Repton was also unable to supervise his scheme after he became ill in March 1815, it was left to Jeffry Wyatt to take over the implementation of his proposals for the garden. It is likely that by the end of 1814 the working relationship between the two designers was far from amicable. After all, Repton had lost the commission for the house to Wyatt, and in drawing up his Red Book proposals he had been highly critical of the arrangement of the walls already under construction, presumably in accordance with Wyatt's design.

Some of Repton's proposals for Endsleigh were simply not acted upon. The most notable omissions were the walled kitchen garden including its conservatory link to the house, the viaduct, the mill on the opposite bank of the river, and the cascade on the hillside behind. Most of Repton's other proposals appear to have been put into effect in one form or another. Surviving detailed drawings by Wyatt indicate that he was responsible for modifying and adapting some of Repton's designs before they were implemented.

To the east of the house, Repton's 'pierced wall' was built along the northern edge of the grass terrace, but in most other respects his proposals relating to the treatment of the bank above this wall appear not to have been

carried out. Instead, two walks – the yew walk and the rose walk – were laid out on the bank, running parallel with the terrace. The rose walk, the lower of the two, terminates in a raised lookout incorporating an arbour, located next to the quarry. The latter feature was laid out precisely in accordance with a detailed construction drawing prepared by Wyatt.

Although Repton's proposal to turn the quarry into a receptacle for geological specimens was not endorsed, a separate building, the Shell Grotto, was designed and built for this purpose by Wyatt, to the east of the quarry, forming an eye catcher and viewpoint at the end of an extended terrace.

Between 1810 and his death in 1840 Wyatt designed a series of picturesque buildings for Endsleigh intended as eye catchers and embellishments in the landscape. Two of these buildings are shown in Repton's proposals, the Dairy and the rustic covered seat in Warm Wood. Although the Dairy was evidently built in the location indicated in two of the Red Book watercolours, it is not certain who was responsible for its siting. Repton's son, John Adey, apparently prepared a speculative 'design for a rustic dairy', but the structure was evidently built to designs drawn up by Wyatt. His first plan is dated 1815 but, curiously, copies of further plans were sent to the Duke of Bedford as late as 5 January 1833. The latter seem to incorporate design modifications to enable the dairy maid to 'reside on the spot'.

Although Repton's proposal for a cascade surmounted by a rustic covered seat on the wooded slopes directly opposite the house appears not to have been effected, it is curious to note that Wyatt prepared a detailed drawing of the 'Rustic Seat for Warm Wood' as late as 2 August 1820. This drawing specifies the means by which the correct picturesque effect was to be obtained: the little structure was 'to be paved with rough stones' and be 'thatched with heather' and supported on 'rough trees'. Alternatively, 'instead of trees, roots might be piled upon each other, having three openings in front – and a wall of roots at the back.'

Of the other minor buildings designed by Wyatt for Endsleigh, the most substantial was the Swiss Cottage, perched high on the summit, and overlooking the Tamar. The building, inspired by the romance of nineteenth-century alpine travel, came complete with 'a sort of Alpine Garden' and Swiss furniture and tableware, all made of wood. It is said that the building was designed c. 1810. However, if this is correct, why did it not feature in Repton's proposals when it offered such splendid reciprocal views of Endsleigh Cottage? On a ledge overhung by a rocky crag, immediately below the Swiss Cottage, Wyatt proposed another elaborate rustic covered seat. A sketch he drew, dated 31 May 1816, shows that the rustic seat was to be roofed with a rock canopy, made to look like part of these cliff and supported by four huge tree trunks. A later pencil sketch, dated August 1819, shows the effect of the two picturesque features high up on the wooded slopes of Leigh Water, as viewed from the river below. One of the Bourne watercolours (1841) confirms that this rustic covered seat was built, and shows that the site chosen by Wyatt offered a magical long-distance view of the Cottage seen across the Tamar Valley.

Another remarkable feature proposed by Wyatt, as part of the overall picturesque scene, was 'an artifical ruin on Castle Hill', located on the distant skyline to the west of the Cottage. Wyatt prepared a series of sketches for this feature between 1832 and 1834, but it would appear that (like Repton and his kitchen garden proposals) he was to be frustrated in his efforts to carry forward this scheme.

The landscape principles advised by Repton were largely adhered to by successive dukes of Bedford, and the picturesque qualities of the landscape were maintained very much as envisaged by Wyatt and Repton right up until the death of the twelfth duke at Endsleigh in 1953. The property was then run as a country hotel by the thirteenth duke's Trustees until it was purchased, in 1962, by the Endsleigh Fishing Club, under whose ownership this use has continued. In its early years the primary interest of the club was naturally the outstanding salmon and sea-trout fishing on the River Tamar. Therefore the gardens, because of a general lack of funds and

in spite of the enthusiastic work of some of the members, became progressively more neglected. Their decline was further exacerbated by the storms that wrought havoc in the early part of 1990.

Ironically, just over a year before the storms struck, Endsleigh became a Charitable Trust with the aim of accelerating the restoration of the buildings, garden and arboretum. Following the storms, Endsleigh was made the target of an English Heritage initiative aimed at restoring our important historic parks and gardens. Aided by grant assistance from English Heritage, a restoration plan was prepared for the Trustees of the Charitable Trust by the Colson Stone Partnership, and restoration work is now proceeding in accordance with the approved plan.

ACKNOWLEDGEMENTS

This chapter is based on research work undertaken by Dr Nigel Temple in the Devon Record Office and elsewhere for the Colson Stone Partnership, as an integral part of the process of drawing up a restoration plan for the historic landscape. The author wishes to acknowledge the generous financial assistance towards this work by English Heritage, as part of their grant initiative to encourage the repair of historic parks and gardens after the storms of 1987 and 1990. The author is also indebted to the Trustees of Woburn Abbey for providing access to the Red Book and other papers and drawings relating to Endsleigh held in the archives of Woburn Abbey, Bedfordshire. He would also like to thank the Trustees and the staff at Endsleigh for their help and encouragement. Particular thanks are due to Mr Philip Thomas and Dr Bill Medd who were responsible for initiating the restoration work at Endsleigh.

SELECT BIBLIOGRAPHY

Carter, G., Goode, P. and Laurie, K. (eds), *Humphry Repton, Landscape Gardener, 1752–1818* (1982).

Hussey, C., *The Picturesque, Studies in a Point of View* (1927).

Hyams, E., *Capability Brown and Humphry Repton* (1971).

Linstrum, D., *Sir Jeffry Wyattville* (Oxford, 1972).

Repton, H., *Observations on the Theory and Practice of Landscape Gardening* (1803).

——, *Fragments on the Theory and Practice of Landscape Gardening* (1816).

Temple, N., *John Nash and the Village Picturesque* (1979).

Chapter Seven

'TO THE NOBILITY AND GENTRY ABOUT TO PLANT': NURSERIES AND NURSERYMEN

AUDREY LE LIÈVRE

The wording used for the title of this chapter, or one of its many variants, was the usual heading of Victorian advertisements for goods and services in the garden. Great opportunities were opening up in nineteenth-century Devon, as elsewhere, for the alert nurseryman and supplier.

The approximately 1.7 million acres of the county included estates that in one form or another went back to Domesday, and others where the mansion had been built in prosperous Elizabethan times or even earlier, often to be rebuilt later – according to whim, or after fire (a frequent occurrence). There were also many unpretentious houses – small manor houses or upgraded farmhouses perhaps – each peacefully occupying its own sheltered valley. Not every large estate remained in the hands of the same family throughout its history, though some did. Families died out; some acquired by marriage more prestigious seats; properties were redistributed throughout a family. Some were bought, or rented, by someone quite unconnected. Perhaps the most stable occupations were those of small houses whose land had developed as a congeries of farms acquired and rented out for the usual three lives.

Though to a Londoner Devon might have seemed impossibly remote before modern transport developed, it was quite remarkable how people got about. By the seventeenth century Exeter, Barnstaple, Tiverton and Bampton had a weekly carrying service with London, probably using pack-horses to start with but later taking both goods and passengers on wagons. The first passenger coach service into Devonshire started in 1658 and took four days for the journey from London to Exeter. By 1835 a duel between two coaches reduced the time to 16½ hours. Though Turnpike Trusts were set up as early as 1753, the poor state of the roads must still have made for very uncomfortable travelling. The arrival of the railways in 1844 – when the Bristol and Exeter reached Exeter – and the spread of the network during the rest of the century, must have made it feel at the time as though the whole country was being opened up and distance, even privacy, annihilated. It would be foolish, moreover, to underestimate the extent and tenacity of other types of communication. A large family and a profession followed over a number of generations forged an important, pervasive network. The employment of servants gave leisure that in turn led to the writing of long letters – and this bound family and friends together in a fashion almost forgotten nowadays, when a swift telephone call is as swiftly forgotten.

W.G. Hoskins, in his *Devon* (1954), sets out the position at the time of the *Return of the Owners of Land* in 1873. Five great estates of 20,000 acres and more were held by the Hon. Mark Rolle (Stevenstone), the Duke of Bedford (Exeter/Endsleigh), the Earl of Devon (Powderham), Earl Fortescue (Castle Hill) and the Duchy of Cornwall (which then, as now, held a large part of Dartmoor). Four further important estates fell into the 10,000 to 20,000 acre category: those of Lord Poltimore (Poltimore), the Earl of Portsmouth (Eggesford), Sir Thomas Acland (Killerton) and Lord Clinton. Most of the old county squirearchy – the Champernownes, Leys, Bullers, Coffins and others – owned estates of between 2,000 and 4,000 acres; some 320 families of the 'squireen' classes owned properties of from 400 to 1,000 acres, and below this were numerous freeholders still living on ancestral farms. In all, 10,162 owners controlled a total of 1,514,000 acres in estates of a size that varied from 1 acre to over 10,000 acres. The *Return* did not break the land usage down into its constituent parts, and thus we simply do not know the total acreage devoted to pleasure grounds, kitchen gardens, woodland, parkland, and so on. But in the case of smaller properties, a larger proportion of the total size would have been devoted to 'garden' – broadly defined.

Quite a large area of Devonshire was thus, in the nineteenth century, 'gardened' in the widest interpretation of the word, and it is well known that planning, planting and maintaining even a small garden is immensely labour- and time-consuming. How was it done in those days? Where did all the supporting services come from?

Then, as now, some owners had very definite ideas of what they wanted: moreover, they had money to spend on making their properties comfortable to live in as well as splendid to show off to visitors. John Loudon, the writer and landscape gardener, who with his wife made a comprehensive tour of Devonshire gardens and nurseries in 1842, wrote in his publication the *Gardener's Magazine* that 'a taste for landscape gardening is the most to be desired in a country gentleman'. Many did have, or soon developed, such tastes, learning as they went. Several of the nobility and gentry had London houses in which they spent varying lengths of time: in London society they were in a prime position to learn of new fashions in gardening, newly discovered plants, and where to get them.

Those landowners who felt that the services of a London landscape gardener would be too prestigious or costly, and who did not themselves feel up to devising a garden plan, had a useful alternative at hand. In Exeter the firm of William Lucombe, founded in 1720 (and which became, sometime before 1828, Lucombe, Pince & Co., until it finally petered out in the 1890s), offered garden design services. At the back of a catalogue thought to belong to the 1860s (few catalogues carried dates in those days) the firm states what it can do:

> Lucombe, Pince & Co. beg to draw the attention of the Nobility and Gentry to the fact that they have for many years been extensively engaged in Designing, Laying out, and Planting Parks, Pleasure Grounds, Ornamental Flower Gardens, Plantations and Cemeteries; also, the formation and planting of Kitchen Gardens. They can refer with much pleasure to the Places of numerous Noblemen and Gentlemen which they have laid out and planted, where an immediate effect has been produced. Their stock of Ornamental Conifers, Hardy Evergreens and Flowering Shrubs, of the most choice and varied description, is unrivalled.

It would be interesting had a list of their commissions survived, but as it is we at least know about Mrs Wells's garden at Cowley House, bordered by the rivers Exe and Creedy, since it was one of those visited by the Loudons – indeed, they had to go there twice, having lost the notes they took on the first occasion. Their report

JAMES VEITCH
JAMES H. VEITCH   JAMES VEITCH, JUNIOR
JOHN VEITCH
HARRY J. VEITCH

JOHN GOULD VEITCH   ROBERT T. VEITCH
ARTHUR VEITCH   P. C. M. VEITCH
JOHN G. VEITCH

The Veitch family, including John Veitch (top right in the left-hand group), the founder of the firm of nurserymen (*Hortus Veitchii,* 1906)

did, however, correctly point out that 'the garden had been judiciously laid out and planted by Mr Pince', but they were soon pulled up sharp by the gardener, Mr Griffin, who reminded them that his employer, 'a zealous patroness of gardening', bought only the best, and thus enabled him to cultivate one of the finest hothouse and greenhouse collections in the county. They must have been infuriating visitors, turning up unheralded and often finding the owners absent.

By the end of the eighteenth century, William Lucombe had begun to encounter rivalry from the firm of John Veitch, which from about 1780 operated on land at Budlake given to him for his lifetime by his employer, Sir Thomas Acland, to start a tree nursery. John Veitch had come south from Jedburgh in Scotland in about 1768 to work for a nursery firm in London, and was sent to Sir Thomas, who wanted to lay out a park at Killerton. Sir Thomas came to think very highly of the young man's work and soon Veitch became steward of all the Acland properties in the West Country. When Sir Thomas died in 1785 work on the park at Killerton ceased, and until it started again under the tenth Baronet, another Sir Thomas, who came of age in 1808, Veitch ran a prosperous business as landscape gardener and tree contractor. His grandson records that during this period he laid out gardens in every county of England except Rutland, as Shirley Heriz-Smith tells us in her interesting series of articles on the Veitches in *Garden History*.[1]

Nearer home, Loudon in his 1842 report mentions work at Luscombe Castle said to have been carried out by John Veitch; he observed, too, that Messrs Veitch and Son were looking after the arboretum at Bicton, 'taking measures to have all the plants correctly named, and all the blanks and deficiencies supplied'. They mowed the surrounding grass, mulched and weeded. The avenue of *Araucaria araucana* (monkey puzzle) was planted in the winter of 1843–4 by James Veitch's men under his direction: the seedling plants came from the nursery of Messrs Loddiges at Hackney. Veitch was responsible, too, for laying out the pinetum at Poltimore House, the Bampfylde property that lay close to Killerton; and he made a short, sensible report to Major Drake on the state of woods and plantations at the Drake property of Nutwell Court in 1819. He recommended a number of remedial measures and volunteered his services part-time to attend to the regulating of the plantations with two or three men to do the pruning and cutting, leaving other jobs 'to the men of the place'.[2] (The pleasure of reading this admirably succinct document is much increased when the authentic voice of John Veitch comes through with a residual Scottish accent, revealed in his spelling of 'prunning'.)

Though Lucombe, Pince & Co. and Messrs Veitch & Co. were the only names listed in James Mangles' *Floral Calendar* (1839) as principal nurserymen, seedsmen and florists in Exeter, the establishment of John Pontey in Plymouth was both efficient and well known in Devon as a whole. Not only did Pontey supply the Duke of Bedford at Endsleigh with a range of trees, plants and bulbs, but he is known to have made an extensive plantation for William Roope Ilbert at Horswell in 1835. So garden design was alive and well in local hands or, as in the case of Veitch, in the hands of foreigners who had settled in Devon. To implement design over the large area so often covered by pleasure grounds, enormous quantities of plants were needed. Of equal importance, though, was someone with knowledge, a good eye, and the ability to organize the work and get it done: in short, a good head gardener.

On a large estate, the head gardener, together with the farm bailiff, clerk of works and head woodman/forester, would report to the steward (or bailiff, or agent). In a smaller place there would, of course, be many variants on this staffing, and on the smaller properties the head gardener, or just gardener, would be directly responsible to the owner. Where this worked well, the end result in terms of purchases and planting could be very happy. Where did head gardeners come from? At Lord Rolle's Bicton, Mr Glendinning was 'sent' by Veitches, who made a point of 'recommending' gardeners both in the South West and also up-country; while Mr Gilpin, who planned the conversion of the old kitchen gardens at Bicton together with other alterations, was an employee of Lord Clinton, Lady Rolle's brother. This was typical of the way in which things worked; at the heart of the system lay personal recommendation. There was also a good deal of co-operation between estates: the agent at Nutwell Court reported to Sir Francis Drake: 'Your Gardiner has been at Mamhead. Mr Vaughan has wrote to his Servant to let Yours have any Thing There.'[3] The appointment of a head gardener was a major commitment for both parties, and an applicant once 'suited' stayed with his employers, if not for life, then certainly for many years. From 1863 the *Gardeners' Chronicle*, first published in 1841, began to carry notices of situations vacant and wanted. The columns soon lengthened and began to appear every week. The present author could find little indication of head gardeners in Devonshire seeking posts, and none sought, but a number of journeymen and under-gardeners were looking for a change, such as A.B.G. of Lophill, near Jump, an 'active' foreman aged twenty-two who had previously served in two noblemen's gardens in south Devon; and a gardener called Harefield from Lympstone with a good knowledge of his profession and a wife who was a good laundress. Gradually rudimentary 'agencies' began to appear. A gardening firm would announce that lists were kept of gardeners suitable for all requirements. Some (including John Downie of crab-apple fame) made a point of the number of Scotch gardeners on their books (no nonsense about 'Scottish' or 'Scots' here, and evidently they were regarded as the most satisfactory of employees). Thus, quite rapidly, the horticultural employment agency grew up.

GARDENER (SINGLE-HANDED, or good Second).—Age 26, single ; seven years' good character. Well up in all branches.—F. C., 33, Torre Square, Torquay, Devon.

GARDENER (SECOND, or good THIRD), in a Gentleman's establishment.—Age 21 ; good experience In and Outdoor.—A. G., Gothic Cottage, Charles Street, Sydenham, S.E.

GARDENER (UNDER), Outside ; could assist under Glass if required.—Age 23 ; good character from present and previous employers.—J. M., 1, Lynton Place, Goat Road, Enfield.

GARDENER (UNDER).—Age 21 ; has had five years' experience in a large Kitchen Garden. Five years' good reference.—R. WRIGHT, The Lodge, Heydon, Norwich, Norfolk.

GARDENER (UNDER), to assist Inside and Out.—Age 21 ; six years' experience. Good character. State wages.—C. GODFRAY, 3, Starke's Cottages, Northwold Road, Upper Clapton, E.

GARDENER (UNDER), to assist Inside and Out preferred—used to both. Six years' experience. Good character.—G. PROSSER, Porthkerry, Cowbridge, Glamorgan.

GARDENER (UNDER).—Has a practical knowledge of Stove and Greenhouse Plants, Flower and Kitchen Gardening. Good character.—McLAREN, 5, Pixholm Grove, Dorking, Surrey.

JOURNEYMAN, in a good establishment.— Age 23 ; five years' experience in best English and Continental Nurseries. Excellent references. — E. H., " Buller's Arms," Crediton, Devon.

JOURNEYMAN, in a large establishment.— Age 21 ; seven years' experience Indoors and Out. Highly recommended. Bothy preferred.—G. FENN, Stocks Gardens, Aldbury, Tring, Herts.

JOURNEYMAN in the Houses.—Age 21 ; eight years' experience Indoors and Out. Six years' good character.—Mr. J. CAMPBELL, Gardener, Mickleover Manor, near Derby.

JOURNEYMAN, in the Houses, in a good establishment.—Age 21 ; five years' experience. Good character. Bothy preferred.—J. DEAN, Lower Eaton, Hereford.

JOURNEYMAN ; age 20.—W. SQUIBB, Gardener, Hooley House, Purley, Surrey, will be pleased to recommend a young man as above to any Nobleman's or Gentleman's Gardener requiring a careful, persevering young man.

JOURNEYMAN, in a Nobleman's or Gentleman's establishment.—Benj. G. STONE, Head Gardener, Eikington Hall, Louth, Lincolnshire, would be pleased to recommend a young man as above ; thoroughly experienced in all branches. Would prefer to be under Glass.—Apply as above.

The names of journeymen and under-gardeners looking for a change of situation frequently appeared in the *Gardeners' Chronicle* notices of situations wanted

Head gardeners made a powerful breed, exercising iron control over their staffs, often disputatious with their fellows, and thirsting for awards at shows. The *Gardeners' Chronicle* provided a useful vehicle for such triumphs – the gardener often being portrayed as a scale object beside some huge plant he had flowered – and a forum for disputes, such as the long-running saga on the origin of the King Pippin apple, on which various giants among head gardeners took a position (Brotherston of Tynynghame, Divers of Belvoir Castle and Molyneux of Swanmore Park among them). In its pages were recorded the results of competitive classes at shows held, not only under the auspices of the (Royal) Horticultural Society but also in various provincial centres, and it was noticeable that the plants, fruit and vegetables that took the prizes were often those that the head gardener most enjoyed growing. As regards the disciplining of staff, the Rules and Regulations drawn up by the head gardener, James Barnes, for use of the Plant Department staff at Bicton in 1842, are interesting. There were twenty-five of them. Each rated its fine, the biggest being 12d. for leaving anything dangerous in or about the stokeholes or furnaces. Others forbade going into any hothouse, greenhouse etc. or walking on any gravel walk with dirty shoes (3d.); neglecting to attend to water fountains, etc. (3d.); and swearing or making use of bad language (for every separate evil expression, 3d.).[4] No wonder that Bicton soon gained a reputation for being one of the best gardens in the county, or that Barnes was sufficiently incensed to take out a libel suit against his employer, who complained about the state in which he had left Bicton garden on his retirement; he won. Staff had to remember that they really needed a 'character' from the head gardener if they wished to move on to better themselves. No state benefits were payable until about the time of the First World War.

A head gardener had a great deal of paperwork to do. James Preece, who worked for Ellen Willmott at Warley Place in Essex, used to stay in his office far into the evening after everyone else had gone home. There

were time-sheets, accounts to settle, orders to place, letters to write, perhaps 'characters' to think about, queries to answer. Running a garden was a sizeable administrative task.

On the choice of plants, owners often had definite ideas, but were not always successful in discussion with the head gardener. There were many new plants coming in from abroad: shrubs from China, South America and Australia; climbers from Chile and Brazil; annuals and perennials from California, Mexico, Russia and the Mediterranean, to suggest only some of the countries of origin that plant hunters were exploring. Sometimes an owner might have contacts – a ship's captain, perhaps, or other travellers – who might bring back plants or seeds from distant parts. It was not of course until almost the end of the nineteenth century that travellers began to realize that there might be long-term disadvantages in continually grubbing up bulbs and roots – and then it was only a beginning.

Meantime, the invaluable *Gardeners' Chronicle* provided an overview of plant availability. The nineteenth century saw an enormous increase in the number of plant nurseries, and pages of advertisements which must have repaid study. Almost any available plant could be bought in this way, but there was a considerable problem in the first half of the century with transport. Four days in a coach, or even longer on a pack-horse, would be enough to defeat even the most resilient plant. Bulbs and seeds, however, were better able to survive. Sometimes plants would be sent by sea: Shirley Heriz-Smith points out that in 1843, among other consignments for Kew, James Veitch sent 100 rhododendrons, two new Lucombe oaks and other shrubs from Topsham to St George's Wharf, Katherine Dock, London to finish their journey by Hiscock's Kew Boat from Hungerford Stairs.[5] Topsham was also used for pears, nuts and potatoes brought in from the Channel Islands, as well as for less perishable items on longer journeys.[6] Barnstaple was also a handy port, much used for shipping timber.

The early nineteenth-century saw an enormous increase in plant availability: Messrs Veitch and Son were in the van (the *Gardeners' Chronicle*, May 1842)

All in all, it must have been a great deal simpler for Devon gardeners to buy plants in the West Country and collect them personally, or have them sent for the relatively short distances by carrier. Devon was in fact very well provided with nurseries, many of them only mentioned in passing in the *Exeter Flying Post* when the nurseryman married, went bankrupt or died. To name a well-scattered selection, nurseries were to be found in Axminster, Bishop's Nympton, Doddiscombsleigh, Kentisbeare, Starcross, Honiton, Torrington, Whimple and Bere Alston. Exeter had its share of small nurseries, too, many of which went out of business after a few years, but we are left with the two important nurseries of William Lucombe and Son (1720–c. 1890) and James Veitch and Son (which moved from Killerton to Mount Radford in 1832; the firm of Veitch finally closed its doors in 1969). Useful too in their time were Joseph and William Ford, related but operating separately, at the end of the eighteenth and in the first half of the nineteenth century. William's business became Ford and Please, and was later taken over by the Quaker family of Dymond, and later still by William Mogridge. It probably closed in the 1830s. Joseph, who died in 1796, inserted an interesting notice in the *Exeter Flying Post* on 30 November 1781. Addressed 'To the Curious in Planting', it offered large quantities of forest and fruit trees; 'five hundred Magnolio's, or Laurel-leaved Tulip trees'; and 'A Variety of curious Exotics, from the South seas, etc. etc.' Charles Sclater, with his son and possibly, later, his grandson, set up a nursery in about 1824, with land in Southernhay and also in Heavitree, which continued until about 1875. He travelled around, returning from Bristol, Bath and London (1824) 'with a great variety of Greenhouse and other Choice Plants'. J. & W. Southwood, in the first quarter of the century, from their nursery opposite the Dunsford Turnpike Gate, offered forest trees, fruit trees, evergreens and flowering shrubs. Each of the nurserymen invited visits from the Nobility and Gentry to the nursery grounds, where every attention and satisfaction was offered, but dogs were to be left at home. Occasionally a spectacle was offered, as when "*Cactus Grandiflora*" flowered at night in the richly supplied conservatory of Mr Chas Sclater. 'Numerous folk flocked to the garden', reported the *Exeter Flying Post*. Nurserymen in the nineteenth century suffered exactly the same trials as do today's – theft, arson, vandalism. There were also disputes over breeding rights: a fierce battle raged between William Lucombe, whose Lucombe oak arose as a seedling in a bushel of 'wainscot oak' sowed about 1765 (according to the *Philosophical Transactions* of the Royal Society), and Joseph Ford, who claimed the right to raise and name an oak, even though it was a product of Lucombe's.

There is no doubt that Devon, and Exeter in particular, benefited enormously from the presence of the Veitch nurseries. The move from Killerton (a necessity because of the limited tenure at Budlake) took place in 1832, John Veitch himself remaining at Killerton until his death in 1839. James Veitch senior, son of John, was soon joined at the Mount Radford nursery by his son James junior. Here they set up orchid houses and grew other exotics, obtained from a number of sources. At about the same time, the Veitches were fortunate in finding an excellent propagator, John Dominy, who had previously worked for Lucombe, Pince and Co. Their next move was to engage their own collectors. In 1840 William Lobb was despatched to Rio de Janeiro: over the years his introductions included *Embothrium coccineum, Lapageria rosea* and "*Tropaeolum azureum*". Thomas Lobb, sent in 1843 to Malaysia and Indonesia, added to the Veitch orchid collection and also obtained a number of pitcher-plants. William died in San Francisco in 1864, and Thomas returned permanently to England in 1860. A third collector, Richard Pearce, who had been working for Pontey in Plymouth, set out for Chile in 1859. These developments, coupled with the move of James Veitch the younger to the premises previously occupied by Messrs Knight and Perry in the King's Road, Chelsea (where henceforth Dominy would carry out all the propagation of exotics), established Veitches as an important nursery countrywide, even internationally. The move took place in 1853, but until 1869 the two firms co-operated closely. James Veitch junior, who already had close links with Kew in the person of the Director, Sir William Hooker, went on to become involved in the detailed affairs of what had become, in 1861, the Royal Horticultural Society. He died in 1869,

and was commemorated by the institution of the Veitch Memorial Medal, set up by subscription by fellow nurserymen and members of the society. But in spite of this grandeur and these preoccupations, the nurseries of Messrs Veitch continued to be available to the people of Exeter and Devon. Messrs Lucombe and Pince, however, despite a period when Veitch appeared to be trying to pre-empt their title of The Exeter Nursery, continued to hold their own by going on steadily with their own type of business, refusing to be hustled, despite the loss of John Dominy to Veitch, and maintaining their own relations with Sir William Hooker at Kew. Theirs was not an easy position, and they deserve credit for handling it well.

The Floral World and Garden Guide (1868) printed an account of a visit to this nursery by a London nurseryman, John Burley, who makes it sound unpretentiously beautiful, the grounds containing many fine specimen trees, including wellingtonias and – a mark of reconciliation – a splendid pair of "*Quercus fordii*". Camellias had been a speciality of the nursery since 1834, and Burley thought that if only half of the plants in the camellia house were to reach flowering stage, they would supply all demands from Edinburgh to Plymouth. The show house contained a splendid *Tacsonia Van Volxemii* (now *Passiflora antioquiensis*), a scarlet lapageria, *Lilium auratum* and other lilies 'capitally in flower', with many other healthy-looking plants. At the gate stood 'the finest specimen of the Lucombe oak in England'.

There were two other important nurseries in Devon at this time, both of them in Plymouth. Pontey, already mentioned, advertised a good deal in the *Gardeners' Chronicle*. He, too, had lost a member of his staff, Richard Pearce, to Veitch, but a 'late foreman' of his, Thomas Corbett, had developed and patented a new apparatus for heating hothouses from water flowing in an open gutter and returning in a pipe, so perhaps he felt that the honours were even. John Loudon spent some time visiting the two Pontey nurseries. The larger, at Vinstone, just outside Plymouth, was apparently run by Mr Pontey senior, 'a most intelligent and intellectual gentleman'. The town nursery was Alexander Pontey's province, and here large collections of greenhouse and hothouse plants had lately been received from South America and the Cape. There was a fine pear orchard, with trees grafted on quince stocks and trained pyramidally. Plants were displayed on either side of a long, straight walk from the entrance. The other nursery belonged to W.E. Rendle. According to Loudon's description, it appeared almost a carbon copy of Pontey's, but two small paragraphs in the *Gardeners' Chronicle* show a rather more inventive turn of mind. The first announces the opening of a 'botanic garden'. Since it appears to have been for the purpose of outdoor entertainment, fireworks, and so on, it was probably more in the nature of a park or winter garden than anything concerned with flowers as such. This was in Union Road. It is possible that the 'botanic garden' ground was later taken over for railway use. Rendle's other idea was an item called 'Rendle's Price Current' – 'a new species of the genus advertisement, and one of the best', commented the *Gardeners' Chronicle*. It included plant and seed lists, an essay competition, a calendar of operations, and 'some miscellaneous matter'. It is interesting because of its hybrid nature – neither catalogue nor magazine – and it was not taken up by other firms. Rendle was, however, a serious nurseryman, and he and Pontey between them were well able to deal with all large orders to be delivered in west Devon.

In nineteenth-century nurserymen's lists, forest trees were prominent. Equally, from the *Exeter Flying Post* and from separately published auctioneers' particulars, it is clear that mature timber was an important sale item. Until 1862, when a naval encounter in the American Civil War first made it starkly clear that wooden ships could not stand up to attack from ironclads, landowners were encouraged to grow as much oak as possible and to allow it to mature sufficiently to supply compass (curved) timber, or straight or great timber, for naval usage. The Royal Society of Arts sought to encourage such activities by presenting medals, and Sir William Templar Pole of Axminster was awarded a Gold Medal for planting ninety-eight bushels of acorns. In practice, landowners were very much tempted to fell oaks at an earlier stage, as they could get a good price for younger

PLYMOUTH NURSERY.

ALEXANDER PONTEY begs to call the attention of the Public to his Stock of Hothouse, Greenhouse, and other PLANTS, especially to his new FUCHSIA TRICOLOR, a beautiful delicate blush white, with sepals tipped with green; a free grower and bloomer; plants of which are now being sent out at 10s. 6d. each. Also the following PELARGONIUMS :—

Lyne's Countess of Mount Edgcumbe .	21s. 0d. each.	
— Diadem, a large white .	. 21 0	—
— Peri of the West . .	. 10 6	—

The sorts named under at 60s. per dozen :—Amethyst, Beauty, Bridesmaid, Corona, King John, Wildfire, Inez de Castro, Nymph, Lady Douro, Prince Albert, Vulcan, Comte de Paris, Sultan, Pince's Zenobia, Jupiter, Matilda, Lifeguardsman, Apex, Wonder, Pride of the Hill. Other good sorts at from 9s., 12s., to 18s per dozen.—Plymouth Nursery, April 4th, 1842.

UNION ROAD NURSERIES, PLYMOUTH.

WILLIAM E. RENDLE respectfully informs the Nobility, Gentry, and the Trade, that he has a few plants left of that favourite Geranium

LYNE'S CIRCASSIAN,

which has gained for itself, by every Florist who has seen it, a first-rate character. Good strong plants, in 60-sized pots, 42s. each.

Lyne's Consort, 21s. each.
„ Magnificent, 21s. „

Lyne's Princess Royal, and Bassett's Glory of the West, (of which W. E. R. possesses the entire stock,) cannot be sent out till about July next, in consequence of the numerous applications for it.

Veitch's Fair Maid of Devon, (just sent out,) 63s. each.
Pansy.—Fox's Cornish Gem, 10s. 6d. each.
Rosa Devoniensis, good strong plants, 7s. 6d. each.
Auraucaria Imbricata, in 48-sized pots, 6s. 6d. each.

W. E. R.'s General Spring Catalogue of Geraniums, Dahlias, Calceolarias, Pansies, Herbaceous Plants, &c. (which contains descriptions of the above-named plants,) can be had on prepaid application.

Agents in London : Messrs. Warner, Seedsmen, Cornhill ; M.W. Bristow, Knightsbridge ; through whom plants of any of the above may be procured.—Plymouth, April 25th, 1842.

Above: an advertisement for Alexander Pontey's Plymouth Nursery (the *Gardeners' Chronicle*, 9 April 1842); below: William Rendle's Union Road Nurseries provided the main competition to Pontey. Between them they were able to deal with all large orders to be delivered in West Devonshire (the *Gardeners' Chronicle*, May 1842)

wood. Charles Vancouver, writing in 1808 on agriculture in Devon, lamented: 'Anyone viewing with an eye to general utility the present state and condition of oak timber in this country, cannot without pain observe so general a destruction of this our principal bulwark.' But in spite of this, many parts of the county were, as John Leland described the South Hams about 1540, 'meatly well woddid', and landowners did plant trees, even if they did not show quite as much enthusiasm about it as Vancouver and others would have wished. As mentioned earlier, a large estate would have had a head woodman who would have dealt with plantations and woods, but the planting of specimen trees in parks often meant that the work of head gardener and head woodman overlapped.

At Ugbrooke, according to Vancouver, Lord Clifford had a red cedar cut which after thirty-five years' growth afforded boards 22 in broad and 12 ft long. At the same time, Lord Lisburne's park at Mamhead had evergreen oak; double-flowering, wainscot or white oak of America; cork oak of Portugal; American red oak; and many others. So forest trees, decorative in the landowner's park, also brought in some income. Even if, in the latter part of the last century, navy timber was no longer required, wood was needed for many other purposes, especially in the country – furniture, tools, fences, hurdles, wagons and so on. The main difficulty with wood had always been transport: sometimes it could take two years to get a load to the other end of the country, and sometimes the whole enterprise just quietly gave up. Timber travelled on wagons called tuggs, and these were used like post horses. It is not difficult to imagine a load, sinking deep into a rutted lane, quite abandoned and wreathed in honeysuckle. In the South Hams, strong horses were specially bred to get heavy loads of navy

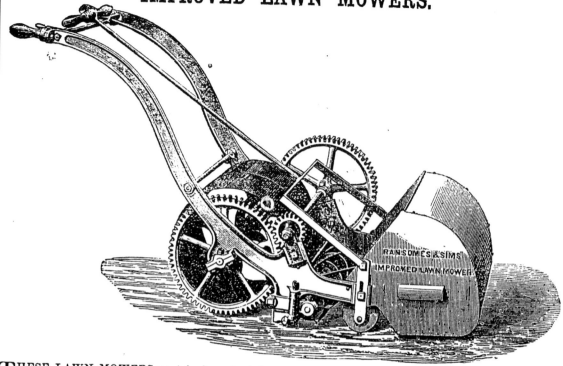

RANSOMES & SIMS, IPSWICH,

MANUFACTURERS OF

IMPROVED LAWN MOWERS.

THESE LAWN MOWERS contain important improvements, rendering them efficient and perfect. They are made from new patterns designed so as to combine strength and lightness with simplicity of arrangement. They are light handy Machines, almost noiseless in work, and so easy to manage that persons unaccustomed to Mowing can cut Grass without any difficulty.

Price:—14-inch, £6 10s.; 16-inch, £7; 18-inch, £7 10s.; 20-inch, £8.

Packing Cases 8s. 6d. each, which will be allowed if returned in good condition, Carriage paid. .

Carriage paid to any Station within 100 miles of London or Ipswich.

Victorian garden suppliers had an inventive turn of mind. Many of their devices were advertised in the pages of the invaluable *Gardeners' Chronicle*. Above: Ransomes' improved lawn mower

timber to the dockyard at Plymouth. Timber felled at Endsleigh went either to Morwellham Quay or to Barnstaple. The coastal trade formed a vital link with the rest of the country.

The mention of tools, fences and hurdles leads us back to the whole question of garden supplies. As usual, whatever anyone was likely to need could be found advertised in the pages of the *Gardeners' Chronicle*. The largest items there were endless diagrams and plans of hothouses and heating systems. But Lucombe and Pince used the back of their catalogue to proclaim their ability to furnish plans and estimates at the shortest notice for conservatories, greenhouses, hothouses, vineries, pine pits, Wardian cases and so on, and 'they point with much satisfaction to the numerous and various constructions they have made, during the last few years, for Noblemen and Gentlemen'. The hothouse for tender exotics and the conservatory attached to a mansion represented perhaps

McNAB'S TRANSPLANTING MACHINE.

ALEXANDER HISLOP

BEGS to acquaint the nobility and gentry that he has been intrusted by Mr. McNab to construct several Transplanting Machines, the same as those now in use in the Royal Botanic Garden, and on several gentlemen's Estates, which have given every satisfaction to the parties using them.

A. H., by the kind permission of Mr. McNab, begs to say that he has made arrangements for the manufacture of these unrivalled TREE and SHRUB TRANSPLANTERS, and can supply them as follows:—

No. 1. To lift a ball 48 inches by 46, complete, with all its gearings, 22*l*. 10*s*.
No. 2. To lift a ball 42 inches by 33, complete, with all its gearings, 19*l*. 15*s*.

N. B. Mr. HISLOP will be happy to supply on application a Prospectus of the method of using the Machine, the same as inserted in the *Scottish Farmer and Horticulturist* by Mr. McNab on the 24th April last.

AGRICULTURAL AND HORTICULTURAL IMPLEMENT WORKS, CANONMILLS, EDINBURGH.

Right: McNab's transplanting machine; below: Richard Read's garden engines, syringes, &c.

MANUFACTURED ONLY BY

RICHARD READ,

INSTRUMENT MAKER (BY SPECIAL APPOINTMENT) TO HER MAJESTY,

35, REGENT CIRCUS, PICCADILLY, LONDON.

CAUTION.—Instruments of the very commonest description being extensively circulated throughout the Kingdom, and sold as "READ'S!" please observe that none are genuine except stamped with the Royal Arms and "READ'S PATENT."

** *A liberal Discount allowed to Seedsmen, Florists, &c., &c.*

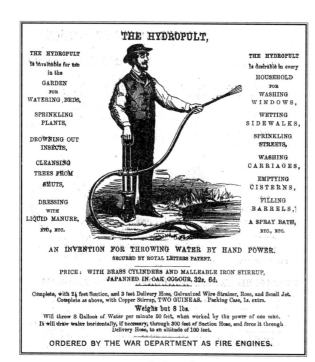

Left: the Hydropult; right: American portable fire annihilator and garden engine

the heaviest expenditure, but there were plenty of others. There were many full-page advertisements for lawn mowers (which came in at the end of the 1830s), rollers, boilers, trellises and arches of all kinds. By the 1850s and 1860s some strange contraptions were to be bought, such as the Hydropult (a 'Portable Fire Annihilator and Garden Engine', looking rather like an old-fashioned stirrup pump), slate cisterns and beehives. Who could resist Hussey's American Reaper, Crosskill's Patent Clod Crusher and Wheat Roller and One Horse Carts, or Fountains for Playing Scented Waters? Salesmen were nothing if not inventive. But there were also a number of down-to-earth items to be purchased. The very first issue of the *Gardeners' Chronicle* advertised quite a range of fertilizers: the London Manure Company offered some fearsome brews, and there were Owen's Animalised Carbon, Odams' Patent Blood Manure for Corn and Roots, Peruvian guano, bone sawdust, and sulphuric acids. Coconut refuse appears to have been in use, 150 years before today's 'new' coconut fibre. Insecticides were slower to come on to the market, but in the mid-century there were Gishurst Compound (against insects and mildew), tobacco tissue for fumigating greenhouses, and Page's Blight Composition. The reader of the *Gardeners' Chronicle* was scarcely kept short of advice, either. Much practical instruction was on offer, the first issue of the magazine listing *The Domestic Gardeners' Manual* by John Towers and *Practical Instruction in Gardening for Ladies* by Mrs Loudon. The *Gardener's Magazine, The Journal of Botany*, and Paxton's *Magazine of Botany* are also mentioned. There were also offers, and Robert Poynter of Taunton, Seed Merchant, advertised 'A Ribbon Border, Six Colours, Post Free, 2s. 6d. Stamps'. The *Gardeners' Chronicle* was certainly a lively, and helpful, read.

The reality, on a Devon estate, was different. At Endsleigh the Duke of Bedford's agent bought bulbs (tulips and crocus); a large consignment of roses of many kinds; and climbers, violets, and heaths – all from Pontey. From Lucombe, Pince and Co. he bought annuals, both hardy and tender, and clumps of primroses; and from W.E. Rendle, a large quantity of seedling thorns, possibly for hedge planting, possibly for growing on in a nursery. The 20,000 three-year oaks must surely have been for direct planting. He also paid a carrier to move

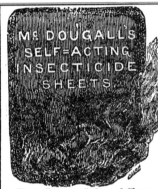
Down to earth items like insecticides and herbicides were increasingly important commodities to nineteenth-century gardeners, a fact reflected in the pages of the *Gardeners' Chronicle*: Richards' weed destroyer, Lethorion, McDougall's self-acting insecticide sheets, lemon oil insecticide

crates of plants to and from Plymouth. At Horswell, William Roope Ilbert also bought from Pontey – flowering shrubs, heaths and pelargoniums, as well as forest trees, which were planted by Pontey's men. But he also bought locally from William Moore – 'White Lelocks',[7] laburnums, red cedars, 'Amarican Arbrovita'; and from Sam Rossiter – thorns, raspberries, and lime trees. There were no fancy fertilizers: only dung, seaweed and lime (much used for the garden, the fields and for the limewash on buildings). Pontey, however, ran a grisly-sounding Bone Manure factory, where imported bones, some of them human and stuffed with old iron to

adulterate them, were used. No insecticides are mentioned: probably they relied on the natural vitality of good plants well tended. Much of the work of a menial kind was done by hourly-paid workers: weeding, digging or planting potatoes, picking up stones. Tools – pruning knives, garden spades and so on – came from local suppliers (Pontey took back two pruning knives, 'as the gardener finds them for himself'). Flower pots were purchased locally, too. Most interesting of all is John Eddy's bill for the erection of a greenhouse at Horswell – 20 ft long, 12 ft wide, equipped with 70 ft of inch board for growing melons, and a stand for plants. The whole cost £34. 2s. 2d.[8] It seems very well worth it, though it was no doubt considered exorbitant at the time.

The impression is that the planting and maintaining of estates and gardens could be carried out very well indeed with the use of local services. Sometimes those 'local' services could be stretched to include either Exeter or Plymouth. Whether this would have been possible without ready back-up from Veitch, Pontey, and Lucombe and Pince is a moot point. Whether, in an increasingly industrial society, when the railway had fully established itself, this would have lasted, is hard to say. But for the early and mid-nineteenth century it worked. And there were advantages, little to be seen today: the Devon and Exeter Horticultural Society, one of several in the county, offered its members a dinner at the New London Inn, 'at which Prize Fruit will form dessert' and one pint of wine was allocated per person. Hours of toil must have seemed well compensated by occasions like these.

ACKNOWLEDGEMENTS

The author is grateful for ready help given by Mr N.D.G. James, and by the staffs of the Devon Record Office, the West Country Studies Library, the Library of the Devon and Exeter Institution, and the Lindley Library (Royal Horticultural Society).

SELECT BIBLIOGRAPHY

Britton, J. and Brayley, E.W., *Devonshire and Cornwall Illustrated* (1832).

Cherry, B. and Pevsner, N., *The Buildings of England: Devon* (2nd edn., 1989).

Brent Elliott, W., *Victorian Gardens* (1986).

Fortescue-Foulkes, R., *From Celtic Settlement to 20th Century Hospital: the Story of Poltimore House* (p.p. 1971).

Hadfield, Miles, *A History of British Gardening* (3rd edn., Harmondsworth, 1985).

Harvey, J., 'Early Nurseries at Exeter', *Garden History Society Newsletter* 24 (1988).

Heriz-Smith, S., 'The Veitch Nurseries of Killerton and Exeter, c. 1780 to 1863', Part 1, *Garden History*, 16, 1 (1988); Part 2, *Garden History*, 16, 2 (1988); 'James Veitch and Sons of Exeter and Chelsea, 1853–1870', *Garden History*, 17, 2 (1989).

Hoskins, W.G., *Devon* (1954).

James, N.D.G., *The History of English Forestry* (1981).

——, *The Trees of Bicton* (Oxford, 1969).

Neale, J.P., *Views of the Seats of Noblemen and Gentlemen* (1847).

Polwhele, R., *History of Devonshire* (3 vols, 1793–1806).

Stroud, D., *Capability Brown* (2nd edn, 1975).

Vancouver, C., *General View of the Agriculture of the County of Devon* (1808).

Veitch, James H., *Hortus Veitchii* (1906).

ORIGINAL SOURCES

Papers in Devon Record Office, as noted

Relevant Nursery Catalogues: Lindley Library, RHS

Relevant numbers of the *Gardeners' Chronicle* and the *Gardener's Magazine,* as noted: Lindley Library, RHS

Relevant numbers of *Exeter Flying Post*, as noted: West Country Studies Library, and Devon and Exeter Institution Library

REFERENCES

1. Heriz-Smith, 'Veitch' (see Select Bibliography).
2. D(evon) R(ecord) O(ffice), Drake Papers, 346M.
3. DRO, 346M.
4. The *Gardener's Magazine*, 17 (1842).
5. Heriz-Smith, 'Veitch'.
6. DRO, Topsham Wharfingers' Journal, Exeter City Archives.
7. DRO, Ilbert Papers (Horswell), 316 add M.
8. DRO, 316 add M.

Chapter Eight

THOMAS MAWSON AT WOOD AND THE EARLY TWENTIETH-CENTURY GARDEN

DAVID MAWSON

Devon must surely be the most satisfying county in the south of England for a landscape architect from the Lake District to work in. I can imagine the delight of my grandfather, Thomas Mawson, when he first saw the site of Wood in 1898, in beautiful rolling countryside near South Tawton, with views to the south and east and a small river at the bottom of the water meadow. There were some mature trees within the 29½ acres, and it was within easy reach of a plentiful supply of local granite. His client was a Mr William Lethbridge, who had in that year purchased the property with a small house on it. Lethbridge wanted to enlarge this and the garden considerably, so that he could entertain in some style.

This was the first commission Thomas Mawson had received in the South West, although he had been in practice since 1884 and had carried out a number of projects in the North West, obtaining a considerable reputation as a landscape architect; he was, in fact, the first garden designer to term himself such. He had had a very difficult start to his life, as his father had died when he, his sister and two brothers were still quite young, leaving their mother to bring them up in straitened circumstances. He was fortunate, however, to have had much help with his education from the local vicar, who encouraged him to read as much as he could. When he left school, an uncle who was an architect took him into his office, but Thomas soon found that he could not stand heights, and decided that a career at ground level was more to his liking.

When Mawson was twelve his family had moved to a smallholding, and he was given his own plot to cultivate despite his age. His uncle gave him a small book entitled *How to Earn £600 a Year from one Acre of Land* – a book he later described as being far from convincing. By the time he reached his early teens he had already decided to become a garden designer, but realized the only way he could achieve this would be by teaching himself. He read any books on gardens and plants he could find in the local library and, when he was a few years older, moved with his brothers to a large firm of nurserymen in London. There he was able to study in specialized libraries in his spare time.

In 1884, aged twenty-three, he met and married a girl from Norfolk and, providentially, was offered a partnership in a firm near London. However, while on his honeymoon, he learnt that this had fallen through. Consequently he made a decision he was never to regret: to set up a new firm with his brothers in Windermere, as garden designers and contractors with their own nursery.

The south front of Wood, *c.* 1907. The garden was designed by Thomas Mawson, the house by his former partner, Dan Gibson

They worked very hard for several years, gaining a good reputation in the area, but Thomas decided that both sides of the firm would prosper better were he to break away and form a separate practice as a landscape architect. Relatively small commissions came in for a year or so, but in 1889 he was asked to lay out a large garden at Graythwaite Hall, Sawtry, near Lake Windermere, and he put into this commission 'all the knowledge I had accumulated so far', as he wrote later in his autobiography. He always held that this project gave him the initial reputation for which he had worked so hard, and it led to many more commissions in other parts of the country, and abroad, over the following forty years. Halfway through his career he added town planning to his other skills, carrying out projects in Britain, Canada and Greece. He was arguably the most prolific landscape architect of the Edwardian period, and towards the end of his life became the first president of the Institute of Landscape Architects, and of the Town Planning Institute; he was also a founder member of the Fine Arts Commission.

His philosophy for landscape architecture (which he termed 'the master art') when laying out a garden, was to relate the garden to the house with great care, and then the house and garden to the surrounding landscape. Wherever possible, he preferred to be called in at the same time as the architect for the house, so that he could discuss with him his ideas for the main features of the garden, and perhaps have some influence over his plans.

As mentioned earlier, Devon must have been a most rewarding county in which to design a garden. For Thomas Mawson, used to working in the Lake District with its superb views, exciting changes in levels,

abundance of stone, high annual rainfall, and mild winters, Devon must have compared favourably with the north of the country. Add to this the reasonably large acreage of the garden, quite probably incorporating running water or an existing lake, the availability of stone and the wealth of the Edwardian client, and the ingredients were present for a very successful outcome. Indeed, several early twentieth-century gardens in Devon incorporate all or the majority of these facets. It would be unreasonable, however, to try to assert that only designers of that period appreciated the great potential of the Devon landscape as the best site for a large country house and garden, as clearly a number of such schemes had been carried out during previous centuries with much success. Perhaps it was the coming of the railways, and later the motor car, making Devon easily accessible from London for the weekend, that encouraged successful businessmen to buy land in the county; that, coupled with the mildness of the winters, particularly in south Devon, made it very attractive. Thus, the number of potential patrons was increased and the scope for garden creation enhanced.

A brief survey will give some idea of the range and variety of Devon gardens, in the years around the First World War.

Tapeley Park, standing just to the east of Bideford and the River Torridge, is an opulent Italianate garden redolent of the high summer of Edwardian England. The 170 acre park and woodland were laid out in the eighteenth century when the house was built, but both were much altered between 1896 and 1916 by Sir John Belcher. He extended the formal garden to the south and planned three Italianate terraces with lawns, borders, a summer-house, dutch-gabled tool-shed, statuary and pond. To the east is an area of ornamental woodland leading to the walled kitchen garden, and on the north side of the stable yard is a thickly wooded valley with a lake at the end of a winding path.

By contrast, Hannaford Manor, near Ashburton, is a much more muscular affair. It was laid out by Thomas Mawson in 1906 for Major Bolitho. It followed only a few years after his work at Wood, and one can find a number of features employed again here. The use of granite for the hard landscaping, and the sloping site, tend to give the gardens a similar character. Hannaford covers 30 acres of formal and kitchen gardens as well as woodland on the high ground to the north, and although it is now, like the house, in divided ownership, the separation has been carefully achieved and is not too obvious.

To the east of the house is a level, square lawn with raised terraces to the north and east. It is interesting to note that on the original plans the lily pond is shown in the centre of the lawn, and not where it is now, on the lower terrace. To the south, as the ground drops away, are more terraces, with lawns and borders. One can still detect the line of the first driveway running east–west at this lower level; it has long since been resited to the north of the house. A most unusual feature at the west side of the house is a thatched stone wall surrounding what was originally the kitchen yard. Like many other gardens in Devon, Hannaford has fine views of the surrounding countryside.

Castle Drogo, Drewsteignton, built between 1911 and 1930 by Sir Edwin Lutyens for Julius Drewe, is arguably the most extraordinary private house designed this century. It stands on a promontory with steeply sloping wooded ground to the south and west. The formal and woodland gardens extend over more than 12 acres, but the estate covers nearly 600 acres in all. Gertrude Jekyll made proposals for terraced gardens on the slopes below the castle but these were rejected, no doubt because they would have been inappropriate to such a type of building. The main gardens were detached from the immediate surroundings of the castle and laid out on rising ground to the north of the approach road and with an east–west axis. They were designed by Lutyens and George Dillistone; the latter was also responsible for the planting. The gardens are surrounded by clipped yew hedges, and were laid out to give a dramatic effect when approached from the

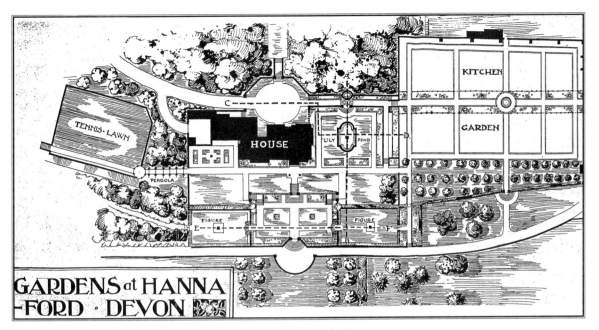

A plan of the garden at Hannaford by Thomas Mawson

A wall fountain at Hannaford

The thatched stone wall surrounding the kitchen yard at Hannaford

lower, western end near the castle. One walks, first, through a tunnel of large beech trees; then through a gateway with a flight of granite steps, into a blaze of colour in the rose garden, on three sides of which are raised terraces with borders. At each corner is an arbour, with *Parrotia* trained over iron frames, and contained within hedges on all sides; they thereby give the appearance of being squared garden houses. Further to the east and still rising, one walks across another terrace and through a shrubbery to an opening in a circular yew hedge and into what is now a well-sheltered croquet lawn. The National Trust, which owns this garden, has built a visitor centre in recent years, and this blends successfully into the environment to the east of the lawn.

Saunton Court, at Braunton in north Devon, is sited on the north side of the River Taw and has long views south over the sand dunes of Braunton Burrows. The house was built in the fifteenth century, but considerably remodelled and extended in 1932 by Sir Edwin Lutyens, who also replanned the 7½ acre garden with Dyber. As one approaches up the drive from the south-west, one is confronted by a high stone wall incorporating a gazebo with clock tower, as well as a gateway porch. Once inside, most of the garden can be seen immediately: beyond the large square lawn are terraces falling down to the south and incorporating long herbaceous borders and a small hill. Further to the south there is a sloping area of grass with shrubs and trees, some of which are recent replacements for the twenty or so lost in the 1991 gale. Near the centre of this 5 acre area is a circular pool.

A typical feature of Lutyens' work (and of this period of garden design generally) is the fine flight of stone steps leading up to a small, higher lawn from near the south-east corner of the house. The lower half of the flight is convex and the upper concave, thus allowing a circular half-landing with a slate-on-edge 'wheel' set flush in the paving. The current owner has restored virtually all the garden to its original design, and maintains it in excellent condition with the help of only one gardener.

The site developed at Castle Tor by Horace Pickersgill from 1928 is on high ground on the west side of Torquay with beautiful views over both the Lyme and Tor bays. It slopes steeply down to the south and although it is 2½ acres in area, there was not enough level ground on which to build the house. The site was therefore terraced, and the house placed at the higher level with, 5½ yards below, a lawn containing a canal-type lily pond. A circular stone turret stands on the south side, and a spiral staircase in it leads down to the next level, where there is a smaller lawn, an archway and a fountain. As the present owner did not want such a large garden, this lower section has recently been separately developed with a sensitively designed house set into the hillside. The two owners share this fine garden, which was laid out by Fred Harrild. Harrild was a pupil of Lutyens, who had originally been approached by Mr Pickersgill on the strength of his work at Castle Drogo.

Lutyens' influence is also apparent in the equally interesting and beautiful garden at Coleton Fishacre, not many miles away near Kingswear, to the west of Paignton. Commissioned in 1925–6 by Rupert D'Oyly Carte (of the Savoy Theatre family), it is now owned by the National Trust. Oswald Milne, another pupil of Lutyens, designed the house and, it is believed, the architectural garden features, such as the two terraces, the gazebo with its fine views out to the sea, and the mill garden. The site extends over 18 acres, and the planting was by Edward White of the firm of Milner White, although Lady Dorothy D'Oyly Carte is thought to have selected most of the shrubs and exotics herself over the course of ten years.

The site must have been chosen most carefully, as it has a very mild micro-climate – so much so, in fact, that South American and Australian plants and shrubs thrive in this sheltered valley leading down to the sea. Since the National Trust took it over it has introduced most successfully even more exotics, making the garden one of the most instructive in the county. Near the house, which is well sited at the higher, northern end of the garden, are dry-stone terraces with herbaceous plants on them. Just to the south-west is a formal rill garden taking advantage of a natural spring-fed stream; the water falls to two rock pools in the informal area of the garden, running down through the shrubbery and woodland to the sea.

Dartington Hall is rather out of the run of Devon gardens so far described, being much larger and having undergone many alterations since the building of the Hall in the fourteenth century. It was in 1927, however, that the present layout was implemented by H. Avray Tipping, with further work in 1933 by Beatrix Farrand, and in 1945 by Percy Cane. The two outstanding features perhaps are, first, the grassed courtyard with a fine swamp cypress to the north-east of the Great Hall, which in character resembles an Oxford or Cambridge college quadrangle. Secondly, the former Tournament Ground to the south-west, which has grassed terraces on three sides; it is a perfect setting for outdoor theatrical and musical performances. Until one walks round the end of the Great Hall, there is no hint of this great feature, nor of the higher ground beyond it, which has many fine mature trees such as Lebanon cedar, Turkey oaks, beech, plane, yew, chestnut and Monterey pines. A long, straight flight of stone steps leads up to a glade in the woodland and near the top of the steps is Henry Moore's 'Reclining Woman'. In the woodland are areas of camellia, rhododendron and hydrangeas. Great care has been taken to site the new buildings and car-parks associated with Dartington's educational use so as not to conflict with the gardens and woodland.

It is in this historical and gardening context that Thomas Mawson's work at Wood, South Tawton, is set. Wood is one of Mawson's finest landscapes, although designed near the beginning of his career and the first so

Wood. The garden entrance in the south front, *c.* 1907

far away from his native Lake District. In 1898, when his client, William Lethbridge, approached him, there was a small house and garden on the site. It seems clear that Mawson saw its considerable potential immediately and felt he could give his client the garden he wanted without too much difficulty.

As he explains in the third edition of his book *The Art and Craft of Garden-Making,* Mawson initially made a complete measured survey incorporating a grid of levels, as the nearly 30 acre site falls appreciably from west to east and from north to south. A stream ran along the east and south sides and there was a lake at the bottom of the south meadow. He was asked to recommend an architect, as his client also wanted to enlarge the house, and Dan Gibson seemed the obvious choice. As Mawson points out in his autobiography, Gibson and he had been in partnership for two years, but had recently dissolved it – paradoxically, because it had been too successful. His initial idea in seeking the partnership had been to secure by their joint efforts a higher degree of architectural expression in the gardens he planned. Mawson had no thought of going beyond the legitimate limits of landscape architecture, but such were Gibson's genius and skill in every area of applied design that, no sooner had he made the round of Mawson's clients, than he was busy

with every conceivable kind of speciality undertaken by an architect. Ecclesiastical, domestic and garden designs along with those for furniture, decorations, bookbinding and jewellery, jostled one another, and as I feared sometimes under pressure of work relegated garden design to a secondary place. In addition, he collected for my clients, china, furniture, silver, pewter, tapestries, prints and miniatures and every other imaginable artistic antique.

The entrance to Wood. Mawson and Gibson agreed that the approach should be imposing

Although Mawson was a keenly interested amateur and would have been delighted to develop this side of their practice, he saw that the motto was 'keep within your compass'. Gardens were his strength, and antiques and horticulture were not, in his view, 'homely companions'. There was, however, a keen bond of sympathy between the two men, and both gained by their collaboration: Mawson by obtaining a wider appreciation of architectural detail, and Gibson by a widened grasp of the fundamentals of composition. Together they planned the house, garden, park, home farm buildings, the decoration scheme and the furniture for Wood; Gibson also selected the silver, china and linen. Mawson's principal contribution to Gibson's work was the preparation of the first ground plan of the house, indicating its relationship to the terraces and garden scheme; while Gibson's contribution to Mawson's work was the alteration of the lodge, to which he added the gate piers, wrought-iron gates and wing walls at a later period. Between them, they planned the main axes of the garden in relation to the doors and windows of the house. There was an east–west axis from the front door terminating in a wooded glade with a semicircular summer-house, and a north–south axis running from the large windows of the hall in the centre of the south face to the circular pool and statue with, in the distance, the water meadow and lake.

Gibson added the north and south wings, making the house symmetrical when viewed from the south, but incorporating to the north extensive servants' quarters and a west wing at the northern end of the west front. He planned a circular-headed arch through this wing to connect the front drive to the stable yard and back

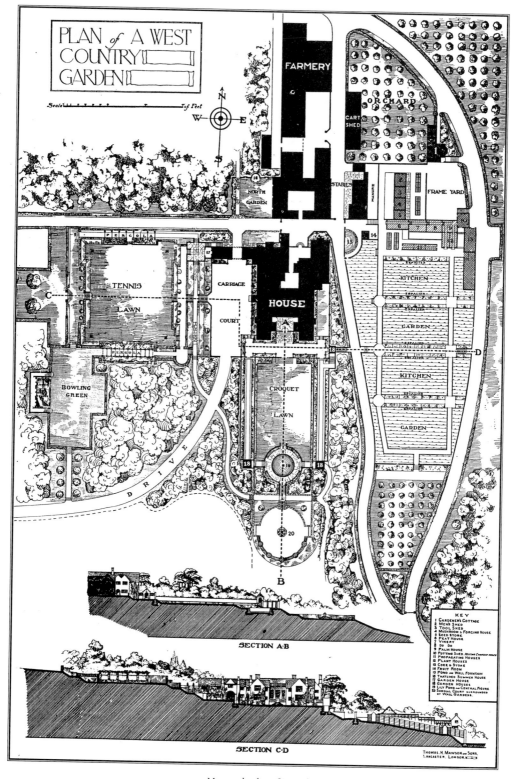

Mawson's plan of Wood

The main (western) door at Wood. The archway in the centre of the west wing led from the carriage court to the stable yard and back drive

drive. The front door of the original house had been on the south front, but Gibson and Mawson quickly decided that it should be moved to the west, in order (as Mawson put it) 'to free the south front for garden developments and, in the near future, privacy, and ensuring that the delightful prospect stretching over rounded hills of such pastoral quality could be viewed across areas of restful lawn unbroken by the turmoil of drives or gravelled spaces'. In addition, as they both felt the existing drive to the south-east of the house gave an uninteresting approach, they agreed that a new drive sweeping down to the carriage court from the south-west should be planned, and that there should be an imposing wrought-iron gateway with stone piers and a lodge. Mawson records that in order to provide a level platform on which the much-enlarged house could sit comfortably, there had to be considerable excavation to form the carriage court on the west side of it, with a drop from the proposed tennis lawn of some 5 yards, as well as the building-up of the ground level on the east side by about 4 yards. To achieve this, a stone retaining wall had to be built above the east drive that runs from the stable yard into woodland and over the stone bridge and beyond; this was in fact the line of the original approach drive.

Steps rise up to the tennis lawn on the east–west axis from the front door, through an intermediate terrace to reduce the height of the necessary retaining wall against the carriage court. On this terrace was planned a stone path flanked by lawns. In the third edition of *The Art and Craft of Garden-Making* (1907) Mawson included a case study of Wood, completed barely two years previously, observing that: 'The grass terraces and tennis courts promise to be the most charming features in the garden but are not presentable photographically until the yew hedges have had two more years of growth.' Since this part of the garden was on the west side of the house and

Wood. The tea-house at the end of the woodland glade

The semicircular thatched loggia in the north garden at Wood

considerably above it, it was decided to keep it quiet and restful, so there were no flower borders, but broad stretches of lawn surrounded by grass slopes and yew trees cut to shape. At the western end of this axis from the front door, but at the highest point of the garden near the road, Mawson terminated the view through the woodland glade with a semicircular pavilion or tea-house.

The two-court tennis lawn was planned to have recessed corners for seats and figures of the four seasons. The plan published in Mawson's book shows pergolas over paths on the north and south sides of this lawn, but today there are no signs of these or of the figures. There is an upper terrace between further yew hedges on the west side of the tennis lawn, and if one sits on the stone bench at the northern end of it one has a fine long vista across the bowling green to the south and the rolling parkland beyond. To the west of this green Mawson placed a stone loggia with a terrace above forming its roof and reached by flights of steps at either side. This was a feature he repeated in later gardens, particularly those at Thornton Manor near Port Sunlight and Roynton Cottage near Bolton, both for Lord Leverhulme.

Before leaving this area of the garden it is worth commenting on its condition in the summer of 1992. The owner, Mr David Peaster, has, virtually single-handed, saved Wood from dereliction; this applies to the house and the garden. He has lovingly trimmed hundreds of yards of 6 ft high yew hedges and cut the large areas of grass over the nine years he has owned the property. Before that it had been a country-house hotel for some years, but the owners, unable to make a financial success of it, were forced to put it on the market. Moreover, it stood empty for some time, causing both the house and garden to fall into a very bad state of repair. As hotels always attract a number of cars, the owners had cleared the shrubbery in the triangle formed by the front drive, bowling green and tennis lawn, putting down gravel to form a car-park. This area has not, so far, been restored by Mr Peaster, which is quite understandable in the circumstances. Mr Peaster is, however, in the process of

The pond at the end of the croquet lawn, looking from the direction of the house at Wood

The wall garden at Wood

The view from the sundial in the wall garden to the centre of the south front at Wood

The lake at Wood. On the far side a path is carried over a weir by a rough wooden bridge

repairing the roof over the semicircular pavilion or tea-house, whose lead has been stolen recently; this illustrates, graphically, a common problem owners of such properties are facing these days.

On the north side of the carriage-court archway is a small, square lawn surrounded by stone walls on three sides, each with semicircular headed niches set in them. In these originally stood small statues, now sadly gone. In the centre of the north wall is a semicircular thatched loggia with a stone seat inside, all making an attractive picture from the billiard-room windows.

Mawson says in his book that the main object, as far as the south front of the house was concerned, was to merge it into its surroundings 'without any harshness or discord, and, looking south from it, to secure a pleasing composition with a rich yet harmonious foreground to the beautiful home landscape beyond'. He erected the two square garden houses at the south-west and south-east angles of the croquet lawn to act as a frame to the 'picture', the fountain and figure being introduced to focus the interest surrounding the circular water-lily pond. The wide paved walk is reached on three sides by steps leading down to the pond. From the gateway, with its fine wrought-iron gate, and still on the main north–south axis, a long flight of steps leads down to what Mawson called the wall garden. This has a wide transverse path on the terrace above the circular lawn where a sundial once stood. Mawson describes this feature as being 'one of the least expensive, but most successful parts of the garden, intended to mark the transition between the formal portion of the grounds and the landscape-garden and park, to which the curved walk leads'.

Walking across the water meadow to the lake, then into the woodland forming a backdrop to it, one enters a different world. A path skirting the far side of the lake has a rough wooden bridge over a weir, which is close to a charming open-fronted stone summer-house with a newly rethatched roof. Early photographs, published in

Mawson and Gibson designed the approach drive bridge at
Wood with unique stone seats set in recesses in the balustrading
at each end

the fifth edition of *The Art and Craft of Garden-Making*, show how open this area was at that time. Now, nearly ninety years later, with the mainly deciduous trees fully mature, one is able to appreciate the effect that Mawson was seeking to achieve. As one carries on in an anticlockwise direction around the lake, one comes across the former main south approach drive with a stone bridge over the river. Mawson and Gibson designed this bridge with unique stone seats set into recesses in the balustrading at each end.

Near the upper end of this drive, where it approaches the house, the garden is retained by a random rubble wall in granite, about 9 ft high. Such has been the growth of the trees and shrubs in the intervening years that sections of the wall have collapsed; they are now being very carefully rebuilt, at considerable expense, as indeed are many yards of the kitchen garden wall to the east. A most interesting feature in the retaining wall near the south-east angle of the house is a flight of steps in a square stone garden house leading down to the back drive. Here again the walls have had to be repaired.

The kitchen garden, which is on a steep slope to the east and about 6 yards below the level of the house, extends over 5 acres. It was laid out with the full range of glasshouses, potting sheds and so forth, common at that period. On an east–west axis from the small garden house noted above was a path with espaliers at each side, dividing the garden into halves, with further parallel paths at either side quartering it. At the higher northern end were the vinery, palm-house and greenhouses, all facing south. Further to the north are the frame yard, mushroom and forcing houses and potting sheds, the orchard and a gardener's cottage. A farm track skirts round the east side of the kitchen garden, leading from what Mawson terms the 'Farmery' on his plan to join the back drive at the southern end of the garden.

Wrought-iron fruit espaliers in the kitchen garden at Wood

The range of glasshouses at Wood

Wood. The granite wall fountain in the kitchen garden

Sadly, it has not proved possible yet for the present owner to do more to the kitchen garden and its buildings than repair the boundary wall, this being a major task on its own. In its heyday, however, when it was no doubt tended by several gardeners whose sole responsibility was this garden and the orchard, it must have been well worth seeing. As Mawson notes:

It is both handy and accessible, adds interest to the garden and promises to be a sought-for pleasurance; it therefore received that attention which always seems to repay so well, when the useful and pleasant are suitably combined. The range of plant and fruit houses, the espaliers, yew hedges and rose borders of hardy perennials, rough granite wall with slate-hooded copings, over which roses and other climbers are allowed to grow, the well-trained fruit trees and borders of sweet herbs, all give interest.

Even eighteen months after Wood was completed, Mawson felt it proved the soundness of certain principles, one of which was that garden designers should not be afraid of stone walls; they do, in fact, present great opportunities for 'garden effects', and local materials and local building methods should invariably be adopted in their erection. Secondly, he held that much ornamental detail is generally unnecessary, and what there is should express simply the character of the constructional material. He observed that this garden in Devon was in a district abounding in rough-grained granite, found lying on the surface amid the surrounding moors and woods; it was always beautifully weathered on the exposed face. The stone split well but was unsuitable for fine dressings or small mouldings, yet was most effective in squared blocks or columns with walls built in rough,

Beginning in 1960, Dr James Smart has created a plantsman's garden, specializing in camellias, around two lakes at Marwood Hill

Luscombe Castle. Humphry Repton's naturalistic planting, surrounding Nash's house, remains essentially as proposed

Dartington Hall. The Tiltyard, possibly used for jousting in medieval times

The University of Exeter enjoys the considerable advantage of being set within an older, well-established landscape. The sculpture, by Barbara Hepworth, stands before the Victorian pinetum

The terrace and pierced wall at Endsleigh Cottage, by Repton for the sixth Duke of Bedford

The moat at Bickleigh Castle, now turned to pacific use as a water garden

Immaculately maintained bedding in the public park at Torre Abbey, Torquay

The Orangery at Saltram, built between 1773 and 1775 and based on a plan by Nathaniel Richmond

The terrace garden at Powderham, developed at the time of the castle's remodelling between 1837 and 1848

Sir John Belcher laid out the three Italianate terraces at Tapeley Park between 1896 and 1916

Lukesland, on the edge of Dartmoor. Informal drifts of colour are provided by shrubs and plants which thrive in the soil and climate of Devon

The path from the garden to the carriage court at Wood,
showing Mawson's fondness for the use of local granite

random rubble. Instead of classic nosings to the steps, the undershadow was obtained by a roughly picked splay rounded over the face of the bead, which was in random lengths laid on a solid rubble core.

In the circular walled garden the stone was not dressed beyond rough scabbling, the crannies being filled with rock plants. He comments: 'the success of this work has inclined me still more towards single retaining walls in preference to expensive pierced work and balustrading, which though necessary to mansions designed in the grand style are not essential to houses of moderate dimensions; the money thus saved could be more effectively spent on good modern sculpture.' It is difficult, even today, to dissent from this view.

Mawson's work for William Lethbridge at Wood was apparently the outcome of a very happy working relationship between them, so much so that on its completion in 1905 he was presented by his client with a copy of *The Praise of Gardens* by A. F. Sievking, handsomely bound with a cover designed by Dan Gibson and inscribed inside:

> To the Author and Begetter
> of the Gardens at Wood
> In grateful appreciation
> From the owner
> 19.9.05

When Lethbridge died in Davos, Switzerland, some years later, Mawson felt he had lost a dear and understanding friend, a man he described as one of the finest type of English gentlemen he had ever met, and a scholar 'withal'.

This chapter has dealt in some detail with Wood, as it makes a significant contribution to the Devon landscape and is a typical example of Thomas Mawson's work and of early twentieth-century garden design. Relating Wood to other Devon gardens of the same period, one finds several common elements. They all tend to show a sensitive appreciation of the site and its surroundings, extending where possible to the planning and placing of the house to connect it to the garden design. The use of local materials such as granite for the house, garden buildings and hard landscaping ensures that they all blend well and jointly fit into the local environment. Where there is a stream running through the property, this is exploited to great advantage in the building of bridges and the formation of rills, small waterfalls, lily ponds and lakes. None of the gardens mentioned is on a level site, so their designers have been able to plan outdoor 'rooms' without the need to wait a number of years for hedges to grow. Terracing has enabled considerable separation at the outset of the parts of each garden.

The social life of the well-to-do of this period called for lawns on which garden parties could be held throughout the summer months, and house parties at weekends meant that there should, if possible, be space for two tennis courts, a croquet lawn and, as at Wood, a bowling green. There had also to be large kitchen gardens growing a wide variety of fruit and vegetables for the household throughout the year. Hothouses were a necessity so that there might always be a supply of potted plants for the house in the winter. One must not forget, either, that if the owner was to keep a good head gardener contented, he had to provide the facilities for him to show his skills at local horticultural society shows.

Good examples of garden design of this period should be conserved along with those of earlier periods. One has to be realistic, however, and face the fact that in virtually no case can the present owners (including the National Trust) afford to employ the number of gardeners who would have maintained these gardens originally; there are many instances where the owner and his family are the sole gardeners.

What can be done, therefore, to overcome this problem? Fortunately, with the invention of electrical hedge trimmers and small tractor-type mowers, owners can, by working extremely hard for most of the week in summer, 'keep the wolf from the door'. Even so, something has to go, and that is usually the labour-intensive care of flower beds and, of course, kitchen gardens. In the shrubberies and woodland, too, there is always work to be done in felling shrubs and trees that are diseased or over-large, and in removing those lost in gales, which seem to be more frequent than in the past. This work usually needs the services of contractors with their specialist equipment, and can be expensive. Gardeners in Devon are fortunate as they are able to avail themselves of services offered by such bodies as the Devon Gardens Trust. Specialist advice, physical work on the ground or simple moral support can help ease the frustrating and even heart-breaking situations with which gardeners are sometimes faced.

NOTE

The photographs in this chapter were taken by Thomas Mawson and used in the 3rd edition of *The Art and Craft of Garden-Making*, 1907.

SELECT BIBLIOGRAPHY

Beard, G., *Thomas H. Mawson* (1976).

Mawson, D., 'T.H. Mawson (1861–1933) – Landscape Architect and Town Planner', *Journal of the Royal Society of Arts*, cxxxii, 5531 (1984), pp. 184–99.

Mawson, T.H., *The Art and Craft of Garden-Making* (3rd edn., 1907).

———, *The Life and Work of an English Landscape Architect* (1927).

Chapter Nine

VANISHED GARDENS

ROSEMARY ANNE LAUDER

Ornate iron gates, rusting gently, hung on noble stone pillars, the tall growth of weeds bearing witness to the passage of time since last they swung open to admit the carriage wheels of visiting gentry. And beyond the gates, the drive – overgrown, blocked by fallen branches, clumps of primroses in the centre, but still leading on through the clinging brambles, past the thicket of overgrown shrubberies. Overhead the tall trees sway – home to innumerable families of sentinel rooks whose evocative cawing is the only sound of life, and the only warning of intruders.

Sometimes the unwary trespasser stumbles on mossy steps, or finds a sad piece of statuary long forgotten. Derelict and rotten summer-houses collapse beneath the weight of ivy – and, just occasionally, some carefully planted shrub still blooms amid the gloom, surviving against all odds. The once-immaculate lawn is now waist-high, and where once were weedless flowerbeds and pleasure gardens, all is overgrown, all gone back to nature. No one gardens here anymore.

This sad scene is repeated throughout the county, where former estates have fallen on hard times, been abandoned to their fate, or await the harsh sentence of the bulldozer as the forerunner to rows of neat little 'executive homes', with the mansion house commemorated in name only on the street signs.

Faded photographs depict those leisured days when the sons and daughters of the wealthy promenaded on the terrace or strolled along the well-kept paths, the ladies in long, elegant gowns, their complexions shaded by frothy parasols, their escorts in boaters and blazers. Tennis parties, gatherings on the croquet lawn, carriage drives to favourite picnic places – and, in the background and never intruding into the photographs, an army of men and boys. The hierarchy of the gardening world was every bit as strict and regimented as the downstairs world 'up at the house'. A large estate could easily employ thirty men to keep the gardens in pristine condition and as the major showpiece decreed by the fashion of the times.

Gardens vanish for a variety of reasons, but these Victorian and Edwardian set pieces were doomed from the start. The closest we get to them today is in the public parks of our towns and cities, where the municipal gardeners put on a colourful display each year. Bedding schemes and seasonal planting are the most ephemeral of all – tiny seeds in the early spring, thrown on the compost heap when their brief moment of glory has passed, to be replaced by another gaudy belle, until the season finishes and bare earth shows through once more. Such displays are only possible with the back-up of greenhouses and plentiful labour.

One such garden would have been found at Poltimore House on the outskirts of Exeter. The house still stands, home of the Bampfyldes from the thirteenth century until the 1920s and the estate from which Lord Poltimore took his title in 1831. But the grounds are sadly decayed and decimated, not least by the cutting of a motorway through the parkland. Until its sale in 1920, Poltimore House had maintained its ancient deer park of some

200 acres, one of the few surviving in the county to be stocked and preserved. The ancient trees and woodlands were part of a familiar landscape, but here as elsewhere the sad story was repeated; the grounds were purchased by a timber merchant, and by the end of the Second World War much of the woodland had vanished. Fortunately the timber merchant must have been more sympathetic than most, for he left the pinetum, and the historic lime avenues. These were possibly planted in honour of the accession of the Hanoverian kings – as a token of loyalty, for their symbol was the linden, or lime, tree. The principal avenue led to the church, and down it Lord Poltimore would process every Sunday, followed by his family and all his servants, in strict order of precedence. The other avenue had at some time been pollarded, and was in poor condition, so in 1956 it was replanted with poplars.

The pinetum was an important feature, for it was planted by John Veitch, the famous Exeter nurseryman, in the early nineteenth century. John Veitch was sending back seeds of the magnificent trees found in California and it would seem probable that some of these found their way to Poltimore, in particular the Wellingtonia, of which five survived in 1971, one of them 137 ft high and with a girth of 22 ft. A description of the grounds as they survived until the 1920s' sale comes from Mr R. Fortescue-Foulkes's book on the history of Poltimore. It also contains a detailed account of the finest trees as they were found in the 1950s, and gives us some idea of the scope and size of the Poltimore pinetum:

In 1957 the pinetum was visited by the Hon. Maynard Greville, at that time one of the country's leading experts on trees . . . in an incredibly short time (he) had listed and measured about 50 of the more important trees. The following are some of the specially interesting ones (C.A. – Central Avenue. L.A. – Lime Avenue):-

Caucasian Fir (*Abiens Normanniana*) in S. bay of C.A. 120ft × 10ft 9in. This is second highest in BI to one at Uplyme, Dorset, which is 126ft, and tying with one at Taymouth Castle, Scotland.
Schrenk's Spruce (*Picea Schrenkiana*) by Kitchen Garden Gate. Greville calls this a superb tree. 81ft × 7ft 11in. Second in height to one at Warnham Court, Sussex, but bigger in girth.
Wellingtonia (*Sequoia Gigantea*) The one already mentioned above as one of Lobb's first seedlings stands with another of about the same height in W. bay of C.A. i.e. 137ft × 22ft.
Lucombe Oak (*Quercus Lucombeana*) near L.A. 129ft × 10ft 6in. This is probably a height record. This tree is a hybrid between a Turkey Oak and a Cork Oak. It was first raised by an Exeter nurseryman called Lucombe in 1765.
Cork Oak (*Quercus Suber*) One parent of the above. This tree is getting near its end and for many years the limbs have been supported by chains. It has the remarkable spread of 67ft and a girth of nearly 15ft, which makes it the stoutest tree of its species in the country.
Sweet Gum (*Liquidamber Styraciflua*) near garden end of L.A. This is a fine specimen of a tree distinguished for its foliage which turns to the most brilliant colours, crimson, orange and bright yellow in the autumn. 80ft × 5ft.
Colorado Douglas Fir (*Pseudotsuga Glauca*), in centre C.A. 110ft × 12ft 7in. This is not the usual form of the Douglas Fir, not growing so tall and having thicker and slightly silvery leaves, with an odour of turpentine. Greville was puzzled by this tree and even Kew was not definite in identification; it may be a variety known as *Pseudotsuga Longifolia*.
Purple Beech (*Fagus Sylvatica purpurea*) at church end of L.A. 108ft × 11ft 2in. This is a particularly fine example of the purple variety of the common beech.
Japanese Umbrella Pine (*Sciadopitys verticillata*) opposite the kitchen garden gate. This curious conifer, first

Poltimore House, by Edmund Prideaux, *c.* 1716. The formal garden, with clipped evergreens, statue and parterre

sent by Lobb from Java and J.G. Veitch from Japan, has no other relatives among others of that order; it is so called owing to the arrangement of the leaves at the end of the shoots giving the impression of an inverted toy umbrella . . . Being one of the five sacred trees of Japan it was extensively planted in the temple gardens.

These few descriptions are given to indicate what was once and could still be an interesting landscaped garden and arboretum on the outskirts of Exeter, and in the future near the projected motorway. It should be a perpetual preserve for plant and bird life; for, besides much else, of the former, orchis of all kinds abound, and of the latter have been seen or heard herons, kingfishers, lapwings, nightjars, woodpeckers, goldcrests and, rarely, the nightingale.[1]

Another charming feature of Poltimore was the Chinese Garden, which was laid out in the design of the fabled willow-pattern plate, with pagoda, wooden bridge and Chinese fencing. Only the fleeing lovers were absent. The garden was made around the River Clyst, which was dammed to form a small pool with an island. This survives, as do clumps of bamboos and other shrubs and trees alien to the lush pasture meadow in which they are sited. Even in 1971, when Fortescue-Foulkes was writing, the pleasure gardens had succumbed to a tangle of laurels, and the rose garden and iris garden were marked only by twisted railings. Many fine rhododendrons were also lost, and he talks of ornamental forest trees, conifers and flowering shrubs. Mention is

Poltimore by Prideaux. The long rectangular pond, flanked with trees

Prideaux's view of Poltimore, *c.* 1727, shows a new front. The trees appear to be the same but the pond has disappeared

The old Elizabethan manor house at Buckland Filleigh in Edmund Prideaux's sketch, dated 1720, showing what was probably an orchard immediately in front of it

made of two mosaic bowls set in the grass at the rear of the house, which were part of an aviary, popular in the nineteenth century when exotic birds were shipped home from the east.

Dotted around the surrounding fields are what could well be lone survivors of the earlier garden, recorded in drawings made by Edmund Prideaux.[2] The earliest, of around 1716, shows the house fronted by a formal garden, with clipped evergreens, a statue, parterre, and with an umbrella-shaped tree in the foreground. A later drawing shows a very different view, with formal rows of trees flanking a long rectangular pond, branching around the house to form a moat. A third drawing, believed to date from around 1727, shows the new front, erected in the early years of the century. The trees appear to be the same, but the lake has disappeared.

Devon is fortunate to have the Prideaux drawings, a major historical resource that provides a record of what the gardens of manor houses were like in the eighteenth century. No poetic licence was used, there are no romantic overtones to confuse the student of architecture and of history. Edmund Prideaux produced a set of topographical drawings, mainly in pen and ink, faithfully portraying the houses and their surroundings. Born in 1693, he was brought up in Norwich, where his father was Dean; in 1728 he inherited Prideaux Place at Padstow, where his descendants still live. He moved down and began important changes there, employing his 'architect's eye'.

The sketches are all of important houses owned by his friends and relations; it would seem that Edmund visited as many as possible in the early 1700s, and that the drawings were either by way of a 'thank you' to his hosts, or for his own amusement. Whatever the reason, they are an invaluable collection. They include Werrington, Stowe (Cornwall), Dunsland, Thuborough and Soldon, Portledge, Buckland Filleigh and Heanton

Netherton Hall. View of the garden front by Prideaux

Netherton Hall at Farway, drawn by Prideaux in 1727

Prideaux's bird's-eye view of Portledge House

Satchville. The drawings are stylized and remarkably detailed – all show a rigid pattern of gardening, with clipped shrubs and trees, planted in rows or around parterre-like paths and beds. There are no flowers, no climbing plants, no lax or exuberant growth. Everything is kept strictly within bounds and nature is firmly outside the garden wall.

In many instances the houses have changed little, most of them being sited in remote rural areas unsuited to the requirements of later generations, who did not fancy spending their winters isolated by a network of muddy lanes. Newer, grander houses were built elsewhere, and the original older buildings left untouched. Soldon Manor, near Holsworthy, is an example. Prideaux would have no difficulty recognizing the house as it is today, but the garden is reduced to a level lawn surrounded by a drive and hedge. Part of the wall survives, but that is all.

Netherton Hall, at Farway near Ottery St Mary, is another example of a house that has been well preserved. It is a beautiful, mellow building, seemingly untouched since Prideaux drew it in 1727. Tucked away in its sheltered valley, the fast-changing pace of the twentieth century seems to have passed it by. This gem of a manor house was built by Sir Edmund Prideaux in the time of King James I, the estate having been purchased from Sir Bernard Drake, who acquired the lands from the Abbot of Canonsleigh after the Dissolution. The owner (the drawing is dated 5 September 1727) was the fifth in descent from the first baronet.

Although Netherton Hall has been preserved almost intact, its garden has not. A plain lawn fronts the house, with not even a path leading to the front porch. There are a few struggling evergreens beyond the grass, which could possibly be survivors of the avenue shown in one of Prideaux's two drawings. Of the ornate clipped shapes and formal layout depicted in the other view, nothing at all survives. There is a charming courtyard garden

Portledge House. The garden front by Edmund Prideaux, 1716

beyond the hedge on the gable end, but the rest has succumbed to 'ease of maintenance'. In recent years attempts have been made to rescue the terraced gardens behind the house, but these are not shown in the drawings.

At Portledge, on the north Devon coast near Bideford, the garden has met with a slightly better fate. The house and estate have been in the possession of the Pine-Coffin family since the eleventh century, and there must have been many gardens on the site before Edmund Prideaux paid his visit. Although both the house and garden have altered considerably, they are recognizable from the drawings. As was so often the case, a new entrance hall was built (sometime after Prideaux's drawing), completely changing the alignment of the house with its grounds. Prideaux showed that what was then the front garden was overlooked by the principal rooms of the house. The symmetrical formal beds are typical, but whether the effect was achieved with grass, low-growing plants or gravel, there is no record.

Today, as the visitor approaches Portledge down the long drive, this elevation of the house is easily recognizable, and very little altered. But the enclosing wall has gone, and the drive sweeps on, through the two beds shown on the left, to take the visitor to the grand new porch with its broad terrace in front. Railings now separate farmland from garden, and the formal beds are simply level grass. A higher garden, also grass, is surrounded by old walling, part cob, part stone, which could be remnants of the buildings shown in the more distant view of Portledge. The two enclosures shown above the house to the left became the walled vegetable garden, and a tennis court. Much of the woodland has survived very much as it is shown, and down on the beach the stream was once dammed to form a sizeable lake. An ancient arched bridge built of stone carried the coastal footpath across the stream, and the sluice gates are visible below. The artist depicts the island of Lundy close to the north Devon shore, and

Above and below: Heanton Satchville, by Prideaux, inscribed 1724. Today all that remains is some terracing and a few stone walls.

presumably the seven vessels shown in the bay would be making for Bideford, then a bustling port of great importance.

Of Heanton Satchville, buried deep in the Devon countryside to the north of Okehampton, nothing at all survives. Here is a prime example of a once magnificent house being abandoned in favour of a more convenient location. In 1724 Heanton Satchville was a notable and noble house. It was of considerable size, and would be considered one of our most important historic houses had it survived. According to Prideaux's drawing inscribed 1724, it had an equally magnificent garden. And today? Nothing. A farmhouse occupies the site, reached down a muddy farm lane. Although it appears from the chimneys to be very old it is doubtful that it was ever part of the Heanton Satchville so tantalizingly portrayed by Prideaux.

Polwhele's *History of Devonshire* sheds some light on the vanishing trick:

This estate was thus advertized in 1782: 'To be sold, a very capital and valuable freehold estate, desirably situate in the parish of Huish . . . with a very capital and large Mansion-house, suited with proper offices, orchards, and gardens, and which for several generations past was the residence of a very genteel family . . . – The manor and advowson of the living were soon after purchased by Sir James Norcliffe Innes, a Scotch baronet, who built a new house on the premises called Innes House.'[3]

Innes House, later named Heanton Satchville, became part of the Clinton Estates and is today the home of Lord Clinton, although the original house was destroyed by fire in the early years of this century. The fate of the original Heanton Satchville is hard to unravel. Remains of terracing and a few stone walls confirm the site of a large and important building, but excavations would be necessary to uncover its full extent. It probably just dwindled into a farmhouse, the stone robbed for barns and other buildings until even the memory of it faded. Prideaux's drawing is virtually all that is left.

Photographs and pictures are all that survive of Dunsland House, near Holsworthy. The formal layout shown in the 1716 Prideaux sketch had long been swept away by the time the property came into the hands of the National Trust in 1954. This formality had itself replaced the parkland shown surrounding the house in an earlier drawing. By the 1950s, all was rough grassland with no trace of the flight of steps or the walled enclosures. The only survivors were the walled kitchen gardens some distance from the house, and the medieval fishponds below in the valley. The Trust had not yet turned their attention to the grounds when Dunsland was totally destroyed by fire in 1967. Today a level grassed area, so seemingly small, marks the site of the house, and all that commemorates it is the name on the crossroads. It has even been erased from the latest Ordnance Survey maps.

The next great era of gardening was the eighteenth century, characterized by its landscapes, when the owner went beyond the immediate confines of the house and included all that could be seen from his mansion. This kind of grand gardening was not for the small squire; not only did he not have sufficient funds, he needed the fields for their proper purpose – farming. Fortunately there are some survivors from this age. Castle Hill near South Molton is an early example, the subject of Chapter Four in this book. Saltram House and Mount Edgcumbe, near Plymouth, are also good examples.

Buckland Filleigh is a property that demonstrates the change. The Elizabethan house remains, but is now overshadowed by a large wing built in the Grecian-classic style. At some time the grounds were landscaped. A ha-ha separates the garden from the parkland, which falls to a lake formed by damming the small stream. An early map shows a hermitage in the woodland, and an ice house, both now gone; to what is now the front of the house (the rear in the Prideaux sketch), the parish road has been sunk between retaining walls, so that it is not visible from the house, which would have had an uninterrupted view across the fields to distant belts of trees.

A distant view of Dunsland. (W. Gauci, *c.* 1850). After a fire in 1967 the National Trust demolished the remains of the house, leaving only a bare platform to mark its existence

Dunsland. Formal enclosures and flights of steps depicted by Edmund Prideaux in 1716

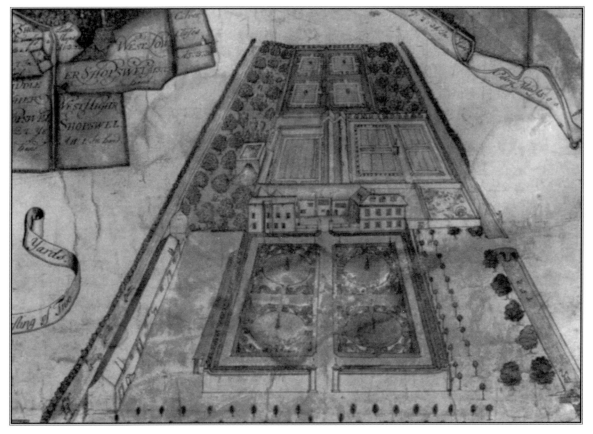

Hartland Abbey and grounds from the west, from a survey after the marriage of Mary Luttrell and Paul Orchard in 1702

There is evidence of the grounds having been 'emparked' with clumps and belts of trees and some fine old specimen trees, although there have been recent losses through old age and gales.

It would be interesting to know what species of tree were used in the gardens of the old manor house as shown by Prideaux. Could it simply have been a neat orchard, planted formally at the front of the house? If so it was unusual, and the trees appear to have been very regularly clipped, yet not drawn as if they were evergreen. There is a strange evergreen of considerable height shown between house and church; strange when it is remembered that the drawing is inscribed 1720 when conifers were far less common than they became after traders and explorers began sending home seeds from abroad towards the end of the century.

The historical sequence of gardening can be clearly seen at Hartland Abbey, on the Atlantic coast of north Devon. Here is a fine example of one of those homes of a county family that has never been sold, where continuity has ensured that much is preserved, and where valuable records exist to show us what it looked like through the centuries. Many changes have taken place, but there has always been an important garden in this fertile and sheltered valley, less than 2 miles from the rugged coastline of Hartland Quay.

The site of the abbey is one of the oldest in the county and has been in continuous cultivation since the foundation of the Augustinian monastery in the twelfth century. The monks would have been the first gardeners, and it was they who shaped the garden that lasted until the end of the eighteenth century. The monastery grounds would have included separate gardens devoted to medicinal and culinary herbs, vegetables, orchards

The front of Hartland Abbey in 1769. Gone are the formal walled gardens, and the planting is confined to narrow beds on the perimeter

and the medieval fishponds that are the sole survivor from this period. At the Dissolution of the Monasteries under Henry VIII, the abbey was awarded to one William Abbott, the keeper of the king's wine cellar, from whom the present owner, Sir Hugh Stucley, can trace his descent.

The monastic tradition and the fashion of the times are clearly demonstrated in an early drawing of 1702, made just after the marriage of the heiress, Mary Luttrell, to Paul Orchard. The bordering stream, the abbey river, is shown confined between straight banks and crossed by a two-arched bridge. This still exists, but the stream follows a more natural, winding course. The observant explorer can still find evidence of the former embankments and weirs by which the water was put to good use. To the west, or seaward side, of the abbey the four formal symmetrical beds appear in the drawings to be surrounded by a garden wall. A long range of buildings borders the lane, and avenues of trees have been planted. Behind, on the inland side, are what would appear to be the vegetable and flower gardens, with mature trees, but all is formality and straight lines.

Three years after the Luttrell/Orchard marriage, extensive alterations were carried out. The son and grandson of Paul Orchard continued the work, during the course of which most of the old abbey disappeared. A drawing made in 1769 from the inland side shows clearly that the changes also affected the gardens. Gone are the formal walled gardens, and the planting is confined to narrow beds on the perimeter. At some stage the gardens on the other side of the house shown in the earlier drawing also vanished. Today the grassland rolls up to the walls of the abbey, with a few fine parkland trees. There are no buildings and no avenues.

An interesting description comes from an article written for *Country Life*:

The bird's-eye view shows the Long Garden up the meadow to the east; a 'wilderness' with a fountain south of the cloister; and a yard to its west, beside the house, full of birds of many sorts including pea-fowl.

Along the whole southern boundary flows the once monastic brook, bridged several times as it is today, with fishponds below the parish church. On the west side of the house was a large formal garden protected by high walls against wind, with stables to its north. By 1769, only its walls remained, but there was a disproportionately large Classic stable hard against it.

An enthusiastic description of the view down from the Pleasure House on The Warren was written by the Rev. James Hervey in 1738: 'Before (the House) is . . . a garden, enriched with fruits and beautiful with flowers. This leads into a curious sort of artifical wilderness made of elms and limes planted in rows, cut into form, and uniting their branches. In the midst is a fountain large enough to swim in, and a little engine playing the waters.' All of these have gone, too, perhaps at the end of the century. The Abbey Meads now recede once more between the woods.[4]

The Victorian garden was perhaps the most vulnerable of all. The county had several important gardens from this rich and exotic era, of which only a handful survive in anything like their original form. The extravagant gardens that the older generation can still remember are as vanished as the way of life that accompanied them: grand houses, grand owners, grand entertaining of large numbers of visiting gentry with little or nothing to do. The gardens were both a status symbol and the pleasure ground that surrounded the house, and it was here that the summer days were whiled away, a kind of respite between the end of the London season and the beginning of the shooting season. Perhaps that was why the emphasis was on bedding plants, because there was no one much around for the rest of the year! The garden had to work, too, and much produce was required to supply the house, not only with vegetables and fruit, but also with cut flowers and pot plants.

Sale particulars of the mid- to late nineteenth century give a valuable insight into this lost world. Membland in Noss Mayo, later the home of Edward Baring, Lord Revelstoke, was sold in 1827. It boasted a pleasure ground, and a capital walled garden, clothed with choice fruit trees and standards, which was 'well stocked and cropped'. There was a melon ground and hothouses and greenhouses with vines, etc.

Also in the South Hams is Combe Royal. This has a notable garden in a deep Devon combe. The lower garden, largely planted with giant rhododendrons, still exists, and is open to the public, but little remains of the elaborate Victorian layout around the house. The garden was featured in the *Journal of Horticulture* in 1871, when its orangery was described as growing varieties of orange, lemons, limes and shaddocks, unprotected except for reed mats in severe weather. This orangery was actually a south-facing wall built with generous recesses, and has survived, although it is now bare of plants.

A similar feature was rediscovered in recent years in the gardens of Roborough House on the outskirts of Barnstaple. Dating any of the garden structures found in the surrounding woodland is chancy, but the house itself was built in the 1700s. Close by the house a large buttressed wall was revealed from underneath a tangle of brambles and saplings, forming one side of the walled garden.

An 1849 description of Pilton House, outside Barnstaple, tells of parterres of flowers surrounded by grounds, margined by full-grown plantations. Walks extended through the park-like grounds for half a mile, and the gardens of 1 acre were partly walled, with a 21 ft conservatory, a forcing house, a pond (with fountain) for gold and silver fish, a gardener's house, sheds, dog kennels, yards and a pheasantry: in fact, everything necessary to support a country gentleman.

Bishop's Court mansion, at Clyst Honiton, sold in 1833, also had its own pheasantry and aviary, together with a commodious covered summer-house, melon and cucumber beds, fruit trees and an orchard, as well as a rookery of noble beeches, elms and oaks, mingled with limes and chestnuts.

The orangery at Combe Royal, from the *Journal of Horticulture* (1871)

The orangery at Combe Royal today, which has survived although bereft of citrus plants

The original house at Stevenstone, surrounded by a deer park, and with a lake in the foreground (J. Bingley, after G.B. Campion, 1831)

Very few gardens of this size have survived; all too many were sold off once their houses became unmanageably large and expensive, and labour too costly. In many instances the valuable parkland trees attracted timber merchants who, once their destructive work was complete, sold the rest for whatever they could get. The house in the meantime had often become an irretrievable ruin.

Stevenstone in north Devon is a good example, and excellent aerial photographs of the extensive grounds survive. Once part of the vast Rolle estates, it was the site of a noble mansion, home of the Hon. Mark Rolle. Records exist of a manor house at Stevenstone from as early as 1304. An old print shows the original house before it was rebuilt in the grand French château style, and also shows that it was surrounded by a deer park, with the lake an important feature. Both elements were frequently found in medieval gardens, providing fresh food throughout the year, in particular the winter months. (Alas, only Powderham Castle still maintains its deer park complete with deer.) Many of the fine trees shown in the print have gone, victims of old age, or of the timber merchant in whose hands Stevenstone ended. A sorry loss was the fine double avenue of yews that led from the house to the parish church of St Giles in the Wood.

The gardens shown in the aerial photograph were contemporary with the Victorian house; the little library building with its accompanying orangery are older. All that remains today is the curving balustrade which separated gardens from parkland, the walls of the walled garden, and the pinetum, albeit somewhat overgrown.

An aerial view of Stevenstone, taken between the wars, showing gardens which are contemporary with the Victorian house

The elaborate parterres, the range of glasshouses, the sunken courtyard and most of the fine trees have gone. Behind the library and connecting it with the orangery was a small garden with a rose-covered pergola of twenty-two arches, which survived until quite recent times, when the Landmark Trust bought the library and restored it for use as an unusual holiday home. The orangery lost its glass roof (supported by a fine cast-iron framework, still to be seen close by), and the area between the two buildings was grassed over.

A description of the formal gardens in the time of Lady Rolle paints a lavish picture:

Beautiful trees of the fir tribe grace the gardens. Attractive is the bed of bamboos and acanthus and near it is a large species of paulonia from seed gathered in the South of France some years ago by Lady Gertrude Rolle, and which flowered for the first time last spring. The avenue of fuchsias look distinctly rich and there is a very good collection of climbing roses and arches and standards of ironwork leading to an open arbour covered with roses and clematis. Fan palms lend a tropical look to the surroundings. The lower flower garden is equally effective with its beds of salvias, fuchsias, begonias, petunias, verbenas, heliotropes etc., while the rockery and fishponds give a finish to this part of the grounds.

The grand new Stevenstone that Mark Rolle built for himself is believed to have been the work of C.M. Barrie – his father was responsible for the Houses of Parliament, and also for several other major commissions –

Stevenstone House was designed by C.M. Barrie. A notable Victorian mansion, it was demolished after the Second World War and its gardens fell into disuse

who frequently included the garden layout in his plans. Stevenstone was separated from its parkland by stone balustrading bounding the formal, level grounds and gardens, and it is quite probable that the architect devised the whole.

On what was once the outskirts of Exmouth was Marley, a vanished Victorian garden *par excellence*. The original site, bounded by Marley Lane, is not easy to find. The estate was sold off and split up into building plots in the 1930s so that it is difficult to envisage the house and gardens as they once existed. The actual site of the house itself is occupied by a pleasant property, also called Marley House but of much more manageable proportions. Surrounding it are the few tangible remains of the gardens – the terrace and balustrading, with steps leading down to what is now a paddock, and to the rear a small length of walling with an arch that once led to the stables, and a small adjacent garden room. One feature carefully preserved by the owners of Marley House is the 'bull ring', a sunken circle once used to exercise horses. It is clearly shown on an Ordnance Survey map of early this century. A large estate is depicted, with forestry, or plantations divided by rides, a large area called 'The Lawn', numerous blocks of outbuildings, two lodges, and the house's own gasometer.

The original Marley House was coeval with the neighbouring Bystock Estate, which was bought by John Bryce on his retirement to Exmouth after amassing a large fortune in South America. Marley was purchased to accommodate his son and six grandchildren. Everything was of the best, with no expense spared. The entrance

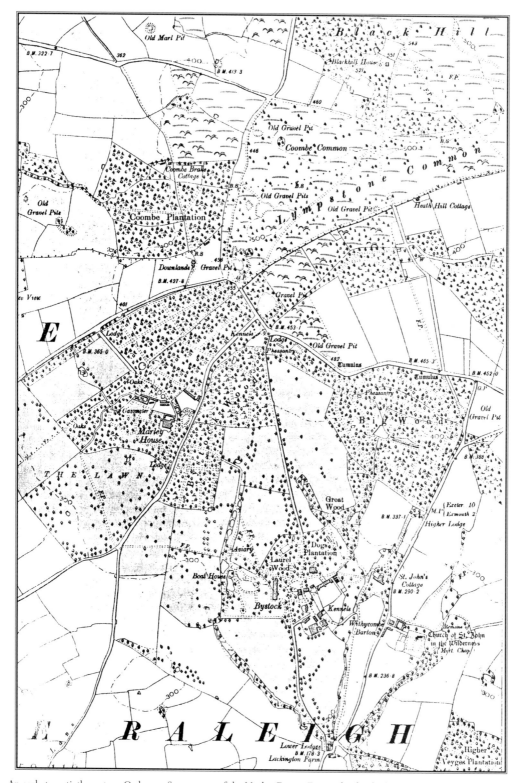

An early twentieth-century Ordnance Survey map of the Marley Estate, Exmouth, clearly showing the 'bull ring', a sunken circle once used to exercise horses

hall had 40,000 Italian tiles and a marble staircase. The drawing room, a mere 79 ft by 39, had furnishings said to have cost £38,000.

The garden was on a similarly large scale. Vanished completely are the sunken Italian gardens, said to have cost £10,000, the greenhouses for growing tropical fruit, the orangery, and the vinery. The sale particulars of 1905 give a very clear picture of the scale of the grounds, and of their glasshouses. From the house one walked out onto the 'imposing ornamental tiled terrace with massive balustrading leading to two flights of broad steps'. There were tennis courts and archery grounds. The glasshouse vinery measured 100 ft by 12½ and the banana house was 40½ ft by 7½. For growing cucumbers, melons and pineapples there was another huge house, 100 ft by 13½; there was a span-roof greenhouse of 62½ ft by 13. The peach and rose house was 162 ft by 11¼ – the whole area must have more than rivalled the Crystal Palace, and the amount of glass required must have been colossal.

Less glamorous were the fruit room, the tool room, potting sheds, mushroom house, stoke hole and boiler room. All in all there were 8 acres of pleasure grounds and 2.2 acres of kitchen gardens. Not a vestige of this survives, with the single exception of the terrace and balustrading.

The house was never lived in. The son for whom it was built died in Paris in 1901 shortly before its completion. The family preferred to live abroad, and after one short let the house was shut up and abandoned. Eventually the property was put up for sale, in 1928, and the builder who purchased it held a demolition sale two years later. Among the 700 lots, after the Italian floor tiles and the brass hinges from the door, were the turfs from the lawns, and the brickwork from the huge walled gardens. By that time, most of the vast acreage of glass had probably fallen prey to vandals and neglect.

What would surely have become one of the county's most important gardens has been lost to industrial expansion. High up on the southern edge of Dartmoor above Cornwood the spoil heaps of the china-clay works grow ever larger. The insidious white dust pervades everything, casting a pall of permanent snow over tree and shrub, choking even the weeds. Yet until the 1960s a beautiful garden existed at Lee Moor, carved out of the granite and clay beds, the pride of its owners and a source of pleasure to the thousand or so visitors who came every year to wander around the ponds and admire the abundance of fine trees and shrubs.

Perhaps the Martins should have realized their days at Lee Moor were numbered, for the Swan Pond that formed a major feature of the garden was the original quarry pit of the early clay workings. The family took a lease in the 1830s on the farmhouse and cottages, which for the next century were used as a holiday home and for shooting parties. Then in the 1930s Lee Moor House became the permanent home of the Martin family, and for many years Mr Martin was chairman of English China Clay. During the next thirty years, three generations created, from a wilderness, a garden that must have been quite outstanding. The nucleus came with the purchase in 1930 of the entire exhibition of Waterer's, the Surrey nursery, from the Royal Show; brought to Lee Moor and planted more or less as it had been exhibited, this became the Waterer Walk.

Rhododendrons are a surprising genus. There doesn't seem to be much resemblance between their native habitat and the exposed uplands of Dartmoor, with the added hazard of the proximity of the clay works. But they thrived at Lee Moor. By the time Nancy Martin, by then Mrs Eric Hare, began to take a hand, there were groves of them so tall that the flowers could only be seen from an aeroplane, and some drastic restructuring had to take place. Many had to be removed, and a large lawn was created with just one white rhododendron in the centre. Mrs Hare's contribution was a rock garden and a two-sided herbaceous border above the lily pond, full of colour and form.

The Martins were fortunate in the help and advice they received from a cousin of the family, Eric Saville of Windsor Park fame. Mrs Hare remembers him having a large hand in the planning and planting, and that there

Lee Moor, above Cornwood. A garden on the southern slopes of Dartmoor, abandoned because of advancing china clay workings

was a two-way traffic between the two gardens. But in 1960 Mr Martin died, and the painful decision was made to abandon the house and its precious garden. Mrs Hare describes it as becoming increasingly difficult to stay – the army were fighting mock battles all around them, there was more traffic, the clay works had become much noisier and were getting closer – and as it had never been her permanent home, she and her husband agreed to sell to the clay company and move back to Slade, below Cornwood, which the family had bought in 1922. An important clause in the sale allowed them a period of five years in which to take anything from the garden they wished. Gradually many of the plants moved down the hill to their new home, and visitors to the Valley Gardens at Windsor who admire *Rhododendron thomsonii* and *R. barbatum* are admiring plants that originated high up on Dartmoor. Lee Moor was abandoned to its fate, but much of it lives on in the splendid gardens created by Nancy Hare and her cousin at Slade.

REFERENCES

1. R. Fortescue-Foulkes, *From Celtic Settlement to 20th Century Hospital: the Story of Poltimore House* (p.p. 1971).

2. J. Harris (ed.), 'The Prideaux Drawings', *Architectural History* 7 (1964).

3. R. Polwhele, *History of Devonshire* (3 vols, 1793–1806), III, p. 414.

4. R. Haslam, 'Hartland Abbey', *Country Life*, clxxiv (1983), p. 605.

Chapter Ten

PUBLIC PARKS AND GARDENS

DAVID RICHARDSON

In the first census, of 1801, Devon was the fourth most populous county after Middlesex and the two industrial counties of Lancashire and Yorkshire. Plymouth, which had flourished on the wars of the eighteenth century, had a population of forty-eight thousand while Exeter, with declining industry and overseas commerce, was a residential city of twenty thousand people. Apart from these two concentrated areas, Devon's population lived in about twenty small market towns, each having between 2,000 and 4,000 people, and a further twenty of between 1,000 and 2,000 inhabitants, the remainder living in many villages, hamlets and isolated farms. Devon remained fourth in numbers among the British counties until 1831, after which the position fell with each successive census – seventh in 1861 and ninth in 1881. By 1901, the county was less than half as densely populated as England and Wales as a whole.

From 1841, each census also showed a steady migration from the Devon countryside to Plymouth, Exeter and the seaside towns, resulting in a decline in importance of the country towns. The spread of railways and rapid increase in tourism after the Napoleonic wars accelerated this exodus all through the century. Exmouth and Teignmouth were already well-established watering-places, from the eighteenth century, but Torquay grew more rapidly after the arrival of the railway in 1848. Retired professional people, convalescing invalids, the middle classes on holiday and the masses of day excursionists, all contributed to the county's economic and social changes.

Agriculture was still the major industry, with fishing, mineral extraction, and the Devonport naval base and commercial port continuing in importance. By this time, however, woollen and textile industries were in decline after their heyday in the previous two hundred years. By the 1920s tourism, with all its ancillary trades and services, had become Devon's largest and most lucrative industry.

The development and changes in the county's economy during the nineteenth century did not create the adverse social conditions that London, the Midlands and the North suffered after the Industrial Revolution. As a result, the demand for public parks and gardens reached the South West late and, to a certain extent, was created by a desire to follow fashion rather than a need to alleviate the appalling working and living conditions of industrialized workers. In addition, holiday resorts saw public parks as an extra facility to offer visitors, and it is not surprising, therefore, that many of the county's significant public parks are located in the seaside towns.

The Institute of Leisure and Amenity Management currently estimates that open space for public recreation and amenity accounts for more than 14 per cent of the land area of the country's urban environment. This

apparently high figure is substantially due to the endeavours of local government during the nineteenth century, in its responsibilities for the towns and cities of the newly urbanized society following the Industrial Revolution.

Open spaces in towns were not a new element of Victorian townscape, as landscaping in the eighteenth century had created not only country estates but also Georgian crescents and squares that frequently included gardens in their design. While these were usually intended for the private enjoyment of those living in the surrounding houses, the Royal Parks in London had long been accessible to the public. Hyde Park, for example, was opened by Charles I in about 1635. However, it is Regent's Park and St James's Park in London, designed by John Nash in 1811 and 1828 respectively, that are generally considered to be England's first major parks specifically intended for public enjoyment. The site of St James's Park had originally been acquired by Henry VIII and laid out as a garden; it remained Crown property after Nash's scheme.

The mid-nineteenth-century preoccupation with public parks transferred the impetus in gardening and landscaping from the private to the public domain. The inspiration for their design and layout derived from their royal and rural predecessors, but the absence of a mansion resulted in major differences of form and vistas. Even so, the new public parks were fenced, with gates guarded by lodges, as if to secure their refuge from an increasingly hostile urbanization. There was only limited scope within the parks for buildings to substitute for a country house, but temples, fountains, statues and obelisks became typical elements of the plan, providing opportunities for architectural style to be displayed and people and events to be commemorated.

Planting in bedding systems proved very popular in public parks from the 1860s, originating in the private gardens of the 1840s. The development of this style was popularized in England by John Gibson (1815–75), who had been apprenticed to Joseph Paxton, then head gardener to the Duke of Devonshire at Chatsworth in Derbyshire. Gibson's layouts at Battersea Park in 1858, and other London parks during the next decade, were major contributions to public park design for the next half century. He obtained both his ideas and his plants direct from Paris, where Barillet-Deschamps had developed the techniques. Partisan supporters of the traditional English landscape were horrified by these gaudy intrusions, but public enthusiasm was evident.

The most popular and enduring of carpet-bedding forms was introduced by John M'Hattie, who was Superintendent of Parks in Edinburgh from the late 1890s. This was a bed laid out in the shape of a clock, with a mechanism set in the ground underneath. The face, numbers, arms and decorative surround were covered with bedding plants and succulents. As with Gibson, however, the idea originated from an exhibition in Paris. While early examples were treated with a certain derision, the floral clock remains to this day a traditional element of park planting, popular with visitors and a challenge to the gardening staff. Three-dimensional floral displays also became popular at this time, made possible by the construction of galvanized wire frameworks into which suitable annual plants were threaded. All these features were extremely labour-intensive, however, and their scale has been reduced considerably during the twentieth century, often resulting in somewhat pathetic displays today, out of scale with other landscape elements in the parks.

Devon has an enormous wealth of public parks and gardens which, if not of national importance through the quality of their design or the reputation of their designers, nevertheless make a major contribution to the quality of life for residents and holiday visitors. The major settlements of Exeter, Plymouth and Torbay provide a significant proportion of the county's total, but nearly all Devon's other towns can claim at least one public park of importance. Many owe their origins to far-sighted local government; donations from benefactors, remembrance of distinguished local figures, memorials to royal occasions, or land claimed by works of engineering – all have provided opportunities for public recreational benefit. All command a high degree of affection in the hearts of local people, as evidenced by the immediate outcry if maintenance standards lapse or any threat of development or erosion becomes apparent. That so many of our public parks remain so delightful

Northernhay Gardens, Exeter, in 1853 (G. Townsend)

and enjoyable, particularly in an age of economic stringency for local government, is a tribute to the endeavours and commitment of the staff who manage and maintain them, and a confirmation of the important role that public parks play in the well-being of local people and in attracting holiday visitors.

Devon is able to claim what is generally recognized as the oldest public park in the country. Northernhay Gardens, in Exeter, were first laid out for public use in 1612, although the main contours of the park were created by the Romans, who quarried the volcanic trap stone for the city wall, and, later, by the Normans, who used the stone for the castle they began in 1068. In Charles II's reign the gardens occupied the outer ditch of the castle, a bowling green having existed under Athelstan's Tower since the days of James I. Fortified in the Civil War and replanted in the late seventeenth century, the present layout results from the construction of the London and South Western Railway along the valley floor in 1860. Today the gardens are renowned for several fine pieces of sculpture, including Sir Joseph Boehm's 'The Earl of Iddesleigh' (1880), and the City War Memorial (1921), by Newton Abbot-born John Angel.

The adjacent Rougemont Gardens, separated from Northernhay and also linked with it by a particularly fine stretch of the city wall, were acquired by the Corporation in 1912. The gardens nestle under the castle walls and occupy part of the moat, with the best-preserved early Norman gatehouse-keep in the country standing at their entrance.

Apart from Northernhay, the other 'Hay' in central Exeter ('hay' meaning a field or enclosure) is Southernhay Green, originally the 'Crolditch' outside the city walls. It was the scene of fairs and exhibitions in ancient times and remained as grazing land until the late eighteenth century. Then, and in the early nineteenth century, the master builder Matthew Nosworthy was responsible for the classic terraces in Southernhay West, as

Remains of Exeter Castle, Rougemont (L. Byrne, after J. Farrington, 1822)

he was for Barnfield Crescent. The central green, originally surrounded by railings, completed an inspired piece of design and represents the most expansive layout of Georgian Exeter, even though the north-western part was destroyed in the last war. Today, Northernhay presents a pleasing combination of lawns, mature trees, roses and bedding plants.

The fourth public park in the heart of the city is the Bartholomew Street Cemetery, a 5 acre extension to the seventeenth-century city burial ground. Thomas Whitaker, surveyor of the Improvement Commissioners, designed the layout in 1836–7, with Egyptian-style catacombs built into the city wall and a terrace walk on top. Opened in 1837, the cemetery was full by 1874 and is now laid out and planted with shrubs as a public open space.

Several other public parks of historic importance are located elsewhere in Exeter. Near the city centre in St Sidwell's, the Belmont Pleasure Ground, opened in 1886, occupies part of the larger area now called Belmont Park. Comparison between Ordnance Survey maps from 1876, 1891 and 1905 reveals an interesting evolution from brickworks and nursery to allotment gardens and today's layout. The City Council claims it to be the first public garden in England with an area specially designed for blind people, the Belmont Scent Garden of 1939. The air of this little-known and rather secluded feature has been sweetened by some of the best fragrant plants that can be grown in Britain, notably shrubs that flower in cold weather.

Bull Meadow, in the St Leonard's part of the city, is a public recreation park of immense value to the surrounding densely populated neighbourhood. It has been claimed that the Meadow takes its name from the Bull Inn, which stood nearby in Magdalen Street until the seventeenth century, but the city archives show the earliest spelling as 'Bole', in 1325. Again, Ordnance Survey maps record how the layout and boundaries have evolved since 1876, when the former Marlborough House had pleasure grounds there and burial grounds and

St Mary Magdalen's Hospital separated the site from Magdalen Street to the north. Bull Meadow was designated a recreation and pleasure ground by Exeter City Council in 1889, under the Public Health Act of 1875. It was the building of Magdalen Bridge in 1832 that largely determined the park's present formation; the City Council has had opportunities to extend the boundaries by acquisition, and has, happily, resisted the temptation to sell parts for development. Although in 1972 the City Council's Development and Public Works Committee approved a scheme for the construction of a multi-million-pound inner bypass junction on Bull Meadow, the scheme was strongly resisted by local people, who mounted a formidable campaign and achieved success after a public inquiry. Today, the most remarkable feature is the huge retaining wall of the bridge, a magnificent example of masonry in Pocombe stone with a coping of Dartmoor granite. Views from here show the full layout of the park, with Dissenters' cemeteries remaining in the foreground.

Bury Meadow, in the St David's part of the city, originally comprised two meadows, known as Little Bury Meadow and Lower (or Great) Bury Meadow. The origin of the name is not clear, but there has been conjecture that it was derived from association with the Bury family, who in 1667 left money for the establishment of a workhouse for the benefit of the poor of Exeter. Sir Edward Seaward was elected first governor of the institution, which was opened in 1701, and it was he who gave Bury Meadow to the Corporation of the Poor in 1703. The Meadow was subsequently leased to the City Council, which developed part of it as a pleasure ground. There was great controversy over the burial of victims of the tragic cholera epidemic of 1832 in the western corner of the Meadow, resulting in a riot by local parishioners. Today, the main access is opposite the magnificent bronze equestrian statue of Sir Redvers Buller (1839–1908), from Downes at Crediton, by the sculptor Adrian Jones, while just inside the park the picturesque Victorian lodge stands in pristine condition. As at Belmont Park, however, the City Council has excelled in a feature-planted area, this time a major herbaceous border, a tradition in public parks sadly lost to mixed shrub borders as maintenance costs escalate. The Bury Meadow border was laid out in 1984, containing sixty-seven species and varieties and designed to give continuity of flower from March to October.

In the St Thomas part of the city, Pince's Gardens commemorate Robert Taylor Pince, who in 1820 joined the famous Exeter nurseries John Lucombe and Son, when they became Lucombe, Pince and Co. There is a fine collection of conifers, and a famous wisteria tunnel. Nearby, the St Thomas Pleasure Grounds, opened in 1891, provide a 4 acre oasis in the built-up area of Cowick Street. Exeter City Council has always taken particular care of its parks and gardens, a policy that brought national and international acclaim in 1981 when the city won the coveted title of European Floral City.

Plymouth's equivalent of Exeter's Northernhay Gardens, in terms of both historical importance and a wealth of sculpture, is The Hoe, which has been a place of recreation for Plymothians since the time of Drake and long before. In the Middle Ages it is known to have had 'Gog Mahog', two giants holding clubs cut into the turf; they survived until the Royal Citadel of Plymouth was built in the seventeenth century by order of Charles II, who personally inspected it in 1670.

The Hoe is often described as the finest natural promenade in Europe, and its development to its present appearance has been long and involved. Hoe Park was laid out in 1817 and extended in the 1880s, after the outworks of the Citadel had been abandoned. Much of the land is technically in the possession of the Ministry of Defence, but it is used by the City Council as a park. The most prominent landmark is the top part of John Smeaton's lighthouse (1756–9), which was presented to the Corporation by the Trinity Board and re-erected on The Hoe after its replacement on the Eddystone Reef in 1882 by the present tower.

The Hoe is especially famous in England's naval history as the starting point of daring enterprises led by Drake, Hawkins, Raleigh and Cavendish. From here, on 19 July 1588, the little fleet of 120 sailed to defeat and

disperse the 'Invincible Armada' of Spain. A memorial statue to Sir Francis Drake, by Sir Joseph Boehm, was unveiled on 14 February 1884, while the Armada Memorial commemorates the tercentenary of the defeat, to designs by the London architect Herbert Gribble and with sculptured work executed by W. Charles May. The crowning figure of Britannia was unveiled by the then Duke of Edinburgh, KG, representing Queen Victoria, on 21 October 1890.

The massive Plymouth War Memorial, dedicated to 7,400 naval men lost in the two world wars, is impressively located on the axis for the layout of the post-war town below. The original design was by Sir Robert Lorimer, with sculpture by W.C. Storr Barber, and was unveiled by HRH Prince George on 29 July 1924. The post-Second World War addition was designed by Maufe, with two bronze groups by William McMillan.

In 1884 the Promenade Pier was completed, its landward end terminating in the Bullring, formalized with a belvedere in 1891. Nearby, on the seaward slopes of The Hoe, some Victorian shelters and seats with delightful ironwork detailing survive, set into the side of the hill and surrounded by shrubs. They now overlook The Hoe Dome Visitor's Centre, designed by the City Architect's Department in 1988.

Central Park in Plymouth is the largest public park in Devon, originally planned as a major lung for the city. The site was formed from a collection of farms, sold cheaply to the City Council by Lord St Levan in 1923 on condition that they remained public open space. The City Council commissioned the landscape architect E. Reuben Mawson to prepare a plan for the park, and his far-sighted report was presented to The Hoe and Parks Committee in October 1928. By 1929 the Ministry of Health had approved the laying out of Central Park as a suitable work of public utility for the relief of unemployment, and works estimated to cost £18,400 were put in hand. It is interesting to note how many of Mawson's recommendations have been implemented, dominated by the Plymouth Argyle Football Club (Home Park) and provision for cricket, tennis, swimming,

This view of Devonport Park in Plymouth, 1865, shows the Swiss Lodge and Napier Fountain, erected in 1858 and 1863 respectively

golf, playing fields, playgrounds and bowling greens, as well as wild gardens and an informal park. In anticipation of an enormous growth in motor traffic, Mawson advocated parking for 700 to 800 cars.

It was not until the 1960s that any major developments took place, and since then there has been acrimony within the City Council and in consultation with the public over the erosion of the landscaped parkland. In 1962 the zoo opened, followed in 1965 by the swimming pool and in 1970 by the Mayflower Centre. By the mid-1970s, only half of the original 234 acres opened by the Mayor in 1931 remained as open space. Argument has continued through the 1980s and into the 1990s, with proposals for hotel and supermarket developments.

In the early nineteenth century Devonport was still ringed by fortifications constructed in 1756 and enlarged in 1783 and 1810. By the mid-nineteenth century, however, part of this area was rented by the Corporation from the War Office and laid out as Devonport Park, as a result of public subscription and a government grant of £500. The opening of the 37 acre park is commemorated on the delightful little Swiss Cottage, designed by Alfred Norman and erected in 1858, with decorative glazed tiles and inscriptions. Nearby is an impressive terracotta fountain erected in 1863 to the memory of Admiral Sir Charles Napier, who commanded the Baltic Fleet in the Crimean War. The park contains a number of military memorials, including a siege gun captured from the Boers during the South African War of 1899–1902. The nearby refreshment house, with two-storey verandas, has recently been converted to an old people's home. Spectacular views of the River Tamar are a feature of the park.

Victoria Park was formed by the filling-in of an arm of Stonehouse Creek, known as the Deadlake, which was purchased from the Earl of Mount Edgcumbe in 1890. Infilling continued for over a decade and work was not completed when the park was formally opened by the Mayor of Plymouth on 8 October 1902. Shelters and a bandstand were constructed in 1903; the latter remained a notable feature in the middle of the park until its demolition in 1971. A pair of lodges dated 1901 and attractively detailed brickwork gate piers are survivals of historic interest. The park is dominated by the sports pitches laid out on the large expanse of grass in the centre, but mature trees and shrubs provide screening from the densely populated areas nearby. Periodic flooding still occurs, a reminder of the park's marshy origins.

There are several other public parks in Plymouth, varying in size but each of local historic importance. Beaumont Park was formerly the grounds of Beaumont House, acquired by Plymouth Corporation in 1890 on the death of the Revd T.A. Bewes and opened in 1892; for a time the house was used as the Borough Museum. The land for Alexandra Park was given by the Rt Hon. John, Lord St Levan, and the park opened on 26 June 1907, exactly five years after the coronation of King Edward VII and Queen Alexandra. Thorn Park (1893) boasts a late Victorian ovoid cast-iron urinal with decorative panels by Macfarlane of Glasgow, hidden in an attractive shrubbery. The lodge, which also marks the entrance to Mutley Park, is now leased by the City Council to the Park Pharmacy Trust, which has created a medicinal garden. Freedom Fields is a small park laid out on the site of the decisive battle in the siege of Plymouth when the Cavalier army was routed on 3 December 1643. The park was extended in 1885 and a memorial to the battle erected in 1891. Hartley Pleasure Grounds were created with mounds of soil excavated from the adjacent Corporation-owned storage reservoirs. To the south-east of the city is Radford Park, once part of the larger Radford Park, dating back to the thirteenth century and owned by the Harris family for over four hundred years. Radford House, where Sir Walter Raleigh was held prisoner before his execution in London, was demolished in 1937, and the park is now owned by the City Council.

While the formal parks and gardens of Plymouth are the major historic landscaped features of the city, mention must be made of the new public areas on the Armada Way axis, from The Hoe to Royal Parade, where every opportunity has been taken to create attractively planted amenities.

Looking west from Rock Walk, Torquay (G. Townsend, 1860)

Further up the Channel, the 'English Riviera' is well known for its mild climate which allows a wide range of exotic plants to thrive. Torbay Borough Council has maximized this benefit and takes pride in caring for its estimated 2,000 acres of parks and gardens, which provide relaxation, enjoyment and entertainment for residents and holiday visitors alike. Nowhere else in Devon can be seen such a sheer density of public planted areas, with over 100 sites identified in the borough's recreational statistics.

The development of Torquay as a seaside resort dates from the end of the eighteenth century, when the south coast of Devon began to be exploited for the new fashion of sea-bathing. Before that, the most important building was Torre Abbey, founded in 1196 by William de Brewer and later becoming an abbey for Premonstratensian canons from Nottinghamshire. The buildings were allowed to collapse and decay after the Dissolution, until Thomas Ridgeway converted some of the domestic ranges to a residence after 1598. From 1662 to 1930, the Cary family were the owners, and enlarged and altered the house from the late seventeenth century onwards.

Today, it is here that Torquay's public gardens are at their most extensive and impressive. The fourteenth-century red sandstone gatehouse effectively divides the various garden amenity areas, each having its own interest and appeal. In 1924 the Council was able to buy the eastern half of the park, stretching from Belgrave Road, and ground levels were raised by the disposal of surplus soil from nearby developments. The layout of the grounds here, an area formerly known as Belgrave Gardens, is extremely pleasant, providing bowls and tennis facilities, fronted by well-maintained planted spaces, an ornamental pool and highly decorative gates, with attractive views of the bay. In 1930 the Council purchased the remainder of the Torre Abbey grounds, and the old kitchen garden at the rear of the abbey was developed as an experimental and demonstration garden with a tropical plant house. Between the mansion and the sea the parkland has been

Torre Abbey, Torquay (J. Salter, 1852)

subject to little alteration and is now used as a miniature golf course, its setting splendidly enhanced by the medieval 'Spanish' Barn. The main entrance drive to the abbey, from Falkland Road at the north-west corner, is through impressive ornamental gates, with great white swans surmounting their stone piers and a picturesque late Victorian lodge nearby.

However, perhaps the most memorable piece of landscape development lies on the sea-front. Plans in the 1870s to construct a railway connection to the harbour by its owners, the Palk Estate, were frustrated in various public meetings and ultimately the Local Board acquired the harbour in 1883. The Board secured parliamentary sanction to build a new stone pier, 550 yards in length, together with a sea wall which enclosed 4 acres of ground in front of Cary Green and the Torbay Hotel terrace. Princess Louise, daughter of Queen Victoria, laid the foundation stone on 6 May 1890, and the pier and the new grounds were named after her.

Using wider powers conferred by its Borough charter in 1892, the Council created Princess Gardens as a notable landmark in the history of the resort. Two hundred thousand tonnes of fill were needed in the 3¼ acres and the gardens, laid out by Mr John Batt Dyer in 1893, were officially opened by the Mayoress on 1 June 1894. Today the gardens occupy a wonderful position on the sea-front, between the Pavilion and the Princess Theatre, and are renowned for their decorative planting. The most eye-catching feature, however, is the cast-iron ornamental fountain, a gift from Mr H. Young of the Torbay Hotel; the Council provided the basin. The War

Memorial was unveiled on St George's Day, 1921. The monument stands about 30 ft high and was designed by Sir Reginald Blomfield, RA. To the east of Princess Gardens is the impressive Pavilion, designed by the Borough Engineer and Surveyor, H.A. Garrett, in 1911. Immediately to the north is Cary Green, which has seen many changes in its history. In the mid-nineteenth century it was a mere beach where the River Fleete flowed through a creek into tidal waters. The creek was gradually filled up by the dumping of building refuse until the construction of the great sewer in 1875–6 allowed the town authorities to level the whole area, with the consent of the Cary and Palk landowners. Cary Green was then laid out as a public garden, with a beautiful avenue of Japanese cherry trees and beds of flowers. In recent years Cary Green has been completely altered by development and changes in highway planning, but the resulting landscape works have continued local traditions for excellence in design.

While Princess Pier and Gardens were under construction, Torbay Road was widened and improved and, below the irregular face of Waldon Cliff, the Royal Terrace Gardens were laid out as a series of steeply climbing paths and bridges. The gardens, popularly known as Rock Walk, are noteworthy for the many subtropical plants and palms, some originally presented by Dr Hamilton Ramsay of Duncan House.

The largest and in many ways the most impressive of Torbay's public gardens is at Cockington Court. The de Cockington family held the manor from 1130 to 1349, some time after which it was sold to Sir William Cary, whose family held the estate for nearly three hundred years. It was sold in 1654 to Roger Mallock, a rich Exeter

Princess Gardens, Torquay, *c.* 1898. The gardens were opened in 1894 and enriched by the gift of the cast-iron ornamental fountain by Mr H. Young of the nearby Torbay Hotel

Princess Gardens, Torquay, *c.* 1930. The Pavilion, seen in the background, was built in 1911

Bowling Green, Princess Pier, Torquay, *c.* 1910

King's Gardens, Torquay, *c.* 1905. Model yacht sailing has always been a popular pastime in public parks

goldsmith whose family in turn occupied the estate until 1932. Parts of the Tudor house survive, but there was extensive remodelling by Rawlin Mallock in about 1673. The whole estate was put up for sale in 1932 and was bought by the Cockington Trust. In terms of local government administration, in 1928 the parish had merged with Torquay, from Newton Abbot Rural District Council. In April 1933 Cockington Court and 223 acres were leased by the Trust for 999 years to the Borough Council, which subsequently bought the freehold for £50,000. The village of Cockington was put up for sale in 1946, when the Prudential Assurance Company bought twenty-seven of the twenty-nine lots on offer.

Today, Cockington Valley is owned largely by the Borough Council and the Prudential. It is managed as a country park, with support from the Countryside Commission, to cater for many visitors and to make sure that this important historical landscape is properly cared for. The grounds are magnificent, both in presentation and in their standards of maintenance. Around the court itself and the nearby church of St George and St Mary are mature avenue and specimen trees, a wide variety of shrubs and a formal walled garden. To the south-east, with tunnel access beneath the Totnes Road, the ornamental parkland is dominated by a series of connected large ponds below Hellinghay Plantation, with colourful displays in season of rhododendrons and gigantic bog plants. At the entrance to the grounds is a picturesque lodge with a rustic veranda on tree trunks supporting the thatched roof. The Devon Rural Skills Trust, founded in 1980, is now based at Cockington Court, where many traditional skills can be seen in action.

It would be tedious to describe the remainder of Torquay's parks and open spaces in detail, but particularly worthy of note – and all, generally speaking, arising from Council initiative or personal gift from major local

landowners – are King's Gardens, Cary Park, Upton Park, Memorial Gardens, Sherwell Park, Victoria Park and Torwood Gardens. The latter formerly contained the Winter Gardens, an iron-and-glass structure opened in 1881; sadly it proved uneconomic to run, and in 1903 it was sold to Great Yarmouth for £1,300 and shipped up the Channel.

Although sometimes regarded, rather unfairly, as Torquay's poor relation, Paignton has a spacious and well laid out late Victorian town centre developed by the local architect G.S. Bridgman, away from today's tourist clutter on the sea-front. As a seaside resort Paignton developed in the late nineteenth century, across the salt marshes and sand dunes that separated the old settlement from the sea. The town enjoys as rich a tradition of public parks and gardens as its neighbour, with Preston Gardens, Preston Park, Torbay Park, Victoria Park, Queen's Park, Hollicombe Gardens, Palace Avenue Gardens, Goodrington Park and the extremely attractive Cliff Gardens figuring in an impressive list.

Formal recognition of the Council's ownership of the site now known as Paignton Green dates from 1866, when public rights on the sand dunes there and at Polsham Green were defended by the Local Board. By May of that year, rights were conveyed to the Board and so Paignton secured its first freehold rights to a public park. The sea wall was constructed by 1868, the cost being partly financed by public subscription, and during the 1870s the layout of Paignton Green was completed, to the mutual benefit of both the sea-front and local developers. Public facilities at the first recreation ground, at Polsham Green, included archery, polo, shooting, cricket and tennis in the early years, while in 1879 the Scarlet Runners Football Club was first permitted to play on the green. The next twenty years saw many improvements and the provision of further amenities, including the construction of the pier from the Esplanade in 1878–9, the Main Shelter, a fountain in 1887 to commemorate Queen Victoria's jubilee, and several small ornamental shelters. Public performances, the Regatta Fair and concert parties became popular in the twentieth century, and the first putting green was

Palace Avenue Gardens, Paignton, *c.* 1910

provided in 1924. It was in this year too that the first suggestion for a concert hall opposite Torbay Road was made, but it was not until 1962 that the Festival Theatre was built, to designs by C.F.J. Thurley. The Victorian fountain disappeared, but in 1975 a new fountain was presented to the Borough of Torbay by the Rotary Club of Paignton to commemorate the club's fiftieth anniversary. Today the area north of the theatre has a rather stark appearance, but to the south ornamental planting and crazy-golf facilities add some interest.

Foremost among Paignton's parks is Oldway Mansion, located on the A379 Torquay road. The American sewing-machine magnate Isaac Merritt Singer fled with his family from Paris to London during the Franco-Prussian War of 1871. He planned a magnificent dwelling in Paignton, and the first stone of the 'Wigwam', now known as Oldway, was laid on 10 May 1873, to designs by Bridgman in a heavy Lombard–Italianate style of brick with terracotta ornament. The mansion remained unaltered until 1904 except for the addition of a large octagonal palm house. Between 1904 and 1907, however, a drastic remodelling was undertaken for Isaac Singer's third son, Paris, inspired by the Palace of Versailles. During the First World War Oldway became an American Women's War Hospital. No longer the permanent home of the Singers, in 1929 the building was adapted for use as the Torbay Country Club; it was again requisitioned during the Second World War. Ministry of Health and local government uses have dominated since 1946, and the site is now offices for the Torbay Borough Council. A major restoration of the grounds and gardens to their former glory was completed by 1951.

The fine formal grounds, including lakes and rock and grotto gardens, were originally laid out to the south of the house by the leading French landscape architect Achille Duchêne. His Italian Garden, to the east of the mansion, is in eighteenth-century style and comprises an intricate parterre of dwarf box hedging interspersed with flower beds and gravel paths. This broad terrace with its retaining wall featuring many ornamental vases is a popular area for visitors, who can also enjoy in season the adjacent wide herbaceous border. Balustraded steps and walls, all in keeping with the architectural style of the mansion, lead to the main lawned terrace, allowing elevated views of the parterre below. The less formal gardens feature two ponds, a waterfall and a wide range of subtropical plants. Two bowling greens, to the north-east, are surrounded by a rich selection of established shrubs.

Preston Green, between Marine Drive and the Promenade, was purchased by the Council from Paris Singer in 1912, the area having been defended from the sea by the Preston Sea Wall, erected by the Singer Trustees in 1876–7. The public acquisition frustrated plans by the Redcliffe Estate to build 'excellent marine residences'. Some thought the £5,067 excessive for 6 acres, which excluded Mr Singer's aeroplane hangar, bought in 1919 for a further £650. The hangar was let at one time to a firm engaged in the production of aerial films and remained until 1939, when the Café was built. Levelling started in 1920, and the shelters and tennis courts were completed in 1923–4. Cars were parked on the green for many years, until the Colin Road car-park was opened in 1936. Today the green is separated from Marine Drive by a hedge of tamarisk, but there is little to commend it as a public open space. Ornamental shelters along the Promenade give some colourful relief.

Apart from Torbay, other seaside towns in Devon have made a significant contribution to their tourist facilities by the extent and quality of their public parks and gardens. Principal among them is Ilfracombe, on the north Devon coast. Up to the end of the Georgian era Ilfracombe was a small fishing town, but in the nineteenth century it became the most popular seaside resort in north Devon. Although efforts to attract visitors began after 1830, it was the arrival of the branch railway line from Barnstaple in 1874 that escalated the status of the resort. As early as 1843 and at the instigation of a group of local residents, Capstone Parade was cut along the sea-front side of Capstone Hill, formerly known as The Capstone, which at the time belonged to the Bouchier-Wrey family. Today the whole of the Promenade area, from the Museum to the Victoria Pavilion, comprises a series of distinctly separate but continuous gardens.

Capstone Parade, Ilfracombe (W. Gauci, after T. Martin)

The opening of the sumptuous Ilfracombe Hotel in 1867, on the sea-front overlooking Wildersmouth and Capstone Hill, provided the key to amenity facilities. In 1877 Capstone Hill itself was purchased as public open space from Sir Bouchier Palk Wrey, who was anxious that it should not be built upon. Then, in 1882, Ropery Meadow was bought for £2,203 by the Local Board of Health, for use as a recreation ground. Queen Victoria's Golden Jubilee of 1887 was celebrated by the completion in the next year of the Victoria Pavilion, designed by W.H. Gould, architect and surveyor to the Ilfracombe Local Board. A glass-and-iron construction some 200 ft long and originally called The Shelter, it was nicknamed 'The Cucumber Frame'. Climbing plants and flowering shrubs made the interior a pleasant venue for the concerts held there. The Pavilion was altered in 1924 to incorporate a concert hall, and in the same year the Council received a grant from the Unemployment Grants Committee for the laying out of the Victoria Pleasure Grounds on Ropery Meadow, with bowling and putting greens surrounded by flower beds and ornamental stone-walling.

The decline of the Ilfracombe Hotel – it was partly converted to municipal offices in 1931, taken over by the army during the Second World War and renamed the Holiday Inn by its new brewery owners after the war – culminated in its eventual demolition in 1976, after lengthy and acrimonious debate. Today's impressive gardens, however, owe their existence in part to its demolition. The Council had already taken over the hotel's former tennis courts in the 1930s and by 1949 had redesigned the area as a public garden, in keeping with the Southern Slope Gardens above. Old prints from the early nineteenth century show Southern Slopes to have been a grassy declivity with grazing sheep, but when the Ilfracombe Hotel was in its heyday the Slopes were cultivated as a kitchen garden. Messrs Veitch of Exeter were commissioned by the Council to landscape the area

Ropery Meadow, with bandstand and Gould's Victoria Pavilion in Ilfracombe, *c.* 1900

in 1931, with allowance to be made for spectators watching tennis below. The site of the hotel itself is now laid out as Jubilee Gardens, and in combination with the adjacent Southern Slopes and Runnymede Gardens creates a magnificent floral and amenity display. A commendable feature of Runnymede Gardens is the recently constructed covered bandstand, on the site of the former fountain. The bandstand in the Victoria Pleasure Grounds was sold in the 1960s, and the area has since been paved in an expansive scheme carried out by the District Council.

St James's Park, on steeply sloping ground off Hillsborough Road, was acquired by the Council in 1925. There is a small gazebo, recently restored, and grotto-like sitting alcoves in the lower footpath, from which expansive views over the harbour, quay, Lantern Hill and beyond to Hillsborough can be appreciated. Behind Adelaide Terrace above High Street, Oxford Park Garden is now merely a small play area for children. Before the construction of the adjacent car-park, however, glasshouses and fishponds provided more interesting garden features.

A mile inland, Bicclescombe Park is a real gem, created originally from part of the town's tip together with marshland and farmland. The park developed slowly between 1906 and the 1930s but has now become a highly maintained landscape offering a wide range of facilities and horticultural variety. The parallel-flowing waters of the mill leat and the Wilder Brook form a particularly attractive feature. The *Ilfracombe Chronicle* on 7 April 1906 reports that the Council decided on tenders for the provision of 1,000 trees and selected that of Mr Gammons, for £2 10s., as his trees were three years old!

The nearby Cairn Pleasure Ground has undergone a transition from Victorian pleasure ground to nature reserve over the past century. Towards the end of 1893 the west side of the Cairn was leased to the Local Board as a public amenity, and in the following year paths and flights of steps were laid out, seats installed and trees

The interior of the Victoria Pavilion, *c.* 1898. The middle section was altered in 1924 to incorporate a concert hall. The end sections remained until the 1960s

planted. In 1899 this side was bought at auction by Ilfracombe Urban District Council, who added the lower part of the east side in 1905 and the upper half in 1911, so that by then it owned all of the Cairn. Its peak, at about 500 ft above sea level, offered fine views of the area and out to the Bristol Channel. By the mid-1950s it was less used by the public, and such neglect made the site more suitable as a nature reserve. The Urban District Council therefore sought advice from the Devon Trust for Nature Conservation (now the Devon Wildlife Trust), and in 1974 this body became the tenant of North Devon District Council.

Sidmouth in east Devon, at the mouth of the River Sid, was also a small fishing town until the early nineteenth century, when its popularity as a holiday resort began to grow. Like Ilfracombe, it today offers a range of attractive public parks and gardens. The most popular of these is Connaught Gardens. Before acquisition by the Council in 1930, the site was the house and garden of Mr Jemmett; known as Sea View, it was in a derelict state and had a sinister reputation. At that time Sea View and its grounds were hidden from sight by high hoardings, but there were a quaint castellated clock tower with belfry, built over old underground lime kilns, and stone steps descending the cliff to the shore. The purchase price was £3,500 and many doubted the wisdom of such expenditure, particularly as the old house had to be demolished and experts found to design and lay out the gardens. However, few today would disagree that the result is magnificent. A series of connected enclosed spaces and glimpses beyond are a constant delight, with a wealth of planting complemented by mature walls of stone, brick and flint. The gardens were formally opened on 3 November 1934 by Field Marshall HRH the Duke of Connaught, named in his honour and dedicated to the use of the public 'for ever'.

As early as 1884 it had been suggested that the Coburg Field, then known as Little Blackmore, should be secured as public pleasure grounds when the site was threatened with development. Nothing was done, but Coburg Field remained as pasture for grazing. The adjacent Blackmore Hall had been built for Mrs Storey in about 1815 and in 1905 Mrs Scott purchased Coburg Field to add to the estate, to prevent it being built upon. After an inquiry by the Local Government Inspector, the Town Council decided to purchase the Blackmore Hall estate, although there were those on the Council who would rather have seen the town benefit financially by development there. Nevertheless, the Council acquired the whole estate in 1914 for £4,400 and opened the Coburg Field portion of it in 1922, with tennis, bowling and croquet facilities; the remainder was resold to two joint purchasers. Subsequently, the old house decayed and was sold again to the Council in 1952, for £3,000. They demolished it, leaving only a tiled area as evidence of its existence. On 18 July 1953, in commemoration of the coronation of Queen Elizabeth II, the grounds were formally opened and renamed the Blackmore Hall Coronation Gardens.

Since 1974, The Knowle in Station Road has been the headquarters of East Devon District Council, surrounded by attractive grounds that are now a public park. The original building was a thatched 'cottage' of forty rooms, built in 1810 under the personal supervision of Lord Le Despenser. It was subsequently rented to the Marquis of Bute, and between 1836 and 1861 it was owned by the collector and connoisseur Mr T.L. Fish, who added picturesque improvements. He also brought exotic trees and plants, animals, birds and fish to the gardens, and on fine Mondays he would open his Marine Villa to the public. Massive rebuilding and conversion in the 1880s into a hotel diminished its architectural qualities, however, leaving little of the early features.

View of the Marble Fountain, Knowle Cottage, Sidmouth. The 'Marine Villa' was owned by Mr T.L. Fish between 1836 and 1861. He introduced exotic plants, animals, birds and fish to the grounds which were open to the public. (After C.F. Williams)

The Den at Teignmouth, showing a game of cricket in progress (G. Townsend, 1853)

Magnificent trees remain in the grounds, particularly specimens of cedar, Wellingtonia and Monterey pine, and the flint summer-house and grotto are picturesque survivals, although in need of restoration.

Elsewhere in Sidmouth pockets of land have been laid out and planted, some funded by donations from benefactors in the nineteenth century, and now add to the floral ambience of the town. On the eastern side of the town, The Lawn is an attractive and tranquil area of grass and trees alongside the River Sid, where The Byes provides a popular walk.

The Lawn, coincidentally, is the name of a park in the seaside resort of Dawlish, where the original village grew up nearly a mile back from the coast. The town began to attract summer visitors as early as the 1790s, and from about 1808 onwards some landscaping in the growing resort took place on the ground between the old village and the sea. Dawlish Water, the stream from which the village took its name, was straightened so that it ran through a broad lawn, and its flow was broken by artifical waterfalls. The Strand and Brunswick Place were laid out on either side and several bridges now provide pedestrian links. Today the stream flows under Jubilee Bridge, past the fountain in York Gardens and under Brunel's railway viaduct at the sea-front. Mature willows are complemented by colourful floral displays in season, with night-time illumination increasing the appeal to visitors.

A few miles to the south, Teignmouth was also a fashionable watering place from the late eighteenth century, and after the arrival of the railway in 1846 it remained popular throughout the nineteenth century. The sea-front was embellished by an esplanade and pier, and The Den now provides a landscaped setting for the Promenade. Before the mid-nineteenth century, The Den was a sandy rise on which fisherman had dried their nets for centuries, formerly in the ownership of the Courtenay family, Earls of Devon. By the 1880s The Den was popular for bicycle-racing and the old Teignmouth Board had invited tenders for its upkeep. After the new Teignmouth Urban District Council was formed in 1894, many changes were made in the following twenty years. The major developments were the provision of sporting facilities for summer entertainment; in 1909 the first bowling green was opened, followed the next year by tennis courts. Floral carpets were a popular feature at

this time, as evidenced by picture postcards from the period. A combination of Second World War damage, highway schemes and car-parking provision, the demise of the grand nineteenth-century buildings in Den Crescent, and the mediocre clutter of late twentieth-century amenities, have robbed The Den of much of its former glory.

Bitton House is well sited on the north slope above the Teign estuary in Teignmouth. The house dates from the late eighteenth century but was remodelled in the early nineteenth century for the naval hero Admiral Pellew, Viscount Exmouth, when the orangery was also built. The spacious grounds were made available for public events, and when archery became popular in the 1850s regular grand archery fêtes and competitions were held there. Private ownership ceased at the turn of the century and the building was used as a hospital, the Isolation Hospital at Lower Bitton being built by the Urban District Council in 1905. In the following year, 5 acres of land at Bitton were purchased by the Urban District Council at a cost of £3,500 and laid out as a public pleasure garden. During the First World War the park was closed to the public because Bitton House was requisitioned by the military authorities; by 1928 it had become council offices. The front of the house now sports two cannon brought home by Lord Exmouth from the Siege of Algiers in 1816 and presented to the Urban District Council by Morgan Giles in 1964. A Friends group was established, and as a result the orangery was restored in 1984. In recent years the old hospital buildings have been demolished by Teignbridge District Council and replaced with modern sheltered housing.

On the opposite side of the estuary, Shaldon has retained much of its Victorian charm and it is here, on the steeply sloping patchwork of fields above the village, that the Homeyards Botanical Garden was created by Maria Laetitia Kempe Homeyard in the late 1920s. She was the widow of William Newcombe Homeyard, the inventor and manufacturer of Liquafruta cough syrup. Their home had been Ness Cottage, at the eastern end of the gardens, and Mrs Homeyard purchased the land for her pleasure ground in the year after her husband's death. The main feature of the gardens is the series of paths and terraces, offering glorious views of Teignmouth and beyond, with a *Cupressus macrocarpa* avenue leading down to a spring-fed pond. A sham castle was built in 1931 and was once used as a summer-house. Now, sadly, it is in a dilapidated state. Mrs Homeyard died in 1944, and in 1950 Teignmouth Town Council purchased the gardens from the Public Trustee. Opened officially in 1955, the gardens are now in the ownership of Teignbridge District Council. Recently, a Friends group has been established and has cleared and restocked the pond, and published a small leaflet setting out the garden's history.

Further south, beyond Torquay and Paignton, Dartmouth is one of Devon's most ancient ports, in a sheltered position on the River Dart. Over the centuries the waterfront has seen many changes in alignment, and the New Quay was built out in 1584–5. Subsequent improvements and reclamation culminated in the building of the embankment in 1885, fronting the river with a long and regular quay in place of a series of jetties. The New Ground was first embanked in 1684 over part of Mill Pool and later extended to provide berths for ships at low water; at first, a small stone bridge connected it with the Butterwalk. South of the New Ground, the boat float maintains access to the harbour under the embankment roadway. Public bonfires on the New Ground were a popular feature of the early years, away from the risk of spreading fire in the town's compact layout. This probably became the excuse for local people to demand the area as public space, resisting attempts by local businessmen to build and develop. Part of the area has now become a public park known as the Royal Avenue Gardens, and these, with the harbour, quay and one of the best groups of seventeenth-century merchants' houses in the county, produce a most picturesque townscape composition. Traditionally, the park plays an important role in the Dartmouth Regatta celebrations. Today the gardens comprise historic features such as a cast-iron Victorian bandstand, a triple-tier stone fountain built in 1897 to commemorate Queen Victoria's

Diamond Jubilee, war memorials and statuary, with pleasantly planted shrubs and floral displays, while trees provide shade for the weary visitor. In 1963, to commemorate the 300th anniversary of the birth locally of Thomas Newcomen, a surviving example of his atmospheric steam engine was erected where visitors could see it working, and a plaque was provided in the gardens. Recently the South Hams District Council has carried out a comprehensive paving scheme to enhance the setting of the bandstand and fountain, at a cost of £110,000, providing an improved axial link to the nearby Butterwalk.

To the north of Royal Avenue Gardens is Coronation Park, occupying a triangular site adjacent to the Royal Naval College and Higher Ferry. This area, too, was reclaimed from the estuary by the construction of the embankment in the 1880s, but remained for many years a dreary expanse of smelly mud and swamp, bordered by old properties in Coombe Terrace. In effect, therefore, the making of Coronation Park represented the completion of the embankment scheme. The park takes its name from the celebrations for the coronation of King George VI in 1937, when thirty-four trees were planted by their donors. The completion of Coronation Park produced a sports ground second to none in the area at that time. Today it also provides facilities for tennis, putting and children's play. There was a proposal by the South Hams District Council in 1977 to convert Coronation Park into the town's major car-park, with a compensatory extension of Royal Avenue Gardens into the New Ground in Mayor's Avenue; fortunately, this idea seems to have been abandoned.

Exmouth, in east Devon, had become a popular place for sea-bathing by the mid-1800s and attracted an increasing number of visitors. Marpool Hall, the major house in the town, had a chequered history during the nineteenth century. As early as 1800 it was in a ruinous state, and was repaired to become the residence of

The Strand Enclosure in Exmouth, *c.* 1902. It was given to the town by the Hon. Mark Rolle in 1870

Manor House Grounds, Exmouth, from East Gate, *c.* 1902

Squire Hull. In 1866 Canon Percy was the occupier, but when he died in 1879 the estate was sold to Sir John Phear, who lived there until his death in 1905. In 1890, however, statutory powers were used to purchase the estate for the construction of the Exmouth to Salterton railway line, and the surplus was sold back to Sir John's children. As a memorial to their parents, they presented the lower portion of the park to the town in 1909; in 1934 Exmouth Council purchased the hall and the remainder of the estate. Although it was used for London evacuees and then as billets for troops during the Second World War, an economic use could not subsequently be found for the hall, which was demolished. Today the main features are the magnificent mature trees and a popular miniature golf course. A plaque on the lodge records the Phears' generosity to the town.

In the centre of Exmouth, the Strand Enclosure is the oldest of the town's recreation grounds, acquired by the Local Board by gift from the Hon. Mark Rolle in 1870. As the name suggests, the Strand was the former quayside, and part of the area now laid out with grass and trees was formerly occupied by the old Market House. The area also includes part of the garden of the former Globe Hotel, demolished to facilitate the construction of Rolle Street. A large granite cross commemorates those who fell in the two World Wars, overlooked by an attractive thatched shelter. The area has recently been enhanced by East Devon District Council with new paving and raised flower beds.

Just south of the Strand Enclosure, behind the Town Council Offices, lies Manor Park, first opened as the Manor House Grounds in 1897. This land had been leased to the town by the Hon. Mark Rolle, laid out and planted at a cost of £1,200 and subsequently given to the town by Lord Clinton. A further 1½ acres were added in 1904 and laid out with an ornamental bandstand at a cost of £1,000. Sadly, the condition of the bandstand

The thatched bandstand in Rock Park, Barnstaple, dated from 1879. Regrettably, it was subsequently demolished, a fate suffered by so many features of this sort

now detracts from the high horticultural quality of the area, and it may be demolished by the District Council. As in the case of so many public parks, mature trees combine well with colourful ornamental planting set in well-kept lawns. In 1992 a floral carpet commemorated the centenary of the Dr Barnado's organization. A novel feature here is the way that privet hedging has been trimmed to provide protective alcoves and canopies to some of the seats. In front of the nearby Imperial Hotel, a Jubilee clock tower was erected on the Esplanade in 1897 to celebrate sixty years of Queen Victoria's reign. At Seaton, also in east Devon, the Diamond Jubilee was similarly celebrated by the erection of a 50 ft high clock tower, at a cost of over £200, on a site donated by Sir A.W. Trevelyan, who had died in 1891.

Barnstaple is the most important town in north Devon and grew up at the lowest crossing point of the River Taw. It has prospered as a port and as a major market centre. Just south of the town centre, Rock Park is now an attractive and popular facility on the eastern bank of the River Taw. When John Roberts Chanter became Mayor in 1859, an area of 3 acres was reclaimed by the building of an embankment, fulfilling his dream for a new pleasure ground by the Taw. In his honour it was named Chanter's Green, and dedicated in 1863. However, the Green was surrounded by derelict brick and timber yards, clay-pits and cottages, with the Coney Gut flowing through. William Frederick Rock financed a more ambitious scheme, buying the surrounding properties and other land along the river, and culverting the stream. By 1879 his scheme was complete and, at Chanter's expressed wish, was named Rock Park. The 32 ft high obelisk memorial was erected in 1884 during the mayoralty of William Avery; two years later, Rock added a further 10 acres for use as a sports ground, and the Ladies Mile drive was created. Today the park is well maintained, sadly having lost its 1879 bandstand but with the obelisk, war memorials and picturesque lodge combining to complement an attractive landscape.

The Square in Barnstaple has seen many changes since the sixteenth century. The construction of the Albert Memorial clock
tower in 1862 added a major architectural feature to the landscape, seen here in 1865

The evolution of the Square in Barnstaple has been well documented and illustrated in local guide and history
books, providing a fascinating comment on the town's social history and the effects of traffic requirements. In
1584 the Square was just a beach crossed (even at low tide) only by a path of raised stones, and an open sewer
ran across the middle. By 1715 the central portion of the Square had been enclosed by a simple bollard and
single iron railing, and in 1875 it was laid out as a garden, crossed by paths meeting at the fountain in the
middle, with more ornate wrought-iron railings around the perimeter. This put an end to the Fair being held
there. In 1862 construction began on the Albert Memorial clock tower, with money subscribed by the
townspeople. The railings were removed during the last war for armaments, and the decline in importance of
Litchdon Street as a main route out of the town, combined with successive requirements of late twentieth-
century highway planning, have radically changed the shape and sadly reduced the importance of this small park.

At nearby Bideford, Victoria Park has also been created from land previously reclaimed. In 1825 tenders were
invited for the embanking of the marsh area north of the Pill, providing a footpath to Northam. After its enclosure
the park was formally opened by the Mayor, Councillor W.T. Coaman, JP, on 9 November 1912. Bideford had lost

its status as a port in 1882, leading to the virtual collapse of the shipbuilding industry. After the First World War, however, Sven Hansen leased a yard to build steel steamships. He presented the town with the adjoining sports field, greatly enlarging the public park. Further large extensions were added in 1952. Today attractive features of the park are the main gates with their historic plaques, recording their presentation by George Oliver Peard in memory of his wife, and the smaller gates and railings erected by the Town Council to commemorate the coronation of King George V. Within the park, on the site of the former bandstand, are eight 'Armada' cannon, for many years used as mooring posts on the quay until its widening in 1890. A tree with a plaque commemorates the stay in Bideford of American troops in preparation for the Normandy landings in 1944. Recent further reclamation, providing much needed car-parking, has been attractively carried out by Torridge District Council, enhancing the setting of the park.

At East-the-Water in Bideford one of the town's three forts, dating from the 1642 Civil War, survives as a public park. Chudleigh Fort, named after Colonel James Chudleigh who was in command of the Parliamentary forces in Bideford at the time, includes a small castellated building commanding the river approaches. It was purchased by public subscription, and a monument was erected in memory of those who fell in the First World War. There is now also a Second World War memorial, standing impressively above the fort. High on the western side of Bideford, Old Town Gardens has been created from part of the former cemetery, the slate headstones being displayed around the perimeter walls.

At Holsworthy, the Stanhope Park Recreation Ground had been rented from Arthur Philip, Earl Stanhope, since 1888, and in 1901 he gave the 8½ acre site to the Urban District Council, subject to certain conditions to protect the cricket ground and its pavilion. The entrance to the park is enhanced by ornamental gates, erected by a grateful town as a mark of esteem towards the donor and to commemorate the coming of age of James Richard, Viscount Mahon, in 1901.

Central Park, behind the Pannier Market in South Molton, does not enjoy the high quality of layout and range of plants so evident in many of the county's town parks. Nevertheless, it provides the setting for the town's swimming, tennis, bowling and children's play requirements. On the western outskirts of the town, the recreation ground provides further sporting facilities, with access through ornamental gates that have commemorative ceramic tiles set in the brick piers, dated 1898.

Simmons Park at Okehampton combines an attractive linear setting in the valley of the East Okement River with mature trees, Swiss-chalet-style almshouses and many commemorative features, all well integrated. The 7½ acre site was presented to the town by Sydney Simmons, a native of Okehampton whose business was in London. The park was officially opened on 8 July 1907 by Sir W.P. Treloar, Bt, Lord Mayor of London, and the memorial plaque gives Sydney Simmons's address at the time as 'Okehampton, North Finchley, Middlesex'. Only the plinth of the bandstand now remains, erected by public subscription to commemorate the coronation of George V in 1911. Separate plaques name Francis J. Worden as the architect, W.J. Avery as the builder and John Cornish as the Mayor at the time. A novel feature of the garden relics is the concrete imitation rustic footbridges that look so realistic among the rockery. A horse trough marking the coronation of King Edward VII and Queen Alexandra in 1902 was moved to the park from the Market Place in the 1960s.

The 4½ mile long Tavistock Canal was built between 1803 and 1817 by the engineer John Taylor, to link the River Tavy with the River Tamar at the old port of Morwellham. The canal is not now used for commercial traffic but provides an attractive historic amenity for The Meadows Pleasure Ground, Tavistock's major public park, located between Plymouth Road and the River Tavy. In 1913 the 14½ acres were acquired by the Urban District Council from the Duke of Bedford and part was laid out for lawn tennis, croquet and bowls. The park featured prominently in the town's celebrations of the Silver Jubilee of King George V in 1935, when there was an unsuccessful move to rename it Bedford Park. The jubilee was marked by an archway entrance from the

The main entrance to Simmons Park, Okehampton, *c.* 1906. Although the scene has changed little in the past ninety years, the similar style gates are lower, and the railings to the right have been removed

Abbey Bridge walk. The many commemorative trees are a feature of the park, and a small sub-garden was designed and planted by Mrs Margaret Wedd in 1990. A covered bandstand remains and there are well-maintained games pitches, but the paddling pool has been grassed over. At the northern end, the Meadowlands Leisure Pool complex provides a family 'tropical paradise'.

People's Park at Tiverton was formed in 1887 to commemorate the Golden Jubilee of Queen Victoria's accession in 1837. The proposed gift of £1,000 by benefactor John Coles from nearby Washfield, who had made his fortune in London, to purchase a suitable site, triggered much local acrimony in public meetings. Sir John Amory opposed the scheme, concerned at the estimated £200 per annum maintenance costs, but the inhabitants of the town at large were strongly in favour. The Misses Carew of Haccombe owned a meadow, already termed The Park, that seemed an ideal location, beautifully sited on elevated ground and surrounded by charming scenery. At first, however, they were reluctant to sell. Eventually all difficulties were overcome, and the People's Park was officially opened on 5 July 1888, an inscription at the main gates recording the fact that funds for the completion of the park were raised by over 1,500 friends of the movement. A notable feature within the park is an ornamental drinking fountain presented by the Revd George Hadow, MA, Rector of Tidcombe, also dated 5 July 1888. Lost, however, are the elegant bandstand with wrought-iron balustrade and the Crimean War gun, which was sent for scrap in the Second World War.

The recreation ground at West Exe in Tiverton is a splendid resource for the adjacent Heathcoat School, with a particularly delightful pond area, well planted with attractive trees and shrubs. Here are also one of the few covered bandstands remaining in the county, and a children's play-pool: so many examples of both have been lost through vandalism and prohibitive maintenance costs.

Discreetly sited in the centre of Crediton is Newcombe's Meadow, which has been the town's main public park since its official opening by the Revd the Earl of Devon in 1931. There had been considerable discussion

and deliberation by the Urban District Council prior to its acquisition, which was facilitated eventually by grants from the Devonshire Playing Fields Association (of which the Earl of Devon was chairman at that time) and the Carnegie Trust. Today the park provides a range of sporting facilities, including a bowling green and a children's play area, while mature oaks and purple beech are of arboricultural interest. A central planting area has been laid out in the park to mark the Silver Jubilee of the coronation of Queen Elizabeth II in 1977. The statue of Crediton-born St Boniface, by the sculptor Alan Durst, was unveiled by Princess Margaret and dedicated by Wilfred, Bishop of Crediton, on 24 July 1960.

People's Park comprises a linear 4 acres on the northern side of the town, originally purchased and laid out as a public park to perpetuate the memory of James Wentworth Buller, MP for north Devon and a resident of Crediton, who died in 1865. The area is now predominantly a grassy slope with mature sycamore, horse chestnut and conifers. A small formal area was laid out in 1957 to commemorate the Jubilee of the Boy Scouts and Girl Guides movement. At the western end of the town, St Laurence's Green was named after a nearby chapel and laid out as a pleasure ground by public subscription in 1897, to mark the Diamond Jubilee of Queen Victoria. In the early part of the last century bull-baiting took place here, and the stone to which the bull was fastened still remains as the centre-piece. Purple beech and horse chestnuts give the green an appearance of maturity, while rose beds provide a splash of colour.

When Wolborough became the Newton Abbot Local Board and, in 1894, the Urban Sanitary District became the Urban District of Newton Abbot, the need for recreational facilities was soon identified. Mr Robert Hugo Montagu Baker, who worked for many years as a clerk to the Wolborough Board and who died in 1894, bequeathed 10 acres to the town for the purpose of a public park. Baker's Park now provides sports facilities on the western edge of the town, and a plaque at the main entrance gates records the historical detail. A military tank and two cannon were presented to the town in 1919, and stood on display in the park until they were taken to help with the scrap-metal campaign in the Second World War. In recent years, the ornamental cast-iron toilets have also been removed.

Also in Newton Abbot, located opposite the railway station, is Courtenay Park, which covers about 20 acres. In the late seventeenth century the nearby Forde House passed by marriage to the Courtenays of Powderham, who in the nineteenth century initiated the rebuilding of the town centre and suburban expansion into Devon Square and towards the station. The park was laid out in 1854 on land belonging to the Earl of Devon and is overlooked by impressive Victorian villas of 1840–60, by local architect J.W. Rowell. There is the plinth remnant of a bandstand, while nearby is an attractive elevated fishpond with stone retaining walls. South of Courtenay Park, off the Torquay Road, is Forde Park, which provides a tranquil setting for sports amid specimen trees. Osborne Street Recreation Ground, with an area of about 6 acres at the eastern end of the town, was purchased by the Urban District Council and laid out for public use in 1900.

Public parks tend to be regarded as an essentially Victorian tradition but, although most owe their origins to the nineteenth and early twentieth centuries, new parks have been and are still being created. Recent designs emphasize natural features and indigenous plant material, with a high regard for the importance of wildlife. They provide a softening green element in the townscape, while affording links to the nearby countryside. Prominent among these in Devon are the five 'Valley' parks designated in Exeter since 1981, at Duryard, Alphington/Whitestone, Ludwell, Mincinglake and Riverside, with grant aid from the Department of the Environment and the Countryside Commission. These form a beautiful necklace around the edge of the city, providing a much needed haven for wildlife and a refuge from the crowds. The valleys have different characteristics and possibilities but each is linked with the surrounding countryside by a series of paths and bridleways. Two of the valleys, Duryard and Ludwell, have been protected from development, while

Mincinglake was formerly a refuse tip. Mincinglake means 'nuns' stream', and the nuns of Polsloe Priory built a dam here six hundred years ago to retain a huge lake to power their corn mill. The lake is long gone, but remains of the dam can still be seen.

Decoy Country Park at Newton Abbot is one of a number of sites managed by Teignbridge District Council for the benefit of recreation, wildlife and the local community. Its 10 acre lake, woodlands, meadows and playing fields provide a wide range of activities for all ages. While not in an urban setting, Stover Country Park at Teigngrace is managed by Devon County Council as a wildlife and recreational facility. James Templer designed and built Stover House in 1776–80 and extensive grounds were laid out, including a large lake with an island, while the Stover Canal was designed to achieve irrigation and drainage.

Woodlands Park is situated within a rapidly expanding residential area of Ivybridge and was developed by the South Hams District Council in the 1980s not only to provide a leisure and recreational area, but also to promote a conservation programme by careful management of the site's existing features. Habitats of wetland, meadow, stream and pond are being preserved or created, and great importance has been attached to access for the disabled.

The Elizabethan Gardens in The Barbican at Plymouth represent a very praiseworthy attempt by the Old Plymouth Society and the Barbican Association to reconstruct a conjectural sixteenth-century garden behind several properties fronting on New Street. On many levels enclosed and retained by high stone walls the gardens, designed by architect Alan Miller-Williams were opened to the public in time for the Mayflower celebrations in 1970.

Other recently constructed parks and gardens have been created at Land of Canaan at Ottery St Mary, Rotary Gardens at Barnstaple, and the George South Memorial Garden at Kingswear. The latter is a delightful little walled garden, implemented by the South Hams District Council and dedicated to the memory of a former councillor who died in 1988.

Several of Devon's other towns have historic public parks and gardens, but no attempt will be made to mention them all in detail. For example, significant parks are located at Beer (Jubilee Memorial Ground), Braunton, Budleigh Salterton (Jubilee Park), Combe Martin (Cobblers Park), Exmouth (The Maer), Holsworthy (Badock Gardens), Kingsbridge (Recreation Ground and Duncombe Park), Newton Abbot (Keyberry Park and Peninn Park), Salcombe (Cliff House Gardens), Totnes (Borough Park and Vire Island) and several in Torbay. All of these contribute to the attractive landscapes of their towns.

Nor should one underestimate the important role that cemeteries have played in the design and provision of public garden areas. The former cemeteries at Bartholomew Street in Exeter and Old Town in Bideford have already been mentioned, but Ford Park in Plymouth, Bideford Road Cemetery in Great Torrington, and many others would deserve a separate study. For this, I would commend reference to Chris Brooks's recent publication *Mortal Remains*.

Parks and gardens are an extremely valuable public resource, even in the late twentieth century when many of the Victorian reasons for their creation are no longer valid. Particularly when designed or utilized as part of an overall landscape strategy for the town, their contribution to the quality of life, whether through active pursuits or relaxed leisure, should be paramount to the local authorities who manage them. Of great concern, however, is the recent trend towards economies of maintenance, placing at risk not only the physical well-being and appearance of the gardens, but also the wealth of expertise built up over the last century in local councils. Of equal concern is the erosion of historic parks by competing demands for land for various aspects of development. Only by a recognition of the social and historic importance of our public parks and gardens can such threats and pressures be minimized.

SELECT BIBLIOGRAPHY

Anon., 'Save Bull Meadow', *Devon Life* (October 1976).

Baxter, J. and J., *Barnstaple Yesterday* (Bristol, 1980).

Beavis, D., *Newton Abbot – The Story of a Town's Past* (Buckingham, 1985).

Bracken, C.W., *A History of Plymouth* (Plymouth, 1931).

Brooks, C., *Mortal Remains* (Exeter, 1989).

Chadwick, G.F., *The Park and the Town – Public Landscape in the Nineteenth and Twentieth Centuries* (1966).

Conway, H., *People's Parks – the Design and Development of Victorian Parks in Britain* (Cambridge, 1991).

Cornelius's Guide – Dawlish (Dawlish, 1880).

Crediton Civic Society, *Crediton Town Trail* (Tiverton, 1991).

Delderfield, E.R., *Exmouth Milestones* (Exmouth, 1948).

——, *Exmouth Yesterdays* (Exmouth, 1985).

Eliot Thomas, W., *Torquay by the Sea* (c. 1930).

Ellis, A.C., *An Historical Survey of Torquay* (Torquay, 1930).

Exeter City Council, *Exeter Garden Trail*, leaflets 9–10, 13–16 (1987–91).

Exeter Civic Society, *Discovery of Exeter*, booklets 1–6 (1981–9).

Fenner, R.A., *Tavistock 1900–1930* (Callington, 1985).

Freeman, R., *Dartmouth – A New History of the Port and its People* (Dartmouth, 1983).

Gill, C., *Plymouth – A New History*, (2nd edn., Tiverton, 1993).

Goaman, M., *Old Bideford and District* (Bristol, 1968).

Grant, A., and Christie, P., *The Book of Bideford* (Buckingham, 1987).

Lamplugh, L., *Barnstaple, Town on the Taw* (Chichester, 1983).

——, *A History of Ilfracombe* (Chichester, 1984).

Lane, R., *Old Sidmouth* (Exeter, 1990).

Lasdun, S., *The English Park – Royal, Private and Public* (1991).

Levine, G., *Secrets of a Garden City – Exeter's Gardens in Words and Pictures* (Exeter, 1990).

de la Mahotière, M., *Tiverton and the Exe Valley* (Chichester, 1990).

Meller, H., *Exeter Architecture* (Chichester, 1989).

Penwill, F.R., *Paignton in Six Reigns – The History of Local Government in Paignton* (Paignton, 1953).

Robinson, C., *Victorian Plymouth* (Plymouth, 1991).

Russell, P., *Dartmouth – A History of the Port and Town* (1950).

——, *A History of Torquay* (Torquay, 1960).

Sutton, A., *A Story of Sidmouth* (Exeter, 1953).

Ward, E.J., Bucklow, H., and Smith, A.E., *Homeyard Botanical Gardens, Shaldon* (Totnes, 1992).

White, J.T., *The History of Torquay* (Torquay, 1878).

Woodcock, G., *Tavistock's Yesterdays – Episodes from her History* 3 (Callington, 1987).

GAZETTEER OF THE MAJOR GARDENS AND PARKS IN DEVON

The following gazetteer does not claim to be exhaustive. It contains all of the landscapes listed in the English Heritage *Register of Parks and Gardens of Special Historic Interest* in Devon, many of the county's other historic sites, and several newer gardens (particularly those that are open to the public). A very large number of gardens of great merit have had to be omitted for reasons of space, but this should not be taken to mean that they are lacking in either quality or interest.

Opening arrangements are indicated where known, but visitors are nevertheless advised to consult the published guides to historic houses and gardens open to the public and the 'Yellow Book' of *Gardens of England and Wales Open to the Public*, produced by the National Gardens Scheme Charitable Trust.

A LA RONDE, EXMOUTH
Listed Grade II on the English Heritage *Register of Parks and Gardens of Special Historic Interest*. The site was purchased in 1795 by the Misses Jane and Mary Parminter, who constructed a unique sixteen-sided *cottage orné* in 1798. Around it they created a complex scheme, including a 'wild walk' and 'bowers, arbours, three obelisks, fountains, glass houses, and rare tropical plants, orangeries'. Little obviously survives. Now owned by the National Trust.

ALLERON, LODDISWELL
Small Regency country house and grounds made remarkable by the existence of a most unusual circular garden, ringed by thatch-topped cob wall (its purpose and date so far not conclusively explained). Open regularly.

ARLINGTON COURT, ARLINGTON
Registered Grade II. An eighteenth-century landscape garden with nineteenth-century formal garden. Severe neo-Grecian house, formerly home of a branch of the Chichester family. The grounds form a typical Jane Austen setting, with shrubberies, winding gravel paths, lake, obelisk, rectory, church and large stable block; fine trees and lawns. Given to the National Trust in 1949 by Miss Rosalie Chichester, the last of her line.

AVENUE COTTAGE, ASHPRINGTON
Formerly part of the eighteenth-century landscape of Sharpham house. Garden of 11 acres, with woodland walks and ponds. Open regularly.

BICKHAM BARTON, ROBOROUGH
Mature garden with a large collection of specimen trees and shrubs. Camellias, rhododendrons and azaleas in woodland setting. Formal gardens with shrub roses and many unusual perennials. Imaginative use of foliage particularly around the old barns and pond, planted with iris and water plants. Open occasionally, and by appointment.

BICKHAM HOUSE, KENN
Garden of 5 acres surrounding a charming, basically early eighteenth-century house. Lawns, mature trees and shrubs, herbaceous borders, impressive kitchen garden and new lake. Open under the National Gardens Scheme.

BICKLEIGH CASTLE, BICKLEIGH
Small, partially moated garden surrounding a fifteenth-century stone castle held by the Courtenays and then the Carews. Water garden, lawns, shrubs and, across the lane, a tiny, cob-walled,

thatched chapel, surrounded by lawn and flower beds. Open regularly.

BICTON, BICTON

Registerd Grade I garden bordered by a leisure park, and Bicton House (now an agricultural college), once the seat of the Rolle family. Formal gardens attributed to Le Nôtre but this is unlikely since Le Nôtre never came to England. Palm House (*c.* 1820) of magnificent design, eighteenth-century orangery, extensive hothouses, *plat d'eau* with central fountain, hermitage with sheep-bone floor, pinetum, American garden with Shell House, Italian garden, several lakes (one of over 12 acres), famous monkey-puzzle avenue worn now by storms and age, and many fine and unusual trees. Open daily all year. The college gardens are also worthwhile and instructive, and open Mon.–Fri. all year.

THE BISHOP'S PALACE, EXETER

Bounded by the great cathedral on one side and the Roman city wall on the other, the garden associated with the medieval Bishop's Palace is perhaps among the oldest in Devon. Extending to around 3 acres, the grounds contain some fine trees, and a wild orchard garden. New planting and the introduction of modern sculpture give added interest. Guided tours by the Corps of Voluntary City Guides.

BRIDWELL, UFFCULME

Registered Grade II. The park was landscaped when the house was built in the late 1770s for the Clarke family. Largely open parkland with widely dispersed mature trees and narrow lake. Not open to the public.

BUCKLAND FILLEIGH, BUCKLAND FILLEIGH

Church and house and lake in heavily wooded rolling hills by William Fortescue in the mid-eighteenth century. Alexander Pope is believed to have advised on planting. The house was rebuilt in a severe neo-Classical style after a fire in the early nineteenth century, and is well matched by the surrounding grass landscape which slopes to a well-positioned lake. Not open to the public.

BURROW FARM GARDEN, DALWOOD

Commercial garden plant centre and tea-house. Begun in 1967, it now covers 5 acres. Glades of mown grass among shrubs and trees, herbaceous borders, pergola, pond, statues, fine views. Open regularly.

CADHAY, OTTERY ST MARY

Informal lakes (medieval fish ponds) and formal pond. Long herbaceous borders. Formal yew trees beside the lawn. Old walls giving shelter to shrubs and climbers. Open regularly.

CASTLE DROGO, DREWSTEIGNTON

Registered Grade II*. Its fame rests in the castle, built 1910–30 for store magnate Julius Drewe by Edwin Lutyens. Gertrude Jekyll initially advised, but Lutyens designed the bones of the garden with stone terraces and steps of granite and walls of yew, with planting the work of George Dillistone. The circular croquet lawn, rose garden and herbaceous borders stand away from the castle with a separate, semi-cultivated wild garden overlooking the River Teign below. National Trust.

CASTLE HILL, FILLEIGH

Registered Grade II*. The ancestral home of the Fortescue family, designed by Hugh Fortescue and his brother Matthew between 1720 and 1760. In its landscaping and profusion of garden building it is a microcosm of Stowe. Magnificent grounds with viewing platform, arboretum including the largest sitka spruce in the country, and shrub-filled valley. Outstanding are the Holwell, Satyr's, Sunrise and Sunset Temples, Sybil's Cave, triumphal arch, and Gothic castle from which the house takes its name. Private, but open occasionally in aid of local charities.

CASTLE TOR, TORQUAY

Registered Grade II. A unique site on three levels overlooking the sea at Torquay, and reminiscent of an Italian garden at Amalfi. Designed by Harrild, pupil of Lutyens, the whole echoes his master's treatment, with stone terraces, steps, walls, a long formal pool with statues, circular lawn and orangery, leading to a barbican with portcullis below, another pool with dragon gargoyles. Open by appointment only.

CHEVITHORNE BARTON, CHEVITHORNE

Garden begun before the First World War by Mrs Ludovic Heathcoat-Amory (of the Knightshayes family). The terraced section adjoining the seventeenth-century house is in three tiers and is Italianate in feeling. Essentially, however, it is an informal garden planted with a wide variety of shrubs and alpines. Open occasionally.

CLIFFE HOUSE, LYNMOUTH

Steeply sloping site overlooking Lynmouth. South-facing slopes of almost bare rock, yet many tender plants thrive here. A paulownia flowers freely; unusual plants from New Zealand, many grown from seed or cuttings. Interesting alpines and rock plants, hollies, pittosporums, acacias, and acid-loving species. Not open regularly to the public.

CLOVELLY COURT, CLOVELLY

Walled garden, now used extensively for market gardening. Fine range of glasshouses. Old roses and shrubs in garden behind house. Terraces with views over Bideford Bay. Parkland extends over 25 acres, with fine views over the sea. Open regularly.

COLETON FISHACRE, KINGSWEAR

Registered Grade II. National Trust. Stream and combe garden leading to the sea, with planting supervised between 1925 and 1937 by Lady Dorothy D'Oyly Carte. Flowering trees, shrubs, rill, paved terrace.

COMBE HOUSE, GITTISHAM

Registered Grade II. Home for several centuries to the Putt family, one of whom developed the eponymous apple. Fourteenth-century house, altered and extended around 1670 and again c. 1815. Woodland and plantations now alternate with open parkland and farmed land, although several built structures survive, including an ice-house, eighteenth-century orangery and the outline of a series of late seventeenth-century (or earlier) walled gardens which extended eastwards from the house. The estate is now in divided ownership and is not open to the public.

THE CROFT, YARNSCOMBE

A young garden full of interesting plants. Island beds crammed with perennials, shrubs and many interesting varieties of iris. Full use is made of a stream with luxuriant planting. Contrast with a dry rocky area, and many climbers. Good range of plants for sale. Open under the National Gardens Scheme, and by appointment.

DARTINGTON HALL, DARTINGTON

Registered Grade II*. Famous garden created by the Elmhirst family as part of their experiment in rural rejuvenation, based on the medieval hall of John Holand, Duke of Exeter. Courtyard garden, tiltyard, twelve apostle yews, Henry Moore statue, huge trees including taxodium, davidia and Lucombe oak. Many celebrated garden designers have worked here including Avray Tipping, Beatrix Farrand, Percy Cane, and Preber Jacobsen who in the 1980s created the herbaceous border overlooking the tiltyard. Open regularly.

DELAMORE, CORNWOOD

House built in 1859 of granite ashlar, and garden with magnolia avenue, unusual rhododendrons and lake reflects this date. Open occasionally.

DOWNES, CREDITON

Fine site crowned by Palladian house with pavilions at each end, the birthplace of Sir Redvers Buller, VC, hero of the Zulu and South African wars. There is a formal terrace below the house and originally serpentine treatment of the River Creedy in the valley below. Attractive wooded park much damaged in the 1990 storm. Various plans for developing terraces and hothouses in the nineteenth century came to nothing. Not open to the public.

THE DOWNES, MONKLEIGH

Sloping site overlooking the River Torridge. Many specimen trees, some mature, some recent planting. Banks of rhododendrons, azaleas, camellias. Interesting climbers and areas of shrubs and perennials with an accent on the unusual. Woodland walk with carpets of bulbs in spring, followed by bluebells in summer. Open regularly, and by appointment.

ENDSLEIGH, MILTON ABBOT

Registered Grade I as befits one of Humphry Repton's most complete creations. Huge *cottage orné* built for the dukes of Bedford by Jeffry Wyatville, becoming their favourite home. There is a spectacular view from the terrace over a Tamar bend to woods beyond; rose, wisteria and yew walks; Swiss Cottage, bothy, ice-house, rockery, grotto, childrens' garden, cascades, dairy, arboreta, 2 mile drive. Now leased by the Endsleigh Charitable Trust and open regularly to the public.

ESCOT, TALATON

Significant eighteenth-century park: 'Perhaps there are no plantations in Devonshire so strong and luxuriant as those at Escot,' said Polwhele in the 1790s. The philosopher John Locke is reputed to have planted some of the beeches. The original house was destroyed in 1808 and rebuilt in an uninspired neo-Grecian style in 1838. Open to the public.

EVERLEY, TOPSHAM

Quite unique 'philosophical garden', symbolizing a quest for the secret of life. The most profound themes are explored in the limited compass of a small town garden. Its creator, Dr Dougal Swinscow, was the author of the remarkable *The Mystic Garden*. Not open to the public.

EXETER UNIVERSITY, EXETER

Main grounds extending to 400 acres, including gardens associated with Thomas Hall (originally Great Duryard House) and Reed Hall (formerly Streatham Hall). Evocative Victorian terracing survives at Reed Hall (c. 1866). More importantly, its environs contain several remarkable trees, some of which must be the oldest in the country and at the time of planting may have been unique in Europe. Some of the Lucombe oaks at Thomas Hall are thought to be original grafted plants. Open to members of the public throughout the year; organized parties by arrangement.

FLETE, HOLBETON

Registered Grade II. Seventeenth-century granite house, remodelled and aggrandized for the Mildmay family by Norman Shaw. Now divided into retirement apartments with each tenant responsible for one part of the large garden. Italian garden; water garden designed by Russell Page in 1925 as his first commission. Notable trees and shrubs positioned on rising ground around house looking down to River Erme. Open regularly.

FORDE ABBEY, THORNCOMBE, DORSET (FORMERLY DEVON)
A detached part of Devon until 1842. The abbey buildings were classicized by Sir Edmund Prideaux, Cromwell's Attorney General, who bought the property in 1649. By the early eighteenth century when Edmund Prideaux, the topographer, depicted the house, the gardens were landscaped in the French taste, with *allées*, clipped evergreens and formal water features. Much of this landscape has been lost; likewise – more fortunately – the 'shrubberized' Victorian garden, apart from some good trees. Much attractive twentieth-century planting: post-war arboretum, herbaceous borders, rock, bog and kitchen gardens. Open daily.

THE GARDEN HOUSE, BUCKLAND MONACHORUM
Built by Lionel Fortescue around a stone tower and walls which recall Sissinghurst and Scotney; now owned by a trust bearing his name. Garden on a steep slope on the edge of Dartmoor, planted on five levels in compartmental style, with herbaceous borders, trees, shrubs and stone paths. Views to Cornwall. Open daily, March to October.

GLEBE COTTAGE, WARKLEIGH
One acre cottage garden, with a great variety of shrubs and herbaceous plants in different situations. Includes a bog garden, stumpery with ferns and a hot dry garden with Mediterranean subjects. Open regularly.

GORWELL HOUSE, BARNSTAPLE
The recent Gorwell housing estate now covers the land that once separated Gorwell House from Barnstaple, but it is still an imposing site with views over the town to the sea. The owners have expanded the garden over the past fifteen years and it now covers some 4 acres. The largest area is at the top where recent plantings include several magnolias, a weeping purple beech, unusual viburnums and many other uncommon species. One area is devoted to cordylines, phormiums, eucalyptus and other semi-tropical species. Tender plants fill the walled garden and smother the walls. Open occasionally.

GREENWAY, KINGSWEAR
Garden of 30 acres around an attractive late-Georgian house (*c*. 1780–90) set on the banks of the River Dart. Many period features including a grotto, and Regency tidal plunge bath with tea-house above. Impressive collection of notable species, particularly from Western China and South America. The estate was bought by Agatha Christie in 1938, and is still owned by her family. Private, but open occasionally under the National Gardens Scheme.

HANNAFORD MANOR, POUNDSGATE
Garden by Thomas Mawson to accompany an Arts and Crafts manor house, 1904–11, by A. Wickham Jarvis, for a Major Bolitho of the banking family. As at Wood, Mawson exploited the

site to create a series of terraces with stone steps and granite balustrading. A semi-circular granite basin with dolphin spout and a lily pond (to Mawson's design but differently sited) contribute to the water features. The house and garden are in divided ownership and not open to the public.

HARTLAND ABBEY, HARTLAND
A valley garden is the most recent occupant of this historic site, although grassy meadows now largely cover the site of the eighteenth-century formal gardens. The wooded valley sides have been planted with rhododendrons, and the late Sir Dennis Stucley created a camellia garden with bog plants, primulas, etc., by the house. The walled gardens higher up the valley are now full of old shrub roses, herbaceous and perennial planting. The walls themselves follow the contours of the valley, giving them an unusual outline. Open regularly.

HAYNE MANOR, STOWFORD
Registered Grade II. Late eighteenth-century landscape, fast reverting to farmland around a Gothic house reminiscent of Strawberry Hill, too long derelict to reveal the past. Remains of a shell-adorned grotto in the wood. Not open to the public.

KILLERTON, BROAD CLYST
Registered Grade II*. The fine park surrounds a hill (Killerton Clump) with the late eighteenth-century house on its southern slopes. The arboretum is one of the earliest, started around 1808 by the celebrated nurseryman John Veitch, who began his career here as gardener to Sir Thomas Acland, seventh baronet. The often illustrated beech avenue was planted at about this time. Further plantings of rare and unusual trees have continued until the present day. To the south and south-west of the house formal borders were laid out around 1900 by the then head gardener John Coutts to a design by William Robinson; the original roses were replaced by herbaceous plants and dwarf shrubs in 1957. The estate was presented to the National Trust by Sir Richard Acland, fifteenth baronet, in 1944.

KINGS GATCHELL, WEST HILL
About two-thirds of an acre sheltered in woodland. Varied herbaceous plants including alpine plants in scree beds and a large collection of ferns. Open occasionally.

KNIGHTSHAYES COURT, TIVERTON
Registered Grade II*. Formal terraced gardens surround the high-Victorian gothic house built within an existing park by William Burges, 1869–74, for the Heathcoat-Amory family. Edward Kemp, a pupil of Paxton, constructed the terraces, created a yew-hedged bowling green and laid out an elaborate kitchen garden in the 1870s. Little change took place until the 1950s, when Sir John

and Lady Heathcoat-Amory simplified the Victorian planting and extended the garden into the adjoining woods with plantings of shrubs, flowers and bulbs. The exquisite lily pond was dug out of the former bowling green at the same time. The house and garden were presented to the National Trust in 1973.

LANGDON COURT, WEMBURY

Registered Grade II. A late seventeenth- to early eighteenth-century garden lies on the south side of the essentially Elizabethan house. Walled terraces, with axial steps and gate piers. The house is now used as an hotel.

LINDRIDGE, BISHOPSTEIGNTON

Registered Grade II. Terraced gardens laid out around a late seventeenth-century house by Edward White for Lord Cable, 1913–14. Formal area with parterre, and circular temple within a moat, to the south side of the house; planned woodlands to east and west. A swimming pool with classical temple added in 1925. All became derelict after the house burnt down in 1962. The building of new houses within the curtilage of the old is being undertaken, with the restoration of the garden progressing at the same time. Not open to the public.

LOWER COMBE ROYAL, KINGSBRIDGE

A combe filled with flowering shrubs and trees. Its south-facing hillside has been planted in recent years with rhododendrons, cytisus, ceanothus, embothrium, and many herbaceous plants. An attractive garden in spring. Open by appointment only.

LUKESLAND, HARFORD

Large garden on the fringe of Dartmoor. Many mature trees and more recent pinetum. Created around a stream, with two ponds and bridges. Water-loving plants, azaleas and rhododendrons, camellias and hydrangeas. Many fine shrubs, including *Cornus* varieties, eucryphias, viburnums. A large davidia tree gives a good display and the monkey puzzle tree is a feature, although the tallest specimen was one of the many losses in the 1990 gale. Open occasionally in aid of local charities.

LUPTON, BRIXHAM

Registered Grade II. Remains of formal gardens and park laid out in the late eighteenth century for the Buller family. The house is now a school and the garden derelict. Fine entrance lodges and railings. Not open to the public.

LUSCOMBE, DAWLISH

Registered Grade II*. House by Nash, garden by Repton (Red Book dated 1799) for the Hoare family who have lived here from 1800 until the present day. Magnificent situation at the head of a combe leading towards the sea; lodges, gravel walks with circular rose garden, and box-edged beds, possibly unaltered in design since the last century; huge trees fringing bowl in which house sits. Not open to the public.

MAMHEAD, MAMHEAD

Registered Grade II*. Park and woodland, now in divided ownership. Fine views, church, obelisk. 'Capability' Brown advised Lord Lisburne on the layout of the grounds in 1772. Salvin designed the house and the barbican-like stable block, from 1826. Formal Victorian beds and terraces were laid out to east of house. Frequent changes of use have resulted in mutilation of original concept. Not open to the public.

MARDON, MORETONHAMPSTEAD

Several acres in a combe with a south-facing slope down to a stream. Artificial small lake with small island. Pleasant rhododendrons and good lawns in a lovely setting. Open occasionally.

MARWOOD HILL, MARWOOD

Over the past thirty years a garden of great merit and renown has been created on an unpropitious site – steeply sloping and exposed to cold sea winds. The work of one man, Dr Smart, Marwood contains a vast collection of plants from all over the world. The garden has grown in two stages. Below the house the small stream was dammed to form two ponds and many fine trees and shrubs were planted. A keen propagator and hybridizer of camellias, Dr Smart's garden is full of good specimens which make a fine showing in the spring together with drifts of bulbs, flowering trees and rhododendrons. Glasshouses in the walled gardens contain tender plants and more camellias, and there is a large plant sales area. Old roses take over in the summer and a raised alpine bed contains many treasures. The garden has been extended with generous plantings along the stream, and a large collection of trees and shrubs, all clearly labelled. It is a professional's garden with what amounts to a tree and shrub library where the amateur can acquire much information. Open daily except Christmas Day.

MIDDLE HILL, WASHFIELD

About half an acre of garden on alkaline soil made by the owners over the last twenty-seven years. Scree beds as well as ordinary flower beds. Lavish planting of herbaceous plants, many of them unusual or rare, all first-rate varieties. Some shrubs and climbers (clematis in variety). Many 'alpine' or small plants in the scree beds. Not open to the public.

MOTHECOMBE, HOLBETON

Delightful Queen Anne house close to the sea with its own hamlet and beach; tree house, stream garden, rockery. Formal walled garden with striated paving on which Lutyens advised when he remodelled part of the house 1922–5. Open occasionally.

MOUNT EDGCUMBE, MAKER, CORNWALL (FORMERLY DEVON)

One of the most famous landscape gardens in England. Part of Devon until the nineteenth century when it was transferred to Cornwall, it was purchased from the estate of the sixth Earl of Mount Edgcumbe in 1971 jointly by Cornwall County Council and Plymouth City Council and is an important 'green lung' for the city. The genesis of the landscape occurred with the formation of a deer park by the Edgcumbes in 1539. The parkland and gardens were laid out between 1740 and 1810, and feature a series of formal areas (French, English and Italian gardens), an orangery, amphitheatre with Ionic temple (Milton's Seat), and a Gothic ruin. The park now contains the national collection of camellias and is being restored vigorously. Open daily all year.

MUSBURY BARTON, MUSBURY

An ancestral home of the Drakes of Ashe. Two good lawns bordered by rose beds and trees (some unusual species). Delightful rustic bridges. Sunny border with colourful annuals by the house – a long, low thatched building that perfectly complements the garden. Not open to the public.

OLD RECTORY, WOODLEIGH

About an acre of ground sloping slightly towards the east. Trees and flowering shrubs, especially magnolias and rhododendrons. Wisteria notably rampant. Wooded walks and glades, with small irregular lawns. Open by appointment.

OVERBECKS (SHARPITOR), SALCOMBE

Registered Grade II. Plantings of exotic trees, shrubs and flowers in a garden first laid out in 1901 by Edric Hopkins. Extended after 1913 by G.M. Vereker and continued by Otto Overbeck between 1928 and 1937, when it was given to the National Trust.

OXTON, KENTON

The creation of the Revd John Swete, the diarist, from 1781. Guided by the principles of the Picturesque, Swete's landscape included a 'ruined gateway', a thatched summer-house, gothic gazebo and informal planting which replaced an older more formal arrangement. An attractive cast-iron bridge was added probably in the early nineteenth century. The estate is now in divided ownership, and the garden is not open to the public.

PLYMPTON, PLYMPTON ST MAURICE

Registered Grade II. A series of early eighteenth-century walled gardens, one with a mount, to the south-west of a spick-and-span Queen Anne house, c. 1700, for the Treby family. The mount, if contemporary with the house, is a remarkable survival. The property is now run as a care home by St Peter's Convent and is not open to the public.

POWDERHAM CASTLE, POWDERHAM

Registered Grade II. The deer park associated with this fourteenth-century fortified manor house was developed in the eighteenth century with extensive tree planting. Triangular castellated belvedere of 1773. At the time of the castle's remodelling, 1837–48, a formal terraced garden was laid out immediately to the east, with geometrical massed bedding; a simplified form of this survives. Open regularly.

PUTSBOROUGH COURT, GEORGEHAM

Water plays an important part in this garden. Huge gunnera and water-loving trees grow around the pond, and moisture-loving plants along the banks of the stream. The water meadow is being developed with a series of bridges, ponds, islands and new plantings of appropriate trees and shrubs. Around the house are mixed borders with arches and an arbour, all covered with climbers. Many roses, and a silver pear avenue. Not open to the public.

PUTSBOROUGH MANOR, GEORGEHAM

Beautiful secluded garden surrounded by high walls, with beds of shrub roses, and perennials. Good stream-side planting, many fine climbers including the unusual feature of myrtle covering the house. Separate garden across the road with mixed borders, roses, shrubs. Not open to the public.

ROBIN HILL, EXETER

Half an acre garden, containing a rock-scree garden, lawn and pond surrounded by a great variety of shrubby and herbaceous plants with winding paths. Open by appointment.

ROCKBEARE MANOR, ROCKBEARE

Registered Grade II. An eighteenth-century house with twin pavilions, fine stable block and excellent model farmyard. The sinuous drive through mature trees, including Lucombe oak, is entered by magnificent gate piers with niches and pediments. Twin lakes are positioned in the rolling landscape to give the impression of a serpentine river. Walled kitchen garden with pool and fountain; small formal terraced garden to south. Not open to the public.

ROSEMOOR, GREAT TORRINGTON

Rapidly becoming a star attraction, this is now the RHS's showpiece of the west. Originally 8 acres of woodland garden surrounding the house, developed by Lady Anne Palmer, VMH, with camellias, rhododendrons, many fine trees and shrubs, old roses and a wealth of border plantings. Since it was given to the RHS a whole new garden has been developed around the visitor centre. Herbaceous borders, rose gardens, a herb and vegetable garden and a new pond and stream planting have greatly extended the range. Open daily all year.

ROUSDON HOUSE, ROUSDON, COMBPYNE

Sir Henry Peek (of grocery fame) bought the entire parish of Rousdon in about 1870 and proceeded to build a house and associated buildings in what W.G. Hoskins calls 'rich man's Tudor', to designs by Ernest George. The gardens included a frame yard with melon, tomato, chrysanthemum and carnation houses; heated greenhouses for peaches, palms, pears, figs and grapes; walled garden, croquet lawn, cricket ground, and ornamental lake. The house is now a school and although the grounds have been adapted for educational use many original features remain. Viewing by written application to the bursar.

ST OLAVES, MURCHINGTON

Late nineteenth-century informal terraces, ending in a dry stone retaining wall 12 to 15 ft high, several hundred yards long, of massive granite blocks. Fine mature trees and, since 1974, extensive shrub planting. Impressive views over the Upper Teign Valley to the high moor. Not open to the public.

SALTRAM, PLYMPTON ST MARY

Registered Grade II*. Landscaped park of the 1770s by Nathaniel Richmond for John Parker, first Lord Boringdon. A number of garden buildings date from this period including an octagonal castle, the garden temple, chapel (formerly a barn), the orangery and the amphitheatre overlooking the Plym estuary. The gardens were remodelled in the 1880s by the third Earl of Morley and his wife, the daughter of R.S. Holford, the creator of Westonbirt Arboretum. Many of the choice specimens at Saltram came from there. The National Trust assumed full responsibility for the property in 1962, since when they have developed the garden and park, introducing a ha-ha, and planting trees to screen views of the urban Plymouth sprawl.

SAUNTON COURT, BRAUNTON

Registered Grade II. Garden remodelled by Lutyens concurrently with restyling the house in 1932. Delightful axial treatment, with formal lawn and gate piers leading to a rill and recessed pool with ram's-head gargoyle. The terrace is approached by concave/convex steps, herbaceous beds flanked by herring-bone walls; pond. Gazebo with clock tower. Not open to the public.

SHARPHAM, ASHPRINGTON

Registered Grade II*. Landscape garden on eminence high above bend of River Dart. Exceptional views from the house built by the noted Sir Robert Taylor for Captain Philemon Pownall out of treasure ship spoils. Mature trees, Henry Moore statue, octagonal boat-house by river. It is believed that 'Capability' Brown may have had a hand in planning a landscape largely unchanged since the eighteenth century. Not open to the public.

SHOBROOKE PARK, SHOBROOKE

Registered Grade II. Magnificent park intersected by River Creedy, with two lakes, innumerable wild fowl and sheep. Fine trees, to an extent ravaged by the 1990 storm which cut a swathe through the park. On one hill a bungalow has been built to replace the burnt mansion, with elaborate terracing and ornamental seats. On another hillside a semi-circular garden seat as eye-catcher. Ornate lodges. Not open to the public.

SIDBURY MANOR, SIDBURY

Large woodland garden surrounding neo-Jacobean mansion built in 1879 for the Cave family who still live there. Walled garden, three lodges, long drive winding picturesquely through the park, valley with stream flanked by many flowering trees and shrubs. Not open to the public.

SILVER COPSE, MARSH GREEN

About 3 acres of lawns with island beds containing a great variety of shrubs and herbaceous plants plus some trees. Reclaimed from scrub over thirty-one years. Small bog garden and ponds, and scree garden. Plants all superbly grown and cared for. A fine example of a plantsman's garden which is at the same time attractive to walk in because well laid out. Many varieties and species. Open occasionally, and by appointment.

SLADE, CORNWOOD

The garden attached to this house and to Slade Barton is all one, but ownership and responsibilities are divided. The whole area comprises several acres of acid soil on a slope towards the south. The garden around Slade is formal, with good lawns, herbaceous beds, some pleasing shrubs (rhododendrons and azaleas), and old walls. Not open to the public.

STOVER, TEIGNGRACE

A large Palladian villa, built 1776–80 by James Templer. He laid out the surrounding landscape, including an extensive lake which is now incorporated within the Stover Country Park (run by Devon County Council). Nearer the mansion, garden buildings include a pedimented temple, an ice-house and an astounding grotto with circular, round-headed and rectangular openings set in a screen of recessed arches. The house has been used as a girls' school since 1932 and it and its environs are not open to the public.

SYDENHAM HOUSE, MARYSTOW

Registered Grade II. Set around a house built in the early seventeenth century for Sir Thomas Wise. Yew hedges, Turtle Grove, canal. Raised herb and formal garden by Simon Irvine in the 1980s; remodelling by Gillian Bauer in 1972 in the canal area. Not open to the public.

TAPELEY PARK, WESTLEIGH

Registered Grade II*. A long winding entrance drive leads to the early eighteenth-century house, in a fine position overlooking the Torridge estuary. Early twentieth-century Italianate garden with three terraces, designed by Sir John Belcher. Formal pool, palm trees, and other exotic trees and shrubs. Holm oak valley. Ice-house and shell grotto. Open regularly.

TAWSTOCK COURT, TAWSTOCK

Huge Strawberry Hill Gothic house built for the Bourchier-Wreys in the late eighteenth century, and now a school. Church full of elaborate funerary monuments. Stable block, sixteenth-century gatehouse, rustic lodge. Small terrace garden in front of the house looking down the valley. Not open to the public.

TORRE ABBEY, COCKINGTON COURT, OLDWAY MANSION, TORBAY

The three major Torbay parks, all formerly the grounds of country houses. They are now managed and maintained by the Torbay Borough Council to an exemplary standard. Open daily all year.

UGBROOKE, CHUDLEIGH

Registered Grade II*. 'Capability' Brown landscape notably unspoiled, begun around 1770. Extending to about 400 acres, it contains the familiar elements of water (three lakes and a fine cascade), carefully planted clumps and a wide expanse of smooth grass. The gardens which immediately surround the house are largely a Victorian creation. To the west an area of lawn, to the north a terrace containing a small box-edged parterre of roses; to the east simple grass terraces with palms and a modest orangery. Open regularly.

WATCOMBE PARK, TORQUAY

Registered Grade II. Intended by Isambard Kingdom Brunel to be his retirement home. Parcels of land were bought but the house was not started before his death in 1869 (the existing house is now a Christian conference centre). Various designers advised Brunel on landscape and planting including William Nesfield, Alexander Forsyth and William Simpson. The arboretum contains many fine, mature trees but all that remains of the planned approach are cobbles for carriage wheels; the whole overgrown by scrub and shrubs. Not open to the public.

WERRINGTON PARK, WERRINGTON, CORNWALL (FORMERLY DEVON)

Werrington House and part of the grounds were in Devon until they were transferred to Cornwall in 1974; some of the park had always been in the Duchy. Three notable periods of landscape development: by Sir William Morice, in the early eighteenth century, when Kent is believed to have had some influence; after 1774, when the property was purchased by the first Duke of Northumberland and the park was laid out; and from 1882 when Werrington passed into the hands of the Williams family of Caerhays, who raised an impressive collection of rhododendrons mainly from Forrest's seed. Not regularly open to the public.

WITHLEIGH FARM, WITHLEIGH

About 3 acres of hillside going down to a stream with an attractive modern bridge. The hillside down from the house is a 'flowery mead' with paths mown through meadow flowers and grasses (rarely seen in Devon). The stream is more or less naturally planted. Open occasionally, and by appointment.

WOLFORD LODGE, DUNKESWELL

Several acres sloping towards the south-west, old established but restored garden on acid soil. Fine views among rohdodendrons, with lawn and glades. Superb when shrubs in flower. Open occasionally.

WOOD, SOUTH TAWTON

Registered Grade II*. Garden designed by Thomas Mawson, an outstanding example of his work, and featured in his often reprinted work *The Art and Craft of Garden-Making*. House by Dan Gibson for William Lethbridge, completed in 1905. This once virtually derelict garden is now being restored. Hidden in dense, wooded country, the gardens boast a lake with thatched summer-house, stone bridge, yew hedges, pavilion, and loggia with platform overlooking croquet lawn; formal garden with pool, fountain and twin garden houses; kitchen garden; dipping tank. Not open to the public.

WOODSIDE, BARNSTAPLE

An amazing collection of grasses, sedges, and monocots has been built up in this unsual garden on a steeply sloping site. Tall trees give protection from the winds and disguise the very close proximity of the town, creating a peaceful atmosphere. Shrubs and trees which seem to struggle in other gardens here reach amazing proportions. Every plant has been carefully chosen and very few are commonplace. Hollies, osmanthus, pittosporums, hebes, low growers and rock plants, some conifers and eucalyptus and the aquilegia 'Woodside' with golden variegated leaves are all specialities. Open occasionally, and by appointment.

YOULSTON PARK, SHIRWELL

Registered Grade II. Parkland probably dating from the mid-eighteenth century, around a Tudor house with *c.* 1700 additions. Attractive late eighteenth-century twin lodges. Not open to the public.

ACKNOWLEDGEMENTS

The editor would like to thank *Country Life* for permission to use the photographs appearing on pages 8, 9 and 17; the Lindley Library of the Royal Horticultural Society for permission to use the illustrations on pages 95, 96, 99, 100, 101, 102 and 103; the Devon Record Office for the document on page 35, the photograph on page 36 and for the Swete watercolours; and Mr P. Prideaux-Brune of Prideaux Place, Padstow, for generously allowing reproduction of the Prideaux drawings. Many of the other illustrations appear by courtesy of the West Country Studies Library and the Devon and Exeter Institution whose assistance is gratefully acknowledged.

With the exception of the photograph of Runnymede Gardens and the Southern Slopes, Ilfracombe, which is by David Richardson, the colour plates appearing in this book are the work of Dougal Swinscow.

Lastly, the editor would wish to record his particular thanks to Mrs Linda Pugsley and Mrs Veronica Lock for typing the consolidated manuscript, and to Mrs Mary Clarke for her invaluable help in compiling the index.

INDEX

References to illustrations are given in italic.